Other Books and Series by Jeff Bowen

Cherokee Intermarried White 1906 Volume I thru X

Applications for Enrollment of Creek Newborn Act of 1905 Volumes I thru XIV

Applications for Enrollment of Choctaw Newborn Act of 1905 Volumes I thru XX

Choctaw By Blood Enrollment Cards 1898-1914 Volumes I thru XX

Oglala Sioux Indians Pine Ridge Reservation 1932 Census Book I
Oglala Sioux Indians Pine Ridge Reservation Birth and Death Rolls 1924-1932 Book II

Census of the Sioux and Cheyenne Indians of Pine Ridge Agency 1896 - 1897 Book I
Census of the Sioux and Cheyenne Indians of Pine Ridge Agency 1898 - 1899 Book II

Northern Cheyenne Tongue River, Montana 1904 - 1932 Census 1904-1916 Volume I

Northern Cheyenne Tongue River, Montana 1904 - 1932 Census 1917-1926 Volume II

Identified Mississippi Choctaw Enrollment Cards 1902-1909 Volumes I, II & III

Sac & Fox - Shawnee Estates 1885-1910 (Under Sac & Fox Agency) Volumes I-VII

Visit our website at **www.nativestudy.com** to learn more about these and other books and series by Jeff Bowen

Portrait of Tecumseh from Lossing's
The Pictorial Field-Book of the War of 1812
is a pencil sketch drawn by Pierre Le Dru,
a young French trader at Vincennes, circa 1808.

Other Books and Series by Jeff Bowen

Compilation of History of the Cherokee Indians and Early History of the Cherokees by Emmet Starr with Combined Full Name Index
(Hardbound & Softbound)

1901-1907 Native American Census Seneca, Eastern Shawnee, Miami, Modoc, Ottawa, Peoria, Quapaw, and Wyandotte Indians (Under Seneca School, Indian Territory)

1932 Census of The Standing Rock Sioux Reservation with Births And Deaths 1924-1932

Census of The Blackfeet, Montana, 1897- 1901 Expanded Edition

Eastern Cherokee by Blood, 1906-1910, Volumes I thru XIII

Choctaw of Mississippi Indian Census 1929-1932 with Births and Deaths 1924-1931 Volume I
Choctaw of Mississippi Indian Census 1933, 1934 & 1937, Supplemental Rolls to 1934 & 1935 with Births and Deaths 1932-1938, and Marriages 1936-1938 Volume II

Eastern Cherokee Census Cherokee, North Carolina 1930-1939 Census 1930-1931 with Births And Deaths 1924-1931 Taken By Agent L. W. Page Volume I
Eastern Cherokee Census Cherokee, North Carolina 1930-1939 Census 1932-1933 with Births And Deaths 1930-1932 Taken By Agent R. L. Spalsbury Volume II
Eastern Cherokee Census Cherokee, North Carolina 1930-1939 Census 1934-1937 with Births and Deaths 1925-1938 and Marriages 1936 & 1938 Taken by Agents R. L. Spalsbury And Harold W. Foght Volume III

Seminole of Florida Indian Census, 1930-1940 with Birth and Death Records, 1930-1938

Texas Cherokees 1820-1839 A Document For Litigation 1921

Starr Roll 1894 (Cherokee Payment Rolls) Districts: Canadian, Cooweescoowee, and Delaware Volume One
Starr Roll 1894 (Cherokee Payment Rolls) Districts: Flint, Going Snake, and Illinois Volume Two
Starr Roll 1894 (Cherokee Payment Rolls) Districts: Saline, Sequoyah, and Tahlequah; Including Orphan Roll Volume Three

Cherokee Intruder Cases Dockets of Hearings 1901-1909 Volumes I & II

Indian Wills, 1911-1921 Records of the Bureau of Indian Affairs Books One thru Seven

Other Books and Series by Jeff Bowen

Native American Wills & Probate Records 1911-1921

Turtle Mountain Reservation Chippewa Indians 1932 Census with Births & Deaths, 1924-1932

Chickasaw By Blood Enrollment Cards 1898-1914 Volume I thru *V*

Cherokee Descendants East An Index to the Guion Miller Applications Volume I
Cherokee Descendants West An Index to the Guion Miller Applications Volume II (A-M)
Cherokee Descendants West An Index to the Guion Miller Applications Volume III (N-Z)

Applications for Enrollment of Seminole Newborn Freedmen, Act of 1905

Eastern Cherokee Census, Cherokee, North Carolina, 1915-1922, Taken by Agent James E. Henderson   *Volume I (1915-1916)*
Volume II (1917-1918)
Volume III (1919-1920)
Volume IV (1921-1922)

Complete Delaware Roll of 1898

Eastern Cherokee Census, Cherokee, North Carolina, 1923-1929, Taken by Agent James E. Henderson   *Volume I (1923-1924)*
Volume II (1925-1926)
Volume III (1927-1929)

Applications for Enrollment of Seminole Newborn Act of 1905 Volumes I & II

North Carolina Eastern Cherokee Indian Census 1898-1899, 1904, 1906, 1909-1912, 1914 Revised and Expanded Edition

1932 Hopi and Navajo Native American Census with Birth & Death Rolls (1925-1931) Volume 1 - Hopi
1932 Hopi and Navajo Native American Census with Birth & Death Rolls (1930-1932) Volume 2 - Navajo

Western Navajo Reservation Navajo, Hopi and Paiute 1933 Census with Birth & Death Rolls 1925-1933

Cherokee Citizenship Commission Dockets 1880-1884 and 1887-1889 Volumes I thru *V*

Applications for Enrollment of Chickasaw Newborn Act of 1905 Volumes I thru *VII*

SAC & FOX - SHAWNEE ESTATES 1920-1924
(UNDER SAC & FOX AGENCY)
VOLUME VIII

TRANSCRIBED BY
JEFF BOWEN

NATIVE STUDY
Gallipolis, Ohio
USA

Copyright © 2022
by Jeff Bowen

ALL RIGHTS RESERVED
No part of this publication can be reproduced
in any form or manner whatsoever
without previous written permission from the
Copyright holder or Publisher.

Originally published:
Santa Maria, California
2019

Reprinted by:

Native Study LLC
Gallipolis, OH
www.nativestudy.com

Library of Congress Control Number: 2022900261

ISBN: 978-1-64968-137-9

Made in the United States of America.

This series is dedicated to
Tanner Tackett
the Constant Gardner
and Friend
and
In memory of
Raina Mae Fulks.

Ab·sen·tee

noun: **absentee**; plural noun: **absentees**

      1. a person who is expected or required to be present at a place or event but is not.

(According to Webster)

Shawnee

noun, plural Shaw-nees, (especially collectively) Shaw-nee.

      1. a member of an Algonquian-speaking tribe formerly in the east-central U.S., now in Oklahoma.

(According to Dictionary.com)

Shawnee Teaching

"Tagi nsi walr mvci-lutvwi mr-pvyaci-grlahkv, xvga mytv inv gi mvci-lutvwv, gi mvci-ludr-geiv. Walv uwas-panvsi inv, wa-ciganv-hi gi gol-utvwv u kvgesakv-namv manwi-lanvwawewa yasi golutv-mvni geyrgi.

"Tagi bemi-lutvwi walr segalami mr-pvyaci-grlahkv, xvga mvtv inv gi bemi-lutvwv, gi bemi-ludr-geiv gelv. Wakv vhqalami inv, xvga nahfrpi Moneto ut vhqalamrli nili yasi vhqalamahgi gelv!"

Translation:

"Do not kill or injure your neighbor, for it is not him that you injure, you injure yourself. But do good to him, therefore add to his days of happiness as you add to your own.

"Do not wrong or hate your neighbor, for it is not him that you wrong, you wrong yourself. But love him, for Moneto loves him also as He loves you!"

Thomas Wildcat Alford
circa 1936

Special Note

You will notice throughout these volumes the author has attempted to duplicate from the original documents places on the page that were destroyed due to water damage. Whole sections of a page could be missing or torn into multiple pieces. In order to duplicate the damage you will find various shapes with a white format to try to represent the damage and the loss of the ability to completely transcribe many of the pages.

INTRODUCTION

The history of the Shawnee is fascinating. Naturally the most famous Shawnee known would be Tecumseh, born circa. 1768, after four other siblings before him. His father was Puckeshinwa, a Shawnee war chief from Ohio. Puckeshinwa crossed the Ohio close to what is now Gallipolis with his fourteen year son Chiksika by his side. As they followed the lead of Chief Cornstalk during the fall of 1774. Tecumseh's famous father was mortally wounded during the fight they would soon encounter. The Shawnees were unexpectedly discovered by a couple of early morning turkey hunters from the settlement called Point Pleasant. These hunters ran as fast as possible back to where the Ohio and Kanawha Rivers meet and sounded the alarm that the Shawnees were coming, the fight lasted most of the day but not without loss to both sides. The Shawnees were badly outnumbered. Pucheshinwa was carried back across the Ohio or as the Shawnees called it the *Spaylaywitheepi*, with the intention to take him back to his village. He must have known his time was short as he laid there telling Chiksika to make sure he devoted his time not only to Tecumseh's but also his younger brothers training in becoming warriors. Pucheshinwa succumbed to his wounds shortly after that request and was secretly buried deep in the forest that day. Chiksika saw his father mortally wounded while defending their home. He had a reverence for his father as a great warrior. He wanted to follow his father's path and not die an average death. In his heart, it had to be on the battlefield as a warrior. Tecumseh followed his brother's every step and planned to die defending his land as his father and brother had. There was no surrendering or giving in to the Americans.

There are several descriptions out there of Tecumseh from his contemporaries, but David Edmunds found one during his research that seems to be the most commanding of any found. "Captain John B. Glegg, Brock's aide-de-camp, who was present at the meetings between Brock and Tecumseh, recorded one of the most vivid descriptions of the Shawnee. According to Glegg, in August 1812 Tecumseh still was in the prime of his life, giving the impression of a man ten years younger. Tecumseh's appearance was very prepossessing; his figure light and finely proportioned; his age I imagined to be about five and thirty [he actually was forty four]; in height, five feet nine or ten inches; his complexion, light copper; countenance, oval, with bright hazle eyes, beaming cheerfulness, energy, and decision. Three small silver crowns, or coronets were suspended from the lower cartilage of his aquiline nose; and a large silver medallion of George the Third, which I believe his ancestor had received from Lord Dorchester, when governor-general of Canada, was attached to a mixed coloured wampum string, and hung around his neck. His dress consisted of a plain, neat uniform, tanned deer-skin jacket, with long trousers of the same material, the seams of both being covered with neatly cut fringe; and he had on his feet leather moccasins, much ornamented with work made from the dyed quills of the porcupine."[1]

There were approximately 39 years that passed between Tecumseh's and his father's deaths. It is hard to believe that the Shawnee's history being as extensive as it was during the early stages of the United States that their descendants' records were so closely guarded under the care of a vegetable bind in an leaky attic. Not only the Shawnee's but also the Sac & Fox, the Pottawatomie and the Kickapoo. There are also many other tribal affiliates to be found in this series, not to mention someone like Jim Thorpe and his family members of the Sac and Fox tribe. Not only was he a gold metal Olympian and multiple sport competitor, but at the time one of America's favorite sons. Thank goodness someone was finally conscious of the situation. The description in the next paragraph explains the neglect of these important documents as given by the Oklahoma Historical Societies Microfilm Catalog.

"In 1933 a survey of Indian tribal records in Oklahoma revealed that the files of the Shawnee and the old Sac and Fox agencies had been sadly neglected, and the lack of space for storing them properly had resulted in much loss. Charles Eggers, Superintendent of the Shawnee Agency, reported that most of the non-current records of his agency were boxed in a storehouse. The papers of the old Sac and Fox Agency were in the loft of a warehouse which was also used for storing vegetables. The roof of the building leaked and the papers were in danger of destruction from moisture. Following the passage of the Congressional Act of March 27, 1934 (H.R. 5631 Public No. 133) which placed the tribal records in the custody of the Oklahoma Historical Society."

As described above the history of the Shawnee people isn't an ordinary history but an extraordinary time in all of our ancestors' lives. Reading Allen W. Eckert's extensive studies taken from what is known as the Draper Papers, a historical record meticulously documented beginning circa 1830. Though Draper covered an approximate time between the 1740's to the 1810's, his collection covered documents and transcriptions concerning Boone, Kenton, Rogers Clark and Joseph Brant, not to mention a considerable amount of Shawnee history from the entirety of the Ohio and Mississippi Valley's. Other authors such as Colin G. Calloway and R. David Edmunds provide an in depth study of the Shawnee people as well as Tecumseh and his life leaving no rock unturned in their research.

As you read different references you find diverse opinions on Tecumseh's mother as to what tribe she came from. Eckert through Draper's work says, "This was

---

[1] Tecumseh, R. David Edmunds Pg. 162-163, Para. 3-4

when Pucksinwah, then twenty-six, led the war party against the Cherokees that had resulted in the capture of Methotasa."[2] Indicating Tecumseh's mother might have been Cherokee. Yet, R. David Edmunds writes, "In 1768, while the Iroquois were selling Shawnee lands at the Treaty of Fort Stanwix, a Creek woman married to a Shawnee man gave birth to a son at Old Piqua, a Shawnee village on the Mad River in Western Ohio. The woman had a difficult labor before giving birth in the small lodge especially constructed for that purpose, some distance from the family's wigwam. The mother, Methoataske (Turtle Laying Its Eggs), had grown up among the Creek villages in Alabama and had met her husband when some of the Shawnee sought refuge among the Creeks during the 1750s. The father Puckeshinwa, remained with his wife's people until about 1760, when the family left Alabama and migrated to Ohio."[3]

You also will find different opinions on how they dressed back then or wore their hair. In Edmunds' book *Tecumseh*, his brother the Prophet Tenskwatawa states, "Warriors should again shave their heads and wear the scalp locks worn by their ancestors." And yet in Thomas Wildcat Alford's *Civilization*, he says, "We boys wore our hair short, very much as the girls of today wear their hair bobbed. This is the way Shawnee men always have worn their hair. Never did they braid it, as some other tribes do."

Alford's book *Civilization* out of the many resources read was likely one of the most informative and enjoyable references in the study. Thomas Wildcat Alford was born in 1860 and belonged to the Absentee Shawnee tribe. He states that he was a descendant of Tecumseh. He spoke about when his family slept under the stars each night and that he never had an English name until his father had him go to school at a Quaker mission. Mr. Alford also talks about two things with real clarity. Alford educates us about clans in the sixth chapter, expounding upon the active history of the Shawnees and the different responsibilities of each as well as divisions among the clans that created tribal changes. These dissensions were nothing new. Anyone that has read extensively about the Shawnee will realize that Alford understood his people and their history. When he wrote about tribal clashes or divisions during the early days, he managed to translate on paper their strength and character. He showed for generations they literally believed they were given an ability to make themselves self-reliant when it came to survival. They traveled far and wide following their own path while installing their own way of life that made them powerful adversaries whether it be against the British, the French or the Americans moving west. Other tribes found them to be awful enemies or potent allies. Then he compares their tribal government

---

[2] A Sorrow in Our Heart, Allen W. Eckert Pg. 22, Para. 3
[3] Tecumseh, R. David Edmunds, Pg. 17 Para. 1

and the clan leaders to being quite similar to the U.S. Presidency and the different government entities. Alford also brings up business committees for the tribe.

He starts with a concise description of the clans, "Originally there were five clans composing the Shawnee tribe, including the two principle clans, Tha-we-gi-la and Cha-lah-kaw-tha, from one of which came the national or principal chief. The remaining three, the Pec-ku-we, the Kis-pu-go, and the May-ku-jay, each had its own chief who was subordinate to the principal chief in national matters, but independent in matters pertaining to the duties of his clan. Each clan had a certain duty to perform for the whole tribe. For instance the Pec-ku-we clan, or its chief, had charge of the maintenance of order and looked after the celebration of things pertaining to religion or faith; the Kis-pu-go clan had charge of matters pertaining to war and the preparation and training of warriors; the May-ku-jay clan had charge of things relating to health and medicine and food for the whole tribe. But the two powerful clans, the Tha-we-gi-la and the Cha-lah-kaw-tha, had charge of political affairs and all matters that affected the tribe as a whole. Indeed, the tribal government may be likened to the government of the United States, in which each state (clan), with it governor (chief), is sovereign in local matters, but subordinate to the president of the United States (principal chief) in national matters. The difference is that the president of the United States must be elected, and may be changed with each election, while the principal chief came to his office by heritage and held it for life, or during good behavior.

At the time of which I write the Shawnee tribe had been divided for many years, and only the Tha-we-gi-la, the Pec-ku-we, and the Kis-pu-go clans were represented in the Absentee Shawnee band. These three clans always had been closely related, while the Cha-lah-kaw-tha and the May-ku-jay had always stood together, and were represented in the group that I have mentioned as living in Kansas at the time of the Civil War."[4]

As referenced earlier Thomas Wildcat Alford brought up their present Indian agent, Thomas, on September 13, 1893, wanting him to present a list of prominent men in their tribe to hold positions on a business committee. This presented a whole new world for the tribe with new pressures through white change so to speak. The government was instilling in their world the destruction of their heritage in tribal customs and culture all to control Indian land through allotment. When he was being told to help form this committee, he was actually being told, what we are doing is we are wiping out your way of life forever. The Congress of the United States was presenting the abolition of all tribal governments so the land could be manipulated through the Curtis Act of 1898. They said, we are splitting the land up. They were allotting so many acres to each tribal member. How much they got depended on

---

[4] Civilization, Alford; Pg. 44, Para. 1-2

whether they planned to farm or raise cattle. If they were building herds they were given double the land for grazing. Alford said, "It was on the thirteenth day of September, 1893 that Agent Thomas informed the Shawnees that he had been directed by the Commissioner of Indian Affairs to submit for approval the names of seven of the most prominent men of the tribe who would constitute a Business Committee to supersede the chiefs and councilors of the old tribal government. The Business Committee was to represent the Absentee Shawnees as a tribe in all dealings with the United States and to act in an advisory capacity to the individual members of the tribe. They were to certify to the identity of grantors of sales of land and to act for the tribe in other matters.[5]

During the study it was noticed that the Curtis Act being enacted on June 28, 1898 and Alford's mentioning its initiation during 1893 became a point of interest or at least premature. It was found that Congress had actually started working in this area of seizure approximately five years prior to the agent's notification, "In 1893 Congress began a special allotment process for the Five Tribes, enacting a number of laws that affect the governmental powers of the tribes. Some of these laws, like the 1889 and 1890 Acts, extended certain Arkansas laws over Indian Territory and expanded federal court jurisdiction; they are relevant today only insofar as they may indirectly affect tribal judicial powers."[6]

Their mention of these laws only being relevant today, though actually not spoken, plead plausible deniability while coinciding with the Indian Reorganization Act of 1934. The government was on a mission. Land and control. The allotment had to take place. They were wanting statehood. They were wanting the Native people to be under one umbrella with everyone else. Tribes were nations. Just like a foreign nation, they were their own government. Originally our constitution was modeled after the Iroquois model, had to start somewhere? So what we did was split up the land among the people that already owned it. Then we took what was left, approximately 90 million acres and sold it at a profit. Who got the money? Only the politicians at the time know? But years after taking the chiefs and councils away there was likely mass chaos like a town hall today. So the government likely was wanting out of the tribal control business. At least enough that they could just control it without being in the bullseye so to speak. Congress and the state had already achieved its goals. So this act was written with the statement that it was a model to make all think we do this for you. "The IRA was intended to provide a mechanism for the tribe as a governmental unit to interact with and adapt to a modern society, rather than to force the assimilation of individual Indians.

---

[5] Civilization, Alford; Pg. 161, Para. 2
[6] Federal Indian Law, Cohen; Pg. 781, Para. 3

The IRA was also an attempt to improve the economic situation of Indians. The Act was intended to stop the alienation of tribal land needed to support Indians, and to provide for acquisition of additional acreage for tribes. Tribes were encouraged to organize along the lines of modern business corporations; a system of financial credit was included to reach this economic objective."[7] Interestingly enough Cohen and Alford both mention this same organizational technique, only one as law and another as a tribal member.

It is disconcerting just in reading a reference from Senator Charles Curtis as he mentioned in his biography that by the time Congress finished rewriting the bill he had submitted he hardly recognized it. "Officially titled the "Act for the Protection of the People of Indian Territory", the Act is named for Charles Curtis, congressman from Kansas and its author. He was of mixed Native American and European descent: on his mother's side -Kansa, Osage, Potawatomi, and French; and on his father's - three ethnic lines of British Isles ancestry. Curtis was raised in part on the Kaw Reservation of his maternal grandparents, but also lived with his paternal grandparents and attended Topeka High School. He read law, became an attorney, and later was elected to the United States House of Representatives and Senate. He served as Vice-President under Herbert Hoover. In the usual fashion, by the time the bill HR 8581 had gone through five revisions in committees in both the House of Representatives and the Senate, there was little left of Curtis' original draft. In his hand-written autobiography, Curtis noted having been unhappy with the final version of the Curtis Act. He believed that the Five Civilized Tribes needed to make changes. He thought that the way ahead for Native Americans was through education and use of both their and the majority cultures, but he also had hoped to give more support to Native American transitions."[8]

The records within this series concern The Absentee Shawnee as well as many other people with different tribal affiliations. Also within these pages are closely related tribes that were under the same agency (The Sac & Fox Agency, Oklahoma) for many years like the Sac & Fox, the Pottawatomie and the Kickapoo. There are likely state recognized Shawnee tribes in the United States, but, "The Absentee Shawnee Tribe of Indians of Oklahoma (or Absentee Shawnee) is one of three federally recognized tribes of Shawnee people. Historically residing in the Eastern United States, the original Shawnee lived in the areas that are now Ohio, Indiana, Illinois, Kentucky, Tennessee, Pennsylvania, and other neighboring states. It is documented that they occupied and traveled through lands from Canada to Florida, from the Mississippi River to the eastern continental coast. In contemporary times, the Absentee Shawnee Tribe headquarters in Shawnee, Oklahoma; its tribal jurisdiction

---

[7] Federal Indian Law, Cohen; Pg. 147 Para. 1-2
[8] Curtis Act of 1898, Wikipedia

area includes land properties in Oklahoma in both Cleveland County and Pottawatomie County." [Today] "There are approximately 3,050 enrolled Absentee Shawnee tribal members, 2,315 of whom live in Oklahoma. Tribal membership follows blood quantum criteria, with applicants requiring a minimum of one eighth (1/8) documented Absentee-Shawnee blood to be placed on its membership rolls, as set forth by the tribal constitution. Though it is not a formal division, there is a social separation within its current tribal membership between the traditionalist Big Jim Band, which kept cultural traditions and ceremonies and has its primary populace in the Little Axe, Norman area, and the assimilationist White Turkey Band, which adopted European ways of the European majority, with many families based in the Shawnee area. Regardless of historical viewpoints, the bands cooperate for the future of the tribe."[9]

When this study was first pursued an old Xerox copy of a catalog that sat on the shelf for twenty five years was the first place searched for a viable source. It was titled, "Catalog of Microfilm Holdings in the Archives & Manuscripts Div. Oklahoma Historical Society 1976-1989". As mentioned in the description from this catalog's Introduction for the Sac and Fox Indian Agencies, it states, "In 1901 the Sac and Fox Agency was divided. The Sac and Fox Agency itself remained at the old site near Stroud with jurisdiction over the Sac and Fox and the Iowa. The Shawnee, Potawatomi and Kickapoo Agency (sometimes simply called the Shawnee Agency) was established about two miles south of Shawnee, Oklahoma. The agencies continued their separate existence until 1919 when they were merged becoming the Shawnee Agency.

Of course today in 2018, everything is digital and on the computer. You have to be thankful for having an old catalog and books on a shelf. There is nothing like the feel of holding a book in your hand. You can pick it up when you want and let your eyes travel to anywhere or any time in history. It has solid print that nobody can manipulate or change. It's just yours to wrap yourself up in without any glowing distractions as Native Americans call them, "Talking Leaves".

Jeff Bowen
Gallipolis, Ohio
NativeStudy.com

---

[9] Absentee-Shawnee Tribe of Indians Wikipedia

Sac & Fox – Shawnee Estates
1920-1924 Volume VIII

DEPARTMENT OF THE INTERIOR

UNITED STATES INDIAN SERVICE

Otoe Sub Agency,
Red Rock, Oklahoma.
January 12, 1920.

Mr. Ira C. Deaver,
   Supt Indian Agency,
      Shawnee, Oklahoma.

Mr dear Mr. Deaver:-

    Amarbe LaDue requests that you draw him a check for the balance of his bank account and send it to this office for delivery to him. Amarbe is a patent in fee Indian and is amply able to blow in what little money he may have on deposit t your office and for that reason I reccommend[sic] that his request be given favorable consideration.

                Very respectfully,

                George A Hoyo
                    Day School Inspector.

GAH

****

                Shawnee Indian Agency,
                Shawnee, Oklahoma,
                January 16, 1920.

Mr. George A. Hoyo,
Day school Inspector,
Red Rock, Oklahoma.

Dear Sir:

    Replying to your letter I am enclosing herewith check No. 3102 - $452.75 in favor of Amarbe LaDue.

                Respectfully,

                  Superintendent.

EB-enclo.

Sac & Fox – Shawnee Estates
1920-1924 Volume VIII

Shawnee Indian Agency,
Shawnee, Oklahoma.
February 17, 1920.

Mr. George A. Hoyo,
    Day School Inspector,
        Otoe Sub-Agency,
            Red Rock, Oklahoma.

Dear Mr. Hoyo:-

Enclosed herewith are the following described checks for the following named Indians under your jurisdiction which I will thank you to deliver:

Name	Check Number	Amount
Mary Harragarra	3476	21.93
John McGlaslin	3471	21.93
Charles McGlaslin	3473	21.93
Walter McGlaslin	3472	21.93
Robert McGlaslin	3471	88.66
Joe Carson	3470	18.62
George Carson	3469	18.07
Charlie Roubidoux	3465	.68
Annie Suck-ko-pe-ah	3484	30.66
Ella Smith	3477	31.92

You may tell these Indians that these amounts represent their shares of the Teresa Big Ear estate.

Very respectfully,

Carbon copy to
Mr. H. O. Decker,
Disbursing Agent,
Pawnee Indian Agency,   Superintendent.
Pawnee, Oklahoma.

[The following letter typed as given]
                    Aullville
                    Mo   3/14.0 70
            Indian Agency Sac Fox
        I here with write you for an application blank for to make a claim for an Indian Homestead write & citizenship claim blank I have all the [illegible] O am a deceant of the Sac Fox Tribe my Grand Father Drew money from the Indians I was advised buy Gabe E Parker to day to write you for an application blank Land 19927/20

Sac & Fox – Shawnee Estates
1920-1924 Volume VIII

3/8/1920TKK
Sac and Fox Citizenship Claim Please give me information Blank for to fill out
I have oil [illegible] all set for to give you   The Land Statement
I close answer soon   [illegible] Ill be on my way to Shawnee now very soon Just as soon as I can hear from Washington

                Your truly
                    S.W.R. Loyd
                    Aullville
                      Mo.

                ****

                Shawnee Indian Agency,
                Shawnee, Oklahoma.
                March 27, 1920.

Mr. S. W. R. Loyd,
    Aullville, Missouri.

Dear Sir:

    Enclosed herewith are application blanks which you asked for in your letter of March 14, 1920.
                Respectfully,

                Ira C. Devaer[sic]
                Superintendent.
G

[The letter below typed as given]

                Seattle Wash.
                Oct 31, 1914

Mr. J.A. Buntin Supt.
    Shawnee Oklahoma.
Dear sir
    Your letter of the 29 recieved and contents noted. I am partly giving you the name of one witness who now is very low sick, now I will give the other names, my mother maiden name was Tennessee
Thomas, by first husband   "   "
Davis   " second   "   "   "
Williams, my fathers name is Wade Wilkins, my grand father's name was Buck William Thomas, I dont know grand ma name. I have one bro. living son by mothers first husband his name is Guss Davis #422 N. Mead Ave, Wichita, Kans.

Sac & Fox – Shawnee Estates
1920-1924 Volume VIII

one sister living by second husband Mr. Mattie Collins #926 Indpendance Ave, Kans City Mo. I have two children living Beanktrice Hallum & Wodard Hallum. My mother died in Kans City Kans Oct 1909, my grand father died long years ago I have other bro and sister died a few years back, Mrs. Cornelia Thomas my mother's sister in law, three cousin Mrs. Susan Philips, Willie Thomas, Cam. Thomas, all living in Miss, the three names underlined are living now at Jackson Miss. they are good witness too the older ones belonged to the same people, Ed, Yeger address of the 3 underlined is R 5, box 18 Jackson Miss. I hope this is the right imfamation if not I will be glad to ans. any question you may ask if I can, I know that I am not on record. This is a new case I am trying to prove any relation to the Shawnees Indians because my grant father was half Shawnee, and as I have good true witness to prove it I will be glad to get my claim in before the old people have passed away. So I may be able to derive some of the benefits what ever it may be. I will give you this address again Mrs. Maria Easdy c/o Taylor Jackson 1141 Armstrong St
   Kans. City Kans.
hopeing this will meet your approval
                    I am very truly
                    Mr. Q. V. Hallum
                       936 Rainer Ave
                       Seattle Wash
P.S. My brother W Henry Williams that died in 1907 have two children living also

---

DEPARTMENT OF THE INTERIOR

UNITED STATES INDIAN SERVICE

Kickapoo Indian Agency,
Horton, Kansas.
March 18th, 1920.

Supt. Ira C. Deaver,
Shawnee, Oklahoma.

Dear Mr. Deaver:

      It appears that the heirs to the Theresa Big Ear estate have been determined by the Department as funds have been transferred here for some of these heirs. Mrs. Lena Morris is entitled to an interest in this estate and I respectfully recommend that the funds to her credit held by you be transferred to this agency. Please make this special as she claims she is in need of money. Her Indian name is Ki-heg-a-ing-a.

                    Very truly yours,
                    A. R. Snyder
ARS/EL   Supt. & Spl. Disb. Agent.

****

Sac & Fox – Shawnee Estates
1920-1924 Volume VIII

Shawnee Indian Agency,
Shawnee, Oklahoma,
March 22, 1920.

Supt. A. R. Snyder,
   Kickapoo Indian Agency,
      Horton, Kansas.

Dear Mr. Snyder;

     Enclosed herewith is my official check No 3791 payable to the order of Mrs. Lena Kihegainga Morris for $99.32.

     This amount represents her share in the Theresa Big Ear Estate.

Very truly yours,

Ira C. Deaver
Superintendent.

G-encl

Shawnee Indian Agency,
Shawnee, Oklahoma,
April 14, 1920.

Mr. Herbert M. Peck,
   United States Attorney,
      Oklahoma City, Okla.

Dear Sir:

     I have your letter of the 5th inst., pertaining to the matter of Thomas C. Lincoln of Perkins, Okla., who makes complaint about the delay in the determination of the heirs of his purported deceased wife.

     The matter of holding hearings to take testimony of the determination of the heirs of deceased Indians is under the direction and supervision of Examiners of Inheritance who travel from one agency to another. Unfortunately the examiner for this jurisdiction resigned a few months ago and I do not believe any ne has been appointed to succeed him.

     I have looked into the matter of the case of Sophia Lincoln with whom Thomas Lincoln was living when she died. It appears that when he was married to Sophia Lincoln, he was not free to marry her, as he was the undivorced husband of another Indian woman who secured a divorce from him after the death of Sophia. It

Sac & Fox – Shawnee Estates
1920-1924 Volume VIII

look to me as though this would bar him from inheriting any of her estate. I am informed that someone attempted to have her estate probated in the County Courts of Payne County and that he was not found to be her legal husband. Of course, the Probate Court had no jurisdiction over a trust estate but it would have its weight before the Secretary of the Interior.

Of course, you are aware that the United States Court has no jurisdiction in determining the heirs of deceased Indian lands and that the Secretary of the Interior has sole jurisdiction over these matters.

Very respectfully,

Ira C. Deaver,
Superintendent.

Shawnee Indian Agency,
Shawnee, Okla., Aug. 6, 1920.

Dr. Jacob Breid,

Supt. Sac & Fox Sanitorium[sic]

Toledo, Iowa.

My dear Doctor:-

I have your letter of the 28th ult., making inquiry about the estate of John McKuck, purporting to be a Sac & Fox deceased allottee.

The records of this office do not show that any man by the name of John McKuck was ever allotted with the Sac & Fox Indians of Oklahoma. The Indian who gave you this information should be questioned further, and if possible, learn the name of the allottee that he claims to be related to and from whom he is supposed to inherit.

Yours truly,

ICD.
EVS.

Superintendent.

****

Dr. Jacob Breid
SUPERINTENDENT AND PHYSICIAN

DEPARTMENT OF THE INTERIOR

UNITED STATES INDIAN SERVICE

SAC & FOX SANATORIUM
TOLEDO, IOWA

July 28, 1920.

Sac & Fox – Shawnee Estates
1920-1924   Volume VIII

Supt. Ira C. Deaver,
    Shawnee, Oklahoma.

Dear Mr. Deaver:

I beg to advise that I have set August 26, 1920, as the date for the hearing, in the estate of Mose Witonesee or Ke-sah-asha, deceased, Sac and Fox of this reservation.

The deceased was an heir in the estate of John McKuck, Sac and Fox Oklahoma, allottee and I would appreciate it very much if you would have the allotment in which she is interested appraised and send me the necessary copies of the appraisement, to-gether with a reference to the office file, declaring her to be one of the heirs and a description of the land in which she was interested.

Very truly yours,
Jacob Breid
Superintendent.

RECEIVED
AUG 1 1920
INDIAN SCHOOL, OKLA.

****

DR. JACOB BREID
SUPERINTENDENT AND PHYSICIAN

DEPARTMENT OF THE INTERIOR

UNITED STATES INDIAN SERVICE
SAC & FOX SANATORIUM
TOLEDO, IOWA

August 13, 1920.

Supt. I. C. Deaver,
    Shawnee Indian Agency,
        Shawnee, Oklahoma.

Dear Mr. Deaver:

In reply to your letter of August 6, regarding the estate of John McKuk, I beg to advise that the records of this office show that John McKuk was an adopted Sac and Fox Indian and was allotted with the Sac and Fox of Oklahoma. The heirs to the estate are William Davenport, John Witonosee, [?]onachequa, [?]esusha, Mameche and [?]ewasamoqua and the rental from this allotment has been distributed to these heirs for several years.

Sac & Fox – Shawnee Estates
1920-1924 Volume VIII

Three of the heirs are now deceased and it was my desire, if the value of their interest in the allotment was more than $250., to hold a hearing at an early date, therefore, my request of July 28, requesting the information.

Trusting that this will enable you to locate the allotment referred to, I am

ery[sic] truly yours,

Jacob Breid
Superintendent.

RD: [?]

RECEIVED
AUG 13 1920
INDIAN SCHOOL, OKLA.

Supt Shawnee
Indian Agency

R. 3875

Detroit Mich
August 9 - 20

Dear sir
as I have changed my add. will notify you so if there is anything coming to me from the Trombla Estate you will know where to send it.

hoping to hear from you soon I am Respt yours

P.O. Leclair

Detroit Mich
1282 Mich Ave

****

Shawnee Indian Agency
Shawnee, Oklahoma,
August 16, 1920.

P. O. Laclair,
1282 Michigan Ave.,
Detroit, Michigan.

Dear Sir:

In reply to your letter of August 9th, in which you advise that you have changed your address and request that if there is any money from, the Trombla estate, you desire your share be forwarded to you.

You are advised that Ozetta Trombla allotment has not been leased through this office and we have collected no money for the heirs as rentals or trespass fees, therefore, can not send you any money.

Respectfully,

Sac & Fox – Shawnee Estates
1920-1924 Volume VIII

IRA C. DEAVER, JHJ/LM
Superintendent.

****

Shawnee Indian Agency,

Shawnee, Oklahoma, May 2, 1919

Mr. Oliver LeClair[sic],
    Care Hotel Central,
        Crestline, [Illegible].

Dear Sir:

    Receipt is acknowledged of your letter of February 14, regarding your present address and I take pleasure in forwarding herewith Treasury check No. 11215 in the sum of $6.87 drawn in your favor which represents lease rental due on the Ozette Trombly[sic], Est.

    Can you give me any information as to the address of Monroe LeClair. The enclosed self-addressed penalty envelope is for your reply.

Very respectfully,

RMM   Superintendent.
Encls.

****

SHAWNEE INDIAN SCHOOL
Shawnee, Oklahoma

Nov. 23, 1916.

Mr. Oliver LaClair,
    Glasgow, Mont. Bx 43.

Dear Sir:-

    There is inclosed herewith U. S. Treasurer check No. 6570 drawn in your favor for $6.87, which is rental derived from, the allotment of Ozetta Trombla, deceased, in which estate you are an heir. This money has just recently been paid into this office.

Sac & Fox – Shawnee Estates
1920-1924 Volume VIII

Very respectfully,

Superintendent.

PEP
Incl. Ck.

****

Shawnee Indian School,

Shawnee, Oklahoma, February 9, 1916.

Mr. Oliver LaClair,
Glasgow, Montana, Box 43.

Dear friend:

This will acknowledge receipt of your letter in which you state that you are one of the heirs of Rosette Trombla, and that if there is any lease money due you from the allotment of this deceased Indian you would like to have it.

I am inclosing, herewith, duly approved check for $6.87, drawn on The First National Bank, Tecumseh, Okla., bank account No. 1505. This check represents your share of the lease money received from this allotment. You should sign this check on the face where checked with a pencil mark, as <u>Oliver LaClair</u>, and endorse it in the same manner before presenting it to a bank for payment

Very respectfully,

JJ/cx
Incl.
8.

Clerk in Charge.

****

[The following letter typed as given]

Glasgow, Mont
Jan. 20 – 16

Mr. O. J. Green
Shawne Okla

Dear Sir

Sac & Fox – Shawnee Estates
1920-1924 Volume VIII

I am one of the heirs of Rozette Trombly and if there is any Lease money there due me Kindly forward same to me at Glasgow Mont and Oblige.

      Yours Respty

        P.O. Laclair
        Box 43
       Glasgow
        Mont

    ****

       Glasgow Mont
       Oct 4 – 13

Mr. J.A. Buntin

      Shawnee Okl

Sir

  have you sent that money of mine due me from the John Moses Laclair Estate to Cody Neb as I wrote you the 20" of last month or not if you have I cant get no word from it and if you haven't sent it yet send it direct to Glasgow Mont as I need it Imeadty to file and a price of land trusting I will hear from you right away   I am

      Resp
        P.O. Laclair
       Glasgow Mont

    ****

       Glascow[sic] Mont
       Sept 29 – 13

Mr. J. A. Buntin

      Sir I am in Mont at Present but will be in Cody Nebraska in a few days and would like for you to send what money is coming to me from the Laclair Estate in full and Oblige.

      Resp
        P.O. Laclair

    ****

Sac & Fox – Shawnee Estates
1920-1924 Volume VIII

Franklin Wash
August 31 – 13

Mr. J.A. Buntin

Sir

If there is any communication you wish to write me my Present address is
Franklin Washington
hoping to hear from you soon I am
Respt
P.O. Laclair

****

Vale Ore
Feb. 24 – 13

Mr. J. A. Buntin
Agent   Shawnee
Okla

Dear Sir

I understand that there is a little Rent money due me at your Office any corspondence[sic] of any kind will reach me at Vale Ore trusting I will [sic] from you soon I am Respt

P.O. La clair

****

Baker Oregon
May 19 – 13

Mr. J. A. Buntin
Shawnee Okla

Sir

I am Informed there is some Rent money due me and is in your care if so wish you would kindly forward same to me at Baker Oregon Box 347 and Oblige

P.O. La clair

****

DEPARTMENT OF THE INTERIOR

UNITED STATES INDIAN SERVICE

SHAWNEE INDIAN AGENCY,

Shawnee, Oklahoma.
April 23, 1912.

Sac & Fox – Shawnee Estates
1920-1924   Volume VIII

Mr. Oliver La Clair,
    La Grande, Union County, OREGON.

Dear Sir:

    The deed you executed to the allotment of John Moses La Clair, your deceased brother, has been found to be invalid in that the description was given wrong. A new deed will therefor be necessary. I wish you would execute this deed as soon as possible and return it here immediately. The present deed reads to the East half of the North-west Quarter whereas it should have been to the North-east Quarter. We regret the error in the matter but assure you the approval of the deed will not be delayed by reason of this fact as the various guardians for the minors must first be appointed and the new deed will be completed before the guardianship matters have been settled.

    Regretting the error,

        Very respectfully,

        J.A. Buntin
RS-1 inclos.   Superintendent.

****

DEPARTMENT OF THE INTERIOR
UNITED STATES INDIAN SERVICE

SHAWNEE INDIAN AGENCY,

    Shawnee, Oklahoma.
    February 7, 1911.

Postmaster,
    White Salmon, Washington.

Dear Sir:

    Some few days ago there was transmitted in your care a letter addressed by this office to Mr. Oliver LaClair, and I now wish to ask that you send this letter to his new address at Arlington, Oregon.

    Thanking you in advance,

        Very respectfully,

Sac & Fox – Shawnee Estates
1920-1924 Volume VIII

RS

Frank A Thackery
Superintendent.
RHS

Feb 11 – 1911

Sir:-

Have no such letter here and don't think their[sic] has ever been one here for that address

Perhaps you have our office mixed with that of White Swan, a post office near here on the reservation.

Resp   [Name Illegible]

****

Shawnee Indian School,
Shawnee, Oklahoma,

January 7, 1915.

Mr. P. O. LaClair,

Glasgow, Montana.

Dear Sir:-

Your letter of December 30th, 1914, with reference to lease money held to your credit at this office has been received. In reply you are advised that the records of this office fail to show that we have any funds of any kind for you. However, I should be glad to have you advise from what source this money you speak of is supposed to have been derived.

Very respectfully,

Superintendent.

FEP

****

Glasgow Mont
Dec 30th – 14

Mr Green
    Supt Indian School

Sir

I understand there is a little Rent Money Due me at your Office if so Please forward same to me at Glasgow Mont and Oblige

Respt yours
P.O. Laclair

Sac & Fox – Shawnee Estates
1920-1924 Volume VIII

****

Shawnee Indian Agency,
Shawnee, Oklahoma,
August 23, 1920.

Commissioner of Indian Affairs,
Washington, D. C.

Dear Mr. Commissioner:

Today a deed has been executed by Rachel Tyner Hood to Davis Tyner, her brother, covering her undivided 1/4 interest in the allotment of Ellen Tyner, deceased. Both the grantee and grantor are heirs in this estate, and the allotment is still under the supervision of the Government. The deed thus executed contains a usual restrictive clause. In accordance with the regulations governing the collection of fees for the work incident to selling and leasing allotted and tribal lands, sales of timber therefrom, etc., effective July 1, 1920, and with order No. 70, $20.00 has been collected from the grantee, Davis Tyner. This deposit has been taken with the understanding that the fees to be collected for such conveyances as this one, is not covered by the regulations and order No. 70, that it is to be returned to the grantee. It does not appear that the regulations promulgated, effective July 1, 1920, cover transactions by the Indian heirs of deceased Indian estates such as this one. Please advise me definetly[sic] on this point so that we may govern ourselves in future similar cases.

Very respectfully,

JHJ/LM

IRA C. DEAVER,
Superintendent.

****

REFER IN REPLY TO THE FOLLOWING:
Land-Sales
71958-20
F I P
Fees.

DEPARTMENT OF THE INTERIOR,
OFFICE OF INDIAN AFFAIRS,
WASHINGTON,
SEP 13 1920

ADDRESS ONLY THE
COMMISSIONER OF INDIAN AFFAIRS

Mr. Ira C. Deaver,

Supt., Shawnee School.

My dear Mr. Deaver:

In response to your inquiry of August 23, 1920, you are advised that Circular No. 1616 does not apply where one heir deeds his portion to another

Sac & Fox – Shawnee Estates
1920-1924 Volume VIII

heir, or where an estate is settled by one heir acquiring the undivided interests of the other heirs.

As a careful reading of the Circular discloses, the charges to be made are to compensate for the time, labor and incidental expenses of appraisement, advertisement, etc.

Very truly yours,
CF Hauke
Chief Clerk.

9 MHF 9

DEPARTMENT OF THE INTERIOR
UNITED STATES INDIAN SERVICE

Shawnee Indian Agency,
Shawnee, Okla., Oct. 2, 1920.

Mr. Walter L. Wilmeth,
Examiner of Inheritance,
Anadarko, Oklahoma.

Dear Mr. Wilmeth:

I have your letter of September 21, pertaining to your coming to this Agency in the near future requesting to be informed the number of cases that should be probated especially those among the Iowas and sac & foxes[sic].

I have to advise you that there are only about four Iowa cases and about 12 or 15 Sac & fox[sic]. There are about as many of the other tribes or about 30 or 40 cases.

There is a Farmer's Station at Cushing which would be nearer to the Iowas and the the[sic] north [illegible] of the Sac & Fox Indian Reserve. I am of the opinion it would be advisable to hold heraings[sic] at the Farmer's station at Cushing for the Iowas and for those Sac & Foxs[sic] who are in the north part of Lincoln County.

A list of the four deceased Iowa allottees follow:
Phoebe Whhitecloud-Black[sic], Iowa No. 81
Sophie Roubidoux-Embler-Lincoln, allotted as Kisn-tah-che-um Iowa No. 15
Mary Grant, Iowa N.[sic] 73
David Tohee, Iowa No. 8.

A complete list of the deceased Sac & Fox whose probate procedures should be held at Cushing will be forwarded you in a few days or as soon as I may consult with the District Farmer at Cushing.

Sac & Fox – Shawnee Estates
1920-1924 Volume VIII

If you desire we call these Iowa hearings before you come here, I will submit to you the names and addresses of the prospective heirs of each so that you may have notices prepared and submitted to this office for service.

> Very respectfully,
> Ira C. Deaver
> Superintendent.

> Shawnee Indian Agency,
> Shawnee, Okla., Oct. 20, 1920.

Mr. A.B. Collins,
District Farmer,
Cushing, Okla.

My dear Mr. Collins:
Enclosed herewith are notices of hearing on which you should report the date of service of these notices. I was of the impression that I had them in the folder I gave you at the Rock Island depot yesterday.

As I remarked to you then, you may send the notices of those interested parties who live at Red Rock, to Mr. Hoyo, Day School Inspector for the Otoes and Poncas, at White Eagle, Oklahoma, who will serve them for you, and when he reports to you, you can complete the blank forms on the bac.

> Yours truly,
>
> Ira C. Deaver,
> Superintendent.

ICD.
EVS.

DEPARTMENT OF THE INTERIOR

UNITED STATES INDIAN SERVICE

> Potawatomi Agency,
> Mayetta, Kansas.
> October 22, 1920.

RECEIVED
OCT 23 1920
SAC AND FOX INDIAN SCHOOL, OKLA.

Ira C. Deaver,
Supt. Indian Agency,
Shawnee, Oklahoma.

Sac & Fox – Shawnee Estates
1920-1924 Volume VIII

Dear Mr. Deaver:

I am in receipt of your letter of October 20, 1920 enclosing findings in the cases of Pah-nah-koh-tho and Wah-que-tah-no-quah, and thank you for the same. I have made copies of these findings, and am returning the originals to you herewith.

Very truly yours,

S.Y. Tutwiler
Examiner of Inheritance.

SYT:EP
enls.

How is everything at Shawnee? Had hoped to be there before long, but guess I'll not get to go there, as I see Wilmeth is there now.

SYT

Shawnee Indian Agency,
Shawnee, Okla., Oct. 25, 1920.

Mr. A.B. Collins,
District Farmer,
Cushing, Okla.

My dear Mr. Collins:

Enclosed herewith are notices of hearing to be held at the Farmer's Station in Cushing, for the purpose of determining the heirs of Edward Matthews and of Emily Johnson, both deceased Sac & Fox allottees.

Please post the notices marked "To whom it may concern", in four different places, and especially one at your station. Please deliver one notice each to the parties interested, and make affidavit on the back of one each, showing that they were delivered.

In the case of Edward Matthews, you will notice that Ann Matthews has been appointed guardian ad litum to represent Annie Matthews, minor. Deliver this paper, with the notice of hearing, to Mrs. Matthews. You may retain the copy showing your delivery and deliver it to Examiner Wilmeth when he arrives.

Yours truly,

Ira C. Deaver,
Superintendent.

ICD.
EVS.
Enclosure.

Sac & Fox – Shawnee Estates
1920-1924   Volume VIII

Shawnee Indian Agency,
Shawnee, Oct. 25, 1920.

Mr. S. Y. Tutwiler,
Examiner of Inheritance,
Mayetta, Kansas.

My dear Mr. Tutwiler:
    I am in receipt of your letter of October 22, returning therewith the findings in the case of Pah nah kah tho and Wah que tah no quah.

I learn from Mr. Snake that the finding of Pah nah kah tho is not the same person as Pah nah koh tho the Kansas allottee. It appears that said Pah nah koh tho had an interest in the estate under this jurisdiction and that Mr. E. A. Upton held a hearing February 6, 1919, to determine the heirs to his estate under this jurisdiction. This hearing is still pending in Washington.

I am enclosing herewith the folder pertaining to this matter for your information and convenience and as soon as it has served your purpose, please return it.

    Yours truly,

    Ira C. Deaver,
    Superintendent.

ICD.
EVS.
Enclosure.

****

DEPARTMENT OF THE INTERIOR

UNITED STATES INDIAN SERVICE

Potawatomi Agency,
Mayetta, Kansas,
October 13, 1920.

RECEIVED
OCT 15 1920
INDIAN SCHOOL, OKLA.

Mr. Ira C. Deaver,
Supt. Indian Agency,
Shawnee, Oklahoma.

Dear Sir:

Sac & Fox – Shawnee Estates
1920-1924 Volume VIII

I am enclosing herewith seven notices of a hearing to be held November 9, 1920 to determine the heirs of Pah-nah-kah-tho, deceased Kickapoo Allottee No. 223. Nah-nim-mik-skuk and Pen-a-tho are here, and I will serve notices on them, and I would appreciate it if you would have a copy served on each of the other persons whose names appear on the notices, and make proof of service to me.

If these persons are unable to attend the hearing, I would be glad to have you take their affidavits showing their relation to the decedent and submit same to me, in duplicate. Please post the extra notice at your office.

                    Very truly yours,

                    S.Y. Tutwiler
                    Examiner of Inheritance.

SYT:EP
encls.

                    This hearing was held here at
                    Shawnee Indian Agcy, Shawnee, Okla
                    by A.E. Upton, Examiner of Inheritance
                                  1919

                    ****

DEPARTMENT OF THE INTERIOR

UNITED STATES INDIAN SERVICE

                    Potawatomi Agency,
                    Mayetta, Kansas,
                    October 20, 1920.

Supt. Ira C. Deaver,   **RECEIVED**
Shawnee Indian Agency,   OCT 22 1920
Shawnee, Oklahoma.   INDIAN SCHOOL, OKLA.

Dear Sir:

A letter has been received from the Indian Office stating that a hearing was held at Shawnee to determine the heirs of Pah-nah-kah-tho, deceased Kickapoo Allottee No. 223 of Kansas, but as the allotment is located here, it will be necessary to hold a hearing at this place. If you have copies of the report and testimony in this matter, I would appreciate it if you would send them to me, and they will be returned to you as soon as I have made use of them.

Sac & Fox – Shawnee Estates
1920-1924 Volume VIII

Very truly yours,

S.Y. Tutwiler
Examiner of Inheritance.

SYT:EP

(Edition of January, 1916.)

****

NOTICE OF HEARING TO DETERMINE HEIRS

DEPARTMENT OF THE INTERIOR

UNITED STATES INDIAN SERVICE.

Kickapoo and Potawatomi Agency,
Mayetta, Kansas, Oct. 6, 1920.

Nah-nim-mik-skuk
Pen-a-tho (Mary Pen-a-tho)
Wah-thah-que
Pah-nah-ke (John Modoc)
Quah-tah-kah-me-sheck
Wah-tho-quah (Wah-thah-ko-ko-quah)
Wah-pah-ko-the-quah

Notice is hereby given that on the 9th day of November, 1920 . 191 , Agency Office, at Horton, Kansas at 9 A.M. , I will take testimony to be submitted to the Secretary of the Interior for the purpose of determining the heirs of Pah-nah-kah-tho, , Kickapoo No. 223 deceased.

All persons having an interest in the estate of the decedent are hereby notified to be present at the hearing and furnish such evidence as they desire. bringing two disinterested witnesses.

Respectfully,

S. Y. Tutwiler
Examiner of Inheritance.

****

Sac & Fox – Shawnee Estates
1920-1924 Volume VIII

PROOF OF SERVICE OF NOTICE OF HEARING IN HEIRSHIP CASES.

I, the undersigned, do certify that I personally delivered a notice of which the within is a true copy, announcing a hearing to determine the heirs of _____
deceased, _____, to be held _____
_____, on the _____ day of _____, 191 ,
to the persons and on the dates hereinafter mentioned, viz:

_____   _____, 191

_____   _____, 191

_____   _____, 191

_____   _____, 191

_____   _____, 191

                                            Name_____

                                            Title_____

Shawnee Indian Agency,
Shawnee, Oklahoma, Oct. 28, 1920

Mr. A.B. Collins,
District Farmer,
Cushing, Oklahoma.

My dear Mr. Collins:

    Enclosed herewith are five sets of notices to be posted for the determination of the heirs of Viola May Crane, Oliver Jackson, Isaac Struble, Samuel Brown and Inos Bass.

    Please post these notices and deliver notices to the persons addressed on each notice. You should complete one of the notices of each set, on the back, showing the date of delivery and return them to this office.

    Yours truly,

    Ira C. Deaver,
ICD.   Superintendent.
EVS.
Enclosure.

Sac & Fox – Shawnee Estates
1920-1924 Volume VIII

Shawnee Indian Agency,
Shawnee, Okla., Oct. 28, 1920.

Mr. Warner L. Wilmeth
Examiner of Inheritance,
Kiowa Agency,
Anadarko, Okla.

My dear Mr. Wilmeth:

Returned herewith is a copy of notice of hearing to be delivered to Thomas K. Oliver, which you request me to serve.

Mr. Oliver lives under the jurisdiction of the Kickapoo and Pottawatomie Agency at Horton, Kansas. I am having the five notices posted under this jurisdiction.

Yours truly,

Ira C. Deaver,
Superintendent.

ICD.
EVS.
Enclosure.

REFER IN REPLY TO THE FOLLOWING:
Probate
14098-19
W H G

RE: Estate Joe Snake
or Snake Man, Shawnee,
Oklahoma.

ADDRESS ONLY THE
COMMISSIONER OF INDIAN AFFAIRS

DEPARTMENT OF THE INTERIOR,
OFFICE OF INDIAN AFFAIRS,
WASHINGTON,
NOV 12 1920

RECEIVED
NOV 13 1920
INDIAN SCHOOL, OKLA.

Mr. Ira C. Deaver,
Supt., Shawnee, Okla.

My dear Mr. Deaver:-

Attention is again invited to Office letter of May 24, 1920 requesting you to furnish a certificate of appraisement in the above named case.

Sac & Fox – Shawnee Estates
1920-1924 Volume VIII

The decedent possessed no allotment of his own, but inherited a 2/33 interest in the estate of Snake Man, deceased allottee No. 386.

Prompt action is requested in this case.

Yours very truly,

EB Meritt
Assistant Commissioner.

11-MH-10

REFER IN REPLY TO THE FOLLOWING:
Probate
16506-19
W H G

Estate of Ah-nah-tho-the, Shawnee, Oklahoma.

DEPARTMENT OF THE INTERIOR,
OFFICE OF INDIAN AFFAIRS,
WASHINGTON,

ADDRESS ONLY THE
COMMISSIONER OF INDIAN AFFAIRS

NOV 12 1920

RECEIVED
NOV 15 1920
INDIAN SCHOOL, OKLA.

Mr. Ira C. Deaver,
Supt., Shawnee, Okla.

My dear Mr. Deaver:-

Referring to the papers in the matter of the heirship to the estate of Ah-nah-tho-the, deceased unallotted Indian who inherited a one-fifteenth interest in the estate of Ah-che-ma-que, deceased Shawnee allottee No. 19-land covering the NW/4 SE/4 and Lot 2. of the SE/4, Section 8, T. 12 N., R. 1 E. I. M., Okla. containing 77.75 acres, you were asked to submit a certificate of appraisement showing the value of said estate for use in the case of Ah-nah-tho-the, deceased.

Your early attention to this matter is urged.

Yours very truly,

EB Meritt
Assistant Commissioner.

11-MH-10

****

Sac & Fox – Shawnee Estates
1920-1924 Volume VIII

CERTIFICATE OF APPRAISEMENT.

Allottee   Ah che ma que   No 19   Agency   Shawnee

I hereby certify that on the 19th day of November, 19 20, I personally visited and made a careful inspection of the following described lands: NW/4 of SE/4, and Lot 2-Sec. 8-Twp. 12S- Rg. 1 E. of I.M. in Oklahoma County, Oklahoma being the allotment of Ah che ma que

That I find the character of the land to be as follows: All bottom, some heavy and some quite sandy. Nearly all is cultivation minerals not considered.

and that it is best adapted for corn, cotton, alfalfa, wheat, etc

That in my best judgment the value of the land is as follows:

Land - - - - - - -	$6,000.00
Improvements - - - - - -	
Total - - -	$ 6,000.00

Chas W Edmister
Farmer   ~~Superintendent.~~

Note: -- The appraisement should be made to correspond with the legal divisions for which bids will be received. The appraisement should be made by the Superintendent, but in cases where it is not possible for him to personally appraise the land, he should appoint an appraiser and fill out the following blank:

I hereby certify that _____ was appointed by me to appraise the land above described; that he is well acquainted with the value of lands in the vicinity of the tract above described, and fully competent to make such appraisement, and that I verily believe the above appraisement is the true value of the land and improvements thereon.

Dated _____ day of _____ 191 .

Superintendent.

Sac & Fox – Shawnee Estates
1920-1924 Volume VIII

REFER IN REPLY TO THE FOLLOWING:
Probate
16500-19
W H G

Estate of Zora Doud
or Beaubien, Shawnee,
Oklahoma.

ADDRESS ONLY THE
COMMISSIONER OF INDIAN AFFAIRS

DEPARTMENT OF THE INTERIOR,
OFFICE OF INDIAN AFFAIRS,
WASHINGTON,

NOV 12 1920

RECEIVED
NOV 18 1920
INDIAN SCHOOL, OKLA.

Mr. Ira C. Deaver,
Supt., Shawnee, Okla.

My dear Mr. Deaver:-

    Referring again to the estate of Zora Doud or Beaubien, deceased, and to Office letter of May 22, 1920, you are again requested to send in the appraisement certificate in this case without delay.

Yours very truly,

11-MH-10

EB Meritt
Assistant Commissioner.

DEPARTMENT OF THE INTERIOR
UNITED STATES INDIAN SERVICE

Kickapoo & Potawatomi Agency
Horton, Kansas
November 17, 1920.

RECEIVED
NOV 22 1920
PAWNEE AGENCY
PAWNEE, OKLAHOMA

Supt. J. C. Hart,
Pawnee Indian Agency,
Pawnee, Oklahoma.

Dear Sir:

I am in receipt of carbon copy of your letter addressed to Mrs. Dora E. Hudson, c.o. Otoe Indian Agency, Red Rock, Oklahoma, with reference to the interest of Minnie May English, at the Kickapoo reservation.

Sac & Fox – Shawnee Estates
1920-1924 Volume VIII

I note you say that you have gotten no information from the Kickapoo Agency but I do not recall having had a letter from you in connection with this case, as I am familiar with the matter and would have so advised you of its status.

Sometime last March, I forwarded to the Office, papers and my report in a hearing to determine the heirs of Katie Roubidoux, dec., but there has not yet been a finding.

You are advised that this child is undoubtably[sic] the sole heir of her mother's interests on the Kickapoo reservation as her husband, Reuben English was legally divorced from her quite a while before her death. The child's mother left a one-tenth interest in an allotment here, valued at $20,000 and $859.42 in money.

As stated above, Minnie May English will be the sole heir of her mother's estate but the funds cannot be used until the Department has rendered its findings.

Very truly yours,
A.R. Snyder A.W.
Superintendent.
ARS:AW

c.c. to Shawnee Agency,
Shawnee, Okla.

****

DEPARTMENT OF THE INTERIOR
UNITED STATES INDIAN SERVICE

Pawnee Indian Agency,
Pawnee, Oklahoma.

November 11th, 1920.

Mrs. Dora E. Hudson,
c.o Otoe Indian Agency,
Red Rock, Oklahoma.

Dear Madam:

  Your inquiry at this Office pertaining to the interest of Minnie May English have so far been unsatisfactorily determined. In a letter to the Kickapoo Agency reveals no interest for her there, and my letter to the Shawnee Agency shows that $11.01 was transferred to this Agency and deposited to the credit of Kate Roubedeaux English, deceased, but we have been unable to find certainty that Minnie May English is the heir of this party.

Sac & Fox – Shawnee Estates
1920-1924 Volume VIII

I am sending a carbon copy of this letter to the Kickapoo Agency and one to the Shawnee Agency with a request that I be advised if either of these Agencies had the record of the heir of Kate Roubedeaux English, deceased, and if so advise me who the heirs are.

Very respectfully,
JC Hart
Superintendent.

C.C./ to Kickapoo Agency,
C.C./ to Shawnee Agency,
WAS:BW

Probate 140-19   ;Probate 16500-19   ;Probate 8912-19   ;Probate 16506 19.
W H G   W H G   W H G   W H G

Shawnee Indian Agency,
Shawnee, Okla., Nov. 24, 1920.

The Commissioner of Indian Affairs,
Washington, D.C.

Sir:

Reference is made to Office letters of November 20, calling my attention to the fact that the Office had heretofore notified me to have certificates of appraisement completed and submitted to the Office covering the estate of

- Snakeman, deceased Shawnee allottee No. 586,
- Ah-che-ma-que, deceased Kickapoo allottee #19,
- Nora Doud, nee Beaubien, deceased Pottawatomie allottee
- Little Doctor, deceased Shawnee allottee No. 422; and
- Martha Little Doctor, deceased Shawnee allottee #423;

In accordance with these instructions, the farmer has visited and appraised these estates and the certificate of appraisement are enclosed herewith.

Very respectfully,

Ira C. Deaver,
Superintendent.

ICD.
EVS.
Enclosure.

Sac & Fox – Shawnee Estates
1920-1924 Volume VIII

Shawnee Indian Agency,
Shawnee, Okla., Nov. 24, 1920.

Mr. S. Y. Tutwiler,
Examiner of Inheritance,
Concho, Okla.

My dear Mr. Tutwiler:

    I have your letter of November 22, returning therewith the papers forwarded to you for your information.

You state that it will probably be necessary, under the circumstances, to have further testimony from Wah-pah-mah-pe-quah to establish the fact that she is the widow of Ec-ah-tah-be-ah. This old lady lives in Mexico but is here on a visit, and I believe she is still here. I will endeavor to learn whether she has remained in the States, and if so, will advise you at the earliest possible date.

In the event she is still here, we would be glad to have you come over and take such testimony as you may desire; and if you will inform me when you can be here, will arrange to have the Indians in interest meet you here at the office.

    Yours truly,

    Ira C. Deaver,
    Superintendent.

ICD.
EVS.

   ****

DEPARTMENT OF THE INTERIOR

RECEIVED
NOV 23 1920
INDIAN SCHOOL, OKLA.

UNITED STATES INDIAN SERVICE

Cheyenne & Arapaho Agency
Concho, Okla., Nov. 22, 1920.

Mr. Ira C. Deaver, Supt.,
Shawnee Indian Agency,
Shawnee, Okla.

Dear Mr. Deaver:

    I received your letters of Nov., 8th and 9th, 1920, enclosing testimony taken by you in the case of Ke-ah-tah-be-ah, Kickapoo Allottee No. 237 of Kansas, also papers in the cases of Ma-nah-the-qua-ah, No. 161, Ah-che-ma-que, No. 19, Sho-wah-kah, No. 29, and thank you for the same.

Sac & Fox – Shawnee Estates
1920-1924 Volume VIII

I am returning herewith the papers relative to findings in the three cases referred to above.

As there is a question about the right of Wah-pah-nah-pe-qua to inherit as the lawful widow of Ke-ah-tah-be-ah. I think it would be well to take additional testimony from her as well as from others at Shawnee, and as I am now located here near Shawnee, it is believed it would be better for me to go to Shawnee and take this testimony. If it is satisfactory with you I could let you know what day to have these people at the office and I could go to Shawnee and take their testimony. There are also some other cases pertaining to the Potawatomi Agency, Kansas, that I would like to see about at the same time.

With best wished for yourself and the others at Shawnee, I am,

Very truly yours,

S.Y. Tutwiler
Examiner of Inheritance.

Shawnee Indian Agency,
Shawnee, Okla., Dec. 3, 1920.

Mrs. Ada Petitt,
Red Rock, Okla.

My dear Madame:
I have your letter pertaining to the notice of hearing called as Cushing to determine the heirs of some estate which you have not designated.

As to this estate being given to other persons, I have no knowledge; and, in fact, I know the Examiner of Inheritance has not yet reported to the Office any of the cases which he has recently held.

Yours truly,

Ira C. Deaver,
Superintendent.

ICD.
EVS.

****

Sac & Fox – Shawnee Estates
1920-1924 Volume VIII

[The letter below typed as given]

RECEIVED
NOV 22 1920
INDIAN SCHOOL, OKLA.

Red Rock Okla
Nov. 18, 1920.

Dear Sir:-

The notice you send me reach me, but I was very sick and I could not be resent although I want to go down there and hear about it

I heard that the alotment was giving to different party if it is I would like to know about it. It is like this there were four brothers and the third one is our father and one of these is Soplia's father, and we have one grandfather but our mothers are different. So I think we are closer than any of them look this over please, and write me right away and I will be down there this is, I will talk to you better when I get there.

Respectfully,

Ada Pettit

Shawnee Indian Agency,
Shawnee, Oklahoma,
December 18, 1920.

Mr. A. R. Snyder,
Supt. Potawatomi Indian Agency,
Mayetta, Kansas.

My dear Mr. Snyder:

In reference to your letter of December 13, regarding the interest of Frank Keesis, Potawatomi, in the estate of I-osh-suck, a Sac & Fox Indian; we have made a thorough search of our records in this matter, and fail to find anything in regard to this estate.

I would suggest that more detailed information be sent us, and we will make further efforts to locate the status of this estate, if there be such a one.

Yours truly,

Sac & Fox – Shawnee Estates
1920-1924 Volume VIII

Ira C. Deaver,
Superintendent.

EVS.

****

DEPARTMENT OF THE INTERIOR

UNITED STATES INDIAN SERVICE

Potawatomi Indian Agency
Mayetta, Kansas
December 13, 1920.

RECEIVED
DEC 15 1920
INDIAN SCHOOL, OKLA.

Supt. Ira C. Deaver,
Shawnee Indian Agency,
Shawnee, Oklahoma.

Dear Mr. Deaver:

Frank Keesis, a Potawatomi, believes that he has an inherited interest in Sac & Fox estate, I-osh-suck. He also tells me that a hearing will probably be held or has been set and that he would like to have a copy of the notice so that he may present his evidence supporting his claim at the proper time. Please hand this to the examiner if he is there now so that he can look it over.

Very truly yours,
A.R. Snyder
Superintendent
ARS:AW

Shawnee Indian Agency,
Shawnee, Oklahoma,
December 28, 1920.

Mr. A.R. Snyder,
Supt. Pottawatomi Indian Agency,
Mayetta, Kansas.

My dear Mr. Snyder:

Sac & Fox – Shawnee Estates
1920-1924 Volume VIII

Reference is made to your letter of November 16, by which I was advised that certain moneys belonging to the heirs of Me-nah-quah were recently transmitted to this office to be deposited to the credit of the heirs of Mi-e-nah-qua.

At this time, Ah-kis-kuck and Joseph Murdock two of the heirs of Mi-e-nah-qua do not have funds sufficient to reimburse these accounts. Joseph Murdock informs me that he had information from the Indian Office that the sale of the allotment of Mi-e-nah-qua was approved November 29, and that your office had been advised of the fact on December 1. If this is a fact you probably could deduct the $30.48 recently paid to each one. If you cannot do this consistently, when the money is transferred to this office, we will have Murdock and Ah-kis-kuck indorse checks for these amounts, and transmit same to you to re-deposit to the credit of the heirs of Mi-e-nah-qua. Mr. Murdock was in my office this morning, and is quite anxious to receive the money due him from the sale of the allotment of Mi-e-nah-qua.

Ah-kis-kuck and Pequa two heirs in this estate reside in old Mexico. During the latter part of next month, I will probably go to the border to deliver lease checks to the Kickapoo Indians residing in old Mexico, and after this money is transferred to this jurisdiction, all, or a portion of it, may be taken to them.

Yours truly,

Ira C. Deaver,
Superintendent.

ICD.
EVS.

****

DEPARTMENT OF THE INTERIOR

UNITED STATES INDIAN SERVICE

Shawnee Indian Agency,
Shawnee, Oklahoma,
Dec 3, 1920.

Mr. A. R. Snyder, Supt.,
   Potawatomi Indian Agency,
      Mayetta, Kansas.

Dear Mr. Snyder:

Enclosed herewith are the following listed checks to reimburse the heirs of Me-nah-quah, also lease checks for Indian[sic] under your jurisdiction:

| No 6155 | $51.48 | Ma-ka-the-quak |
| 6156 | 30.48 | Pequa |

Sac & Fox – Shawnee Estates
1920-1924 Volume VIII

6157	30.48	Roy Kickapoo
6173	11.50	Dan Whitecloud
6172	18.75	Susan Whitecloud
6174	5.62	Sarah Whitecloud
6175	22.39	Louise Whitecloud
5394	5.62	Sarah Whitecloud

There are no funds at the present time to the credit of Ah-kish-kuk and Joseph Murdock.

Very truly yours,

Ira C. Deaver
Superintendent.

MPG-encls

****

DEPARTMENT OF THE INTERIOR

UNITED STATES INDIAN SERVICE

Potawatomi Indian Agency
Mayetta, Kansas
November 16, 1920.

Supt. Ira C. Deaver,
Shawnee, Oklahoma.

Dear Mr. Deaver:

It has been found that the heirs of Mi-e-nah-quah were, through error, sent money belonging to the heirs of Me-nah-quah and if any of the following have funds to their credit, I would thank you to transfer same to this agency to reimburse the rightful heirs. The names of these Indians are:

Ah-kish-kuck   no funds
Pe-quah
Joseph Murdock   no funds
Meck ke the quah and
Roy Kickapoo, $30.48 in each case.

Very truly yours,
A.R. Snyder
Superintendent,
ARS:AW

Sac & Fox – Shawnee Estates
1920-1924 Volume VIII

DEPARTMENT OF THE INTERIOR

UNITED STATES INDIAN SERVICE

Shawnee Indian Agency
Shawnee, Oklahoma
Jan. 13, 1921

Mr. A. B. Collins
U. S. Farmer
Cushing, Oklahoma

Dear Mr. Collins:

The inclosed carbon copies of letters to Dr. Breid, Supt. Sac & Fox Sanatorium, Toledo, Iowa, are self explanatory as to the appraisement certificates he desires.

Phis-tau-na-ha, who is now dead, has a 2/9 interest in the allotment of Andrew Barker, deceased. It will be necessary then for you to appraise the allotment of Andrew Barker.

Ke-sha-sah, Mo na-che-qua, and Ke-wa-so-no-qua, each have 1/12 interest in the allotment of John McKuk, deceased. It will be necessary for you then to appraise the allotment of John McKuk. SW 32-12-6

Thomas Chuck, who is now dead, has a 1/7 interest in the allotment of Jim Scott, deceased. Appraise the allotment of Jim Scott, deceased.

Arthur Brown has a 1/3 interest in the estate of Pa-phis-na; Pa-phis-na has a 3/10 interest in the allotment of Henry Cora Sha-que-quot, deceased. Then Arthur Brown has 1/10 interest in this allotment through Pa-phis-na, deceased. It will then be necessary for you [sic] appraise the allotment of Henry Cora Sha-que-quot.

When you complete the appraisements submit the certificates of appraisement of each allotment involved to this office so that we may furnish them to Dr. Breid.

                              Very truly yours,
                              Ira C Deaver
                              Ira C. Deaver

CC to Dr. Breid   Superintendent
JJ

****

Sac & Fox – Shawnee Estates
1920-1924 Volume VIII

Shawnee Indian Agency
Shawnee, Oklahoma
January 13, 1921

Dr. Jacob Breid
Supt. Sac & Fox Sanatorium
Toledo, Iowa

Dear Dr. Breid:

Your letter of Dec. 28, 1920 is at hand wherein you request certificates of appraisement of the share of Ke sha sah, Mo na che qua and Ke wa so no qua in the estate of John McKuk, deceased; Thomas Chuck in the estate of Jim Scott, deceased; and Arthur Brown who is an heir in the estate of Pa pa nine (Pa-phia-na), deceased, who has a 3/10 interest in the estate of ~~Henry~~ Cora Sha que quot.

The Farmer, Mr. Collins is being requested to appraisement[sic] the estates involved and execute certificates of appraisement and when completed, we will forward them to you.

Phis-tau-na-ha, has 2/9 interest in the estate of Andrew Barker. Ke-sha-sah, Mo-na-che-qua and Ke-wa-so-no-qua each have 1/12 interest in the estate of John McKuk estate. Thomas Chuck has 1/7 interest in Jim Scott estate. Arthur Brown has a 1/3 interest in the estate of Pa-phia-na, who has a 3/10 interest in the ~~Henry~~ Cora Sha-que-quot estate, which makes Arthur brown have 1/10 interest in the estate of ~~Henry~~ Cora Sha-que-quot.

Very truly yours

cc to Collins:
JJ

Ira C. Deaver
Superintendent

****

Sac & Fox – Shawnee Estates
1920-1924   Volume VIII

Shawnee Indian Agency
Shawnee, Oklahoma
Jan. 13, 1921

Dr. Jacob Breid
Supt. Sac & Fox Sanatorium
Toledo, Iowa

Dear Dr. Breid:

In compliance with your request of the 28th of Dec. last, I herewith inclose herewith my official check No. 6472 for $40.59, drawn on account of Phistaunaha, acct. P-99, who is dead and is one of the heirs in the Andrew Barker estate under this jurisdiction.

This Indian had 2/9ths[sic] interest in the estate of Andrew Barker, deceased. I have taken up the matter of having the allotment of Andrew Barker appraised. When the appraisement certificates have been executed by the Farmer, Mr. Collins, I shall forward them to you.

Very truly yours

Ira C. Deaver
Superintendent

CC to Collins

JJ

****

DEPARTMENT OF THE INTERIOR

UNITED STATES INDIAN SERVICE

Shawnee Indian Agency
Shawnee, Oklahoma
Jan. 13, 1921

Mr. A. B. Collins
U. S. Farmer
Cushing, Oklahoma

Dear Mr. Collins:

The inclosed carbon copies of letters to Dr. Breid, Supt. Sac & Fox Sanatorium, Toledo, Iowa, are self explanatory as to the appraisement certificates he desires.

Sac & Fox – Shawnee Estates
1920-1924 Volume VIII

Phis-tau-na-ha, who is now dead, has a 2/9 interest in the allotment of Andrew Barker, deceased. It will be necessary then for you to appraise the allotment of Andrew Barker.

Ke-sha-sah, Mo na-che-qua, and Ke-wa-so-no-qua, each have 1/12 interest in the allotment of John McKuk, deceased. It will be necessary for you then to appraise the allotment of John McKuk. SW 32-12-6

Thomas Chuck, who is now dead, has a 1/7 interest in the allotment of Jim Scott, deceased. Appraise the allotment of Jim Scott, deceased.

Arthur Brown has a 1/3 interest in the estate of Pa-phis-na; Pa-phis-na has a 3/10 interest in the allotment of ~~Henry~~ Cora Sha-que-quot, deceased. Then Arthur Brown has 1/10 interest in this allotment through Pa-phis-na, deceased. It will then be necessary for you [sic] appraise the allotment of ~~Henry~~ Cora Sha-que-quot.

When you complete the appraisements submit the certificates of appraisement of each allotment involved to this office so that we may furnish them to Dr. Breid.

                                  Very truly yours,
                                  Ira C Deaver
                                  Ira C. Deaver
CC to Dr. Breid   Superintendent
JJ

****

Shawnee Indian Agency

                                  Shawnee, Oklahoma
                                  Jan. 13, 1921

Dr. Jacob Breid
Supt. Sac & Fox Sanatorium
Toledo, Iowa

Dear Dr. Breid:

      In compliance with your request of the 28th of Dec. last, I herewith inclose herewith my official check No. 6472 for $40.59, drawn on account of Phistaunaha, acct. P-99, who is dead and is one of the heirs in the Andrew Barker estate under this jurisdiction.

      This Indian had 2/9ths[sic] interest in the estate of Andrew Barker, deceased. I have taken up the matter of having the allotment of Andrew Barker appraised. When

Sac & Fox – Shawnee Estates
1920-1924 Volume VIII

the appraisement certificates have been executed by the Farmer, Mr. Collins, I shall forward them to you.

Very truly yours

Ira C. Deaver
Superintendent

CC to Collins

JJ

****

Dr. Jacob Breid
Superintendent and Physician

Department of the Interior

UNITED STATES INDIAN SERVICE
Sac & Fox Sanatorium
TOLEDO, IOWA

December 28, 1920.

Supt. Ira C. Deaver,

Shawnee, Oklahoma.

Dear Mr. Deaver:

We are holding several reports on heirship, pending receipts of certificates of appraisement from your jurisdiction. Among these are the estates of Ke-sha-sah, Mo-no-che-qua and Ke-wa-so-no-qua, heirs to the John McKuk estate, Thomas Chuck, an heir in the Jim Scott estate, deceased, and Arthur Brown, and Pa-pa-hine one of the heirs in the estate of Sas-que-quot.

I would appreciate it very much if you would have these interests appraised and certificate forwarded to me at the earliest practicable moment so that I can forward my reports to the Indian Office.

Very truly,
Jacob Breid
Superintendent.

RL:MC

RECEIVED
JAN 3 1921
SHAWNEE INDIAN AGENCY
SHAWNEE, OKLA.

****

Sac & Fox – Shawnee Estates
1920-1924 Volume VIII

CERTIFICATE OF APPRAISEMENT.

Allottee   Susie Scott.   No. 357   Agency Shawnee Okla.

I hereby certify that on the   28   day of   Jan, 1921   , 191
I personally visited and made a careful inspection of the following described lands: North 1/2 of the South West 1/4 of Sec. 18, Township 17.N Range 6 E.I.M. in Payne Co Oklahoma.   being the allotment of Susie Scott, Deceased

That I find the character of the land to be as follows:

  Dark Sandy loam 35 acres in Cultivation. 40 acres bottom bal. is taken up by Creeks and draws.

and that it is best adapted for   Corn Cotton and Alfalfa.

That in my best judgment the value of the land is as follows:

    Land $3500.00

    Improvements... 0000.00

                  Total.......................... $3500.00

                                Arza B. Collins
                                U.S. Farmer.   Superintendent.

Note: --The appraisement should be made to correspond with the legal divisions for which bids will be received. The appraisement should be made by the Superintendent, but in cases where it is not possible for him to personally appraise the land, he should appoint an appraiser and fill out the following blank:

I hereby certify that   Arza B. Collins.   was appointed by me to appraise the land above described; that he is well acquainted with the value of lands in the vicinity of the tract above described, and fully competent to make such appraisement, and that I verily believe the above appraisement is the true value of the land and improvements thereon.

Dated   day of   191 .

                                            Superintendent.

****

Sac & Fox – Shawnee Estates
1920-1924 Volume VIII

CERTIFICATE OF APPRAISEMENT.

Allottee Andrew Barker   No 42   Agency Shawnee Okla.

I hereby certify that on the 18 day of Jan 1921 ~~191~~
I personally visited and made a careful inspection of the following described lands:
W 1/2 of N.E. 1/4 & E. 1/2 of N.W. 1/4 of Sec 25 Twp. 14 E Range 6 E.I.M. in Oklahoma. being the allotment of Andrew Barker, Deceased
That I find the character of the land to be as follows:
Rough Sandy Land partially covered with Timber. 40 acres in cultivation.

and that it is best adapted for Corn Cotton and Gorage[sic] Crops.

That in my best judgment the value of the land is as follows:

Land $4000.00

Improvements....................................... 0000.00

Total........................... $4000.00

Arza B. Collins
U.S. Farmer. ~~Superintendent.~~

Note: --The appraisement should be made to correspond with the legal divisions for which bids will be received. The appraisement should be made by the Superintendent, but in cases where it is not possible for him to personally appraise the land, he should appoint an appraiser and fill out the following blank:

I hereby certify that _____ was appointed by me to appraise the land above described; that he is well acquainted with the value of lands in the vicinity of the tract above described, and fully competent to make such appraisement, and that I verily believe the above appraisement is the true value of the land and improvements thereon.

Dated _____ day of _____ 191 .

Superintendent.

****

Sac & Fox – Shawnee Estates
1920-1924 Volume VIII

CERTIFICATE OF APPRAISEMENT.

Allottee Cora Sha-que-quot.   No 334   Agency Shawnee Okla.

I hereby certify that on the   17   day of   Jan, 1921   ~~191~~

I personally visited and made a careful inspection of the following described lands:

North West 1/4 of Sec. 17 Township 16, N Range 6 E.I.M. in Oklahoma.

being the allotment of   Cora Sha-que-quot.

That I find the character of the land to be as follows: Rooling prarie[sic]

Land. Dark sandy loam. 30 acres in Cultivation.

and that it is best adapted for   Grazing and Small Grain.

That in my best judgment the value of the land is as follows:

Land $4000.00

Improvements... 500.00

Total........................ $4500.00

Arza B. Collins
U.S. Farmer.   ~~Superintendent.~~

Note: --The appraisement should be made to correspond with the legal divisions for which bids will be received. The appraisement should be made by the Superintendent, but in cases where it is not possible for him to personally appraise the land, he should appoint an appraiser and fill out the following blank:

I hereby certify that   Arza B. Collins   was appointed by me to appraise the land above described; that he is well acquainted with the value of lands in the vicinity of the tract above described, and fully competent to make such appraisement, and that I verily believe the above appraisement is the true value of the land and improvements thereon.

Dated   day of   191 .

Superintendent.

****

Sac & Fox – Shawnee Estates
1920-1924   Volume VIII

Shawnee Indian Agency
Shawnee, Oklahoma
January 13, 1921

Dr. Jacob Breid
Supt. Sac & Fox Sanatorium
Toledo, Iowa

Dear Dr. Breid:

Your letter of Dec. 28, 1920 is at hand wherein you request certificates of appraisement of the share of Ke sha sah, Mo na che qua and Ke wa so no qua in the estate of John McKuk, deceased; Thomas Chuck in the estate of Jim Scott, deceased; and Arthur Brown who is an heir in the estate of Pa pa nine (Pa-phia-na), deceased, who has a 3/10 interest in the estate of ~~Henry~~ Cora Sha que quot.

The Farmer, Mr. Collins is being requested to appraisement[sic] the estates involved and execute certificates of appraisement and when completed, we will forward them to you.

Phis-tau-na-ha, has 2/9 interest in the estate of Andrew Barker. Ke-sha-sah, Mo-na-che-qua and Ke-wa-so-no-qua each have 1/12 interest in the estate of John McKuk estate. Thomas Chuck has 1/7 interest in Jim Scott estate. Arthur Brown has a 1/3 interest in the estate of Pa-phia-na, who has a 3/10 interest in the ~~Henry~~ Cora Sha-que-quot estate, which makes Arthur Brown have 1/10 interest in the estate of ~~Henry~~ Cora Sha-que-quot.

Very truly yours

cc to Collins:
JJ

Ira C. Deaver
Superintendent

****

Sac & Fox – Shawnee Estates
1920-1924 Volume VIII

Dr. Jacob Breid
Superintendent and Physician

Department of the Interior

United States Indian Service

Sac & Fox Sanatorium
Toledo, Iowa

December 28, 1920.

Supt. Ira C. Deaver,

Shawnee, Oklahoma.

Dear Mr. Deaver:

I beg to advise that Phia-tau-na-na, one of the heirs to the estate of Andrew Barker, died to-day and I am requesting that any funds you have on deposit to the credit of this woman, or which are received in the future, be transferred to me as I will need part of them to settle her funeral expenses.

I would also be very glad if you would have her interests in this estate appraised and forward certificate to me at the earliest possible date, so that i may have same to submit with my report on heirship cases.

Very truly,

Jacob Breid
Superintendent.

RL:MC

RECEIVED JAN 3 1921 SHAWNEE INDIAN AGENCY SHAWNEE, OKLA.

****

Shawnee Indian Agency
Shawnee, Oklahoma

Feb. 1, 1921

Dr. Jacob Breid, Supt.
Sac & Fox Sanatorium
Toledo, Iowa

Dear Dr. Breid:

In accordance with your request for appraisement certificates covering certain allotments in which some of the Indians under your jurisdiction were interested and who are now dead, I am sending herewith to you the certificates:

Sac & Fox – Shawnee Estates
1920-1924 Volume VIII

One covering the allotment of Cora Sha que quot, in which Arthur Brown is interested through Pa phia na, 1/3 of 3/10 or 1/10.

One covering the allotment of Andrew Barker, in which Phia tus na ha has a 2/9 interest.

One covering the allotment of Susie Scott in which Thomas Chuck is interested through Jim Scott.

and[sic] another one covering the allotment od[sic] John McKuk in which Ke sha sah, Mo na che qua and Ke wa so no qua, each have a 1/12 interest.

Very truly yours

Ira C. Deaver
Superintendent

Incls.
JJ

[The letter below typed as given]

RECEIVED
MAR [?] 1921
SHAWNEE INDIAN AGENCY
SHAWNEE, OKLA.

Mayetta Kansas
March 4 1921

Dear Sir:-
It has been very long time since I've been wanting to trace an air land by the name of Mah-see-was wife of John Cadue that the nearest I can spell it.
That is my grandma name.
Please let me know if she had any land their by that name. I wanted Mr Snyder to look that matter up but he said he is to busy it has been about two years I have been after him to trace it for me.
Please do that much for me and I will be very much please.

Yours Respt
Mary Delg.

Please Answer soon

Mah the was 1181
N^2 SW-29-7-5 80 ⎰sold 3-27-1901
N^2 SE-30-7-5 80 ⎱ "   5-14-1902
216

45

Sac & Fox – Shawnee Estates
1920-1924 Volume VIII

Mah cha wa 986
W1/2 of NW 30-6-5- Cancelled and
Homestead patent issued

****

Shawnee Indian Agency,
Shawnee, Oklahoma,
March 19, 1921.

Mary Delg.
Mayetta, Kansas.

Dear Madam:

In reply to your letter of March 4, in which you inquire about some heirship land in the name of, as you give it, Mah-see-was, who was the wife of John Cadue, you are advised that the nearest the name you give we have on our allotment schedule of the Citizen Pottawatomie Indians, is allottee No. 1181, which appears on the schedule as Mah-the-was, who was allotted the N/2 of the SW/4, Section 29, Township 7, Range 5, East, 80 acres, which the record shows was sold on March 27, 1901. This allottee also received as an allotment, the N/2 of the SE/4, Section 40, Township 7, Range 5, East, 80 acres. This was sold and approved May 14, 1902.

We have another allottee whose name was Mah-cha-was, No. 986, the W/2 of the NW/4, Section 30, Township 6, Range 5, East, was tentatively allotted to this Indian, but the record shows that this allotment was cancelled and a homestead patent issued thereon. I trust that this is the information that you desire.

Very truly yours,

JHJ/LM

IRA C. DEAVER,
Superintendent.

Shawnee Indian Agency,
Shawnee, Okla., April 20, 1921.

Mr. A. R. Snyder,
Supt. Pottawatomi Indian Agency,
Mayetta, Kansas.

Dear Mr. Snyder:-

Sac & Fox – Shawnee Estates
1920-1924 Volume VIII

Philip Lee and Frank Smith who claims[sic] to be heirs to the estate of who they call Qua to a deceased Pottawatomi allottee, requests me to write you about the status of the sale they claim has been made on this allotment.

I do not like to bother you with this matter, but you are familliar[sic] with the Indian and knew that if he thinks there is a dollar coming to him, he begins asking about it long before it becomes available for distribution.

       Very respectfully,

       IRA C. DEAVER
       Superintendent.

       Shawnee Indian Agency,
       Shawnee, Oklahoma,
       August 3, 1921.

Mr. Peter W. Lightfoot,
Ft. Thomson, So. Dakota.

Dear Sir:

This is to acknowledge the receipt of your letter of July 16th requesting information relative to two Indian estates.

I have to advise you that Sac and Fox Agency is no longer a separate agency, and that Mr. Johnson has been transferred to Espinola[sic], New Mexico. Sac and Fox Agency was combined with Shawnee Agency with offices at Shawnee, Oklahoma, during the summer of 1919.

The Indians mentioned by Mr. Cooper to you are not allottees. Their names do not appear in any of our records. Since Mr. Cooper is an allottee of the Prairie Band of the Potawatomi of Kansas I suggest that you make this inquiry at Potawatomi Indian Agency, Mayetta, Kansas, A.R. Snyder, Supt.

       Very truly yours,

8 od[sic] 3.   Supt & Spec. Disb. A.

    ****

Sac & Fox – Shawnee Estates
1920-1924 Volume VIII

Peter W. Lightfoot,
Lease Clerk
Fort Thompson, S. Dak.

RECEIVED
JUL 28 1921
SHAWNEE INDIAN AGENCY
SHAWNEE, OKLA.

Fort Thompson, South Dakota.

July 16, 1921.

Mr. Horace J. Johnson,
Supt. Sac & Fox Agency,
Stroud, Okla.

Dear Mr. Johnson:

   Joseph Cooper, a Pattawatamie[sic] Indian enrolled on the Pattawatamie reservation, at Horton, Kansas, but married to Ellen How, of this reservation, requested that I write you relative to two estates that he claims to be heir to on your reservation, namely, No-de-no qua and Koh-ze-qua, both now deceased.

   Mr. Cooper states that these allottees were aunts of his mother, who was known as Ah-she-nek, or Angeline Ah-cha-co-geesh. He further states that he has been advise that two persons who were related to his mother as follows: John Batiste, first cousins, and Ke-se-nah, nephew, both having the same aunt.

   Mr. Cooper further states that he had a sister, now dead, who has a surviving husband and several children who he believes should also be heirs to these estates.

   From the meager information given above, you may be able to give Mr. Cooper some information as to the present status of these estates which will be greatly appreciated by him. You may address him at Grosse, South Dakota, or in my care as it is very likely that he will come to me for an explanation of your letter even if you was to write to him direct.

   From this you will see that I am still holding down the fort at Fort Thompson, South Dakota. I am the only one, with the exception of Mr. O'Shea, of the old force that is still here. I lost Mrs. Lightfoot, last November, and the work of caring for the children is very hard in spite of the fact that Cynthia is now very near a grown woman, and doing all that she can to take her mother's place.

   With kind personal regards to yourself and Mrs. Johnson, and all others of your immediate family that I knew here who may still be with you, I am,

        Very respectfully,
        Peter W. Lightfoot

Sac & Fox – Shawnee Estates
1920-1924   Volume VIII

Shawnee Indian Agency
Shawnee, Oklahoma
October 26, 1921

Mr. Leonard Coon
Emporia, Kansas
Con. Dol.

My dear sir:

It has been reported to me that you are a brother of Benjamin F. Coon of Hand, Oklahoma R.F.D. #2, and that you have an interest in an allotment of Indian land at the Shawnee Indian Agency, Shawnee, Oklahoma. It is desired that some disposition of this allotment be made at an early date, and I would be pleased to have you either write to your brother at the address given above or to myself at Shawnee, stating what your desires are, in this matter

Very respectfully

J. L. Suffecool
Superintendent

JLS/JC

****

Shawnee Indian Agency
Shawnee, Oklahoma
October 24, 1921

Post Master
Emporia, Kansas

My dear sir:

Will you please inform me if there is a man by the name of who receives mail from your office? The last knowledge we had of his where-abouts was, that he was in Emporia, Kansas. This information is desired in order that property, in which he is an heir and which is under the jurisdiction of the United States, can be disposed of.

An immediate reply is requested.

Very respectfully

J. L. Suffecool
Superintendent

JLS/JC

Sac & Fox – Shawnee Estates
1920-1924 Volume VIII

Shawnee Indian Agency,
Shawnee, Oklahoma,
October 26, 1921.

Mr. Walter L. Luthye,
R. # 8,
N. Topeka, Kansas.

Dear Mr. Luthye:

This is to acknowledge the receipt of your letter of the 17th instant in regard to your inherited interests.

There is enclosed by official check No. 2103 for the sum of $64.58 which was transferred from the account of your brother Fred Luthye. There are also enclosed application blanks which you should fill out, acknowledge, and return to this office.

Very truly yours,

10 cd 36

J.L. Suffecool,
Superintendent.

Shawnee Indian Agency,
Shawnee, Oklahoma,
Oct. 27, 1921.

Mrs. Sarah F. Starr,
1501 S. 1st St.,
Terre Haute, Indiana.

Dear Madam:

I have your letter dated Oct. only concerning inherited interests you claim to have here.

In connection with this matter you are advised that although there has been some prospecting but to date there has not been any great discovery of oil.

Sac & Fox – Shawnee Estates
1920-1924 Volume VIII

The Hon. Cato Sells is not the Commissioner of the Indian Affairs now. A change has been made and the present Commissioner is Chas H. Burke. However, a letter addressed The Hon. Commissioner of Indian Affairs, Washington, D. C. will answer your purpose.

You did not give sufficient information in your letter as to who your grandmother was, and for that reason we are unable to furnish you the information you desire. Let us hear from you in this matter further.

       Very truly yours,

10 cd 27.   J. L. Suffecool
        Superintendent

     Shawnee Indian Agency
      Shawnee, Oklahoma
      October 27, 1921

Stanard & Ennis
Attorneys at Law
Shawnee, Oklahoma

Gentlemen:

Some time ago your Mr. Ennis was in this office, concerning the estate of Catherine Griffenstein, deceased, and filed a brief for consideration of the Department.

We agreed to send the brief to Washington, if you would submit sworn affidavit from the physician who attended upon Mr. Griffenstein, and what these physicians knew about the care of her by her daughter in law, Mrs. Emma Griffenstein. We are still holding the paper in this office, pending the receipt of the affidavit, which we requested to be filed in order that we may include such affidavit with our report to Washington.

       Very respectfully

       J. L. Suffecool
JJ/JC   Superintendent

Shawnee Indian Agency,
Shawnee, Oklahoma, Oct. 28. 1921.

Mrs. Marie Anderson,
Sapulpa, Okla. R#1 Box 129.

Dear Mrs. Anderson:

Referring to your letter of the 1st instant, written to Thompson Alford, Lease Clerk, relative to the allotment of Mrs. Chas. Lewis, deceased. I have to advise you that this land is not leased for the year 1922. This has been referred to Chas. F. Edmister, U. S. Indian Farmer under this Agency.

Relative to the patent in fee. I have to advise you that it was sent to the Indian Office January 27, 1921 and was faborably[sic] recommended by Mr. Ira C. Deaver, Supt., then, but it was found necessary to write the Superintendent for some additional information. This was referred to the Field Clerk at Tulsa and in his report he recommended that patent in fee be not issued to the heirs.

Very respectfully,

J. L. Suffecool,
Superintendent

TBS

DEPARTMENT OF THE INTERIOR

UNITED STATES INDIAN SERVICE

Shawnee Indian Agency
Shawnee, Oklahoma
November 2, 1921

NOTICE

Joe Kaseca
Norman, Oklahoma
Route #7

Sac & Fox – Shawnee Estates
1920-1924 Volume VIII

George Kaseca
Norman, Oklahoma
Route #7

Angeline Williams
Ft. Cobb, Oklahoma
c/o Peter Williams

The department of the Interior determined the heirs originally April 28, 1914 subsequent to this date, particularly on Oct. 7, 1916, re-opening of the case was had in which further testimony was taken. On October 8, 1920, the Department of the Interior made a finding in this case and modification determed[sic] Angeline Williams to be a daughter and one of the heirs to the estate of Kaseca, but through error, the Department determined said heirs to Kaseca under the laws of Arkansas, whereby the findings should have been in accordance with the laws of the Territory of Oklahoma. It will be, then necessary to modify the findings and bring such findings of the heirs under the proper laws and to re-open the case. To do this, it is necessary to notify all the parties in interest of such action; that it is proposed to amend the modified findings to conform to the laws of Oklahoma, as herein above set out.

Thirty days from the receipt of this notice is hereby given to each party in interest within which to show cause, if any there be, why the said proposed amendment should not be made.

J. L. Suffecool
Superintendent

JJ/JC

Land-Sales

124446-13
12342-21

Shawnee Indian Agency,
Shawnee, Oklahoma
Nov. 2, 1921.

The Honorable
Commissioner of Indian Affairs,
Washington, D. C.

Dear Mr. Commissioner:

Sac & Fox – Shawnee Estates
1920-1924 Volume VIII

Reference is made to Office letter bearing above caption in regard to the issuance of patents in fee to trust lands in which the allotment of Joe Vetter, Iowa allottee No. 16 is particularly considered.

The Office is respectfully requested to consider the following resume of the entire matter contained in Office correspondence bearing captions as follows, with recent actions taken in the matter:-The heirs of Joe Vetter were determined in Law-Heirship 60508-14 FE. According to the declaration Nesojame Vetters[sic] inherited 1/3 interest. The heirs first requested for a patent in fee which was denied them, Land-Sales 26874 MAP, due to the fact that one of the heirs could neither read nor write English. It appears that Nesojame Vetter willed her 1/3 interest in the estate to Clarence Z. Spurlock and Lizzie Spurlock, husband and wife, and the Department approved the will November 27, 1918. Both of the Spurlocks are white persons; Land-Sales 54200-20 attempted to convey their 1/3 interest to R.A. Brooks. In Land-Sales 124446-13, 8149-21 MAP Hon. J. W. Harrold M.C. requests report at non-issuance of patent in fee, and report thereto in full was made. Finally in Land-Sales 124446-13, 12342-21 NR the Superintendent was directed to ask Mr. R.A. Brooks to give a quit-claim deed to the United States in trust for the heirs of Joe Vetter. There is on file with the records of this case in this office such a deed properly executed with the exception that it is signed by Mr. R.A. Brooks alone, dated June 21, 1921.

In connection with this matter Mr. R.A. Brooks appears to be desirous that a full investigation be made. He appears willing to comply with every reasonable requirement of this office in the matter. He has offered to pay the other heirs equal to 2/3 of the appraised value of the allotment if the Office will consent to the settlement. The heirs have expressed their willingness to accept this offer by signing form 5-110c, acceptance of sale and affidavit of vendor.

Annie Perry Tohee for whose protection the heirs were denied the patent in fee is an old lady. She is an heir the whole of David Tohee's allotment, 1/3 of Townsend allotment No. 64, and 1/3 of the allotment in question. Her share in this allotment if sold would be disbursed under supervision.`

It seems to appear that the Office may take advantage of one of two propositions in the settlement of this matter. First, according to plan outlined in Office Land-Sales 124446-13, and 12343-21, by removing the cloud that has apparently been made by the sale to Mr. R.A. Brooks of the Spurlock interests by accepting the quit-claim deed signed by both himself and wife. Second, by authorizing special sale, waiving regulations governing land-sales, and accepting the offer made by Mr. Brooks to the other heirs and accepted by them.

After a full consideration of the matter by the Office I respectfully request that I be given such instruction as it deems proper in view of the foregoing mentioned conditions.

Sac & Fox – Shawnee Estates
1920-1924 Volume VIII

Very respectfully,

J. L. Suffecool,
Supt. & S.D.A.

Shawnee Indian Agency,
Shawnee, Oklahoma,
November 2, 1921.

Commissioner of Indian Affairs
Washington D.C.

Dear Mr. Commissioner:

Benjamin West who died about 1904 has a little balance of $31.63, account number 9-79. The amount has been on the books for several years. Harry or Aaron Wilson has come to the office and claims to be one of the heirs in this estate.

It appears that the deceased has no other property under the jurisdiction of this office only the funds to his credit. We have prepared for the heirs an affidavit which George Pecan and Jim Warrior have signed, and the affidavit is enclosed herewith to be used in connection with authorizing me to pay to the heirs of Benjamin West, the amount herein shown.

Very truly yours

J. L. Suffecool
Superintendent

JJ/JC

Probate
6355-1919
  L L

Shawnee Indian Agency
Shawnee, Oklahoma
November 3, 1921

Commissioner of Indian Affairs
Washington D.C.

Sac & Fox – Shawnee Estates
1920-1924 Volume VIII

Dear Mr. Commissioner:

Transmitted herewith is a Brief filed by Stanard & Ennis, attorneys of Shawnee, Oklahoma, concerning the claim of Emma Griffenstein against the estate of Catherine Griffenstein, deceased, together with the affidavit of Emma Griffenstein supporting her claim of $1,450.00, for the care of the said Catherine Griffinstein[sic] during the last years of her life time. There are also enclosed herewith affidavits of Anna Weiss, Lena Mason, Dr. Thor Jager, Helen Mason, Mrs. Catherine Riggs, Mrs. Dorothy Jocelyn and Mrs. Osie Thuma, in support of the claim.

Emma Griffenstein is the divorced wife of Chas. J. Griffinstein, who has a 1/3 interest in the Catherine Griffinstein estate.

No information is on file in this case; that Emma Griffinstein presented her claim against this estate at the time of the hearing.

Catherine Griffinstein, deceased Citizen Pottawatomie, allottee number 246, was allotted the N/2 of Section 22, Township 9, Range 2E, I. M., Oklahoma, containing 320 acres under the act of February 8, 1887 (24 Stats. L., 388). Patent in fee for the SE/4 of the NE/4 and the NE/4 of the NE/4 and 282.78 acres on the East side of SW/4 of the NE/4 of the above 1/2 section, was issued November 3, 1910 (54330-10). The SW/4 of the NW/4 of the original allotment was sold and deed approved August 28, 1907 (70946-1907). The heirs to this estate were determined by the Department August 5, 1919. The claim of Emma Griffenstein against this estate was not presented, it appears, either at the hearing or with the Department, hence no mention of such a claim is made in the Department's findings.

The attorneys, Stanard & Ennis presented this matter to this office and it was promised that the Brief and Affidavits filed with this office in the case would be presented to the Office for such consideration as it may deem necessary in view of the record in the case, hence this letter and enclosures.

                                Very respectfully

                                J. L. Suffecool
                                Superintendent

JJ/JC

Sac & Fox – Shawnee Estates
1920-1924 Volume VIII

Shawnee Indian Agency
Shawnee, Oklahoma
November 3, 1921

Benjamin F. Coon
Maud, Oklahoma
R.F.D. #2

My dear Sir:

When you were in the office recently, you requested this office to find out where your brother, Leonard Coon was located. In complying with your request, we wrote to the Post Master, Emporia, Kansas and we have a reply at the bottom of our letter from the Post Master, Harrison Parkman, stating that Leonard Coon is working at Art's Café, 422 Commercial St., Emporia, Kansas.

Our letter and his answer at the bottom is enclosed herewith for your information.

Very truly yours

J. L. Suffecool
Superintendent

JJ/JC

Shawnee Indian Agency
Shawnee, Oklahoma
November 3, 1921

Pete Pahmahmie
c/o Mashno
Mayetta, Kansas

Dear Sir:

Replying to your letter of November 27, wherein you state that you should be the only heir to the estate of Ke-tum-wah, you are advised that the report on this estate, as stated before, has been made to the Indian Office in Washington by the Examiner of Inheritance, and if the report made, includes people who should not be heirs in the estate and you were left out in the evidence adduced at the hearing, it will be necessary for you to file

Sac & Fox – Shawnee Estates
1920-1924 Volume VIII

with this office, affidavits, concretely setting forth what relationship to the deceased you claim to be and why you believe yourself to be an heir.

Upon receipt of such affidavits as you may desire to submit, we will forward them to the Indian Office for such consideration as may be necessary to obtain a re-hearing in the case.

Very truly yours

J. L. Suffecool
Superintendent

JJ/JC

Prob. 6355-1919
    L L

Shawnee Indian Agency
Shawnee, Oklahoma
November 5, 1921

Commissioner of Indian Affairs
Washington D.C.

Dear Mr. Commissioner:

On November 3, to transmitted a Brief from Stanard & Ennis, attorneys of Shawnee, Oklahoma, together with certain affidavits in connection with the claim of Emma Griffenstein in the sum of $1450., against the estate of Catherine Griffenstein.

Since, Stanard & Ennis have filed the affidavit of Mrs. Gertrude Tankersley, which is transmitted herewith to be filed with the other papers, which were forwarded as stated above.

J. L. Suffecool
Superintendent

JJ/JC

Shawnee Indian Agency,
Shawnee, Oklahoma,
Nov. 9, 1921.

Mr. Osmond Franklin,
Avery, Oklahoma.

Sac & Fox – Shawnee Estates
1920-1924 Volume VIII

Dear Sir:

This is in reply to your letter of the 7th instant about Christian Mohee's allotment.

You are informed that this allotment was sold in the year of 1905 while your tribe was still under the Sac & Fox Agency, Stroud, Okla., and the papers concerning the sale may still be there.

No record of your heirship to the Mohee estate other than Charley Mohee can be found here.

When you come to this office talk this matter with me so that we may be able to get all your reasons for the way you think.

Very truly yours

J. L. Suffecool
11 od 9. Supt. & S.D.A.

Land-Sales
79080-21
8-905-21
J T H

Shawnee Indian Agency,
Shawnee, Oklahoma.
Nov. 10, 1921.

Messrs. Youngblood & Deister,

Tecumseh, Oklahoma.

Gentlemen:

Reference is made to your request to the Indian Office, Washington, for a copy of trust patent covering the allotment of Lilly Forman, Shawnee allottee No. 322 and copy of finding of the Business Committee.

You are informed that a copy of the Office reply bearing caption as above is at hand. In conformity therewith there is enclosed the Certificate of Business Committee requested for by you.

You are further informed that there is a Departmental finding, viz. Law-Heirship 7935[?]-15 F E, in which the following are recognized as heirs with their proportionate shares, as follows:

Sallie Tyner - - - 1/4

Sac & Fox – Shawnee Estates
1920-1924 Volume VIII

Webster Alford - - 1/4

Sco-nay-se - - - - 1/4

A copy of the above mentioned finding will be mailed you if you so desire.

Very truly yours,

11 od 10.   J. L. Suffecool
                                                         Supt. & S.D.A

Shawnee Indian Agency
Shawnee, Oklahoma
November 10, 1921

Mr. Peter Deichman
U. S. Probate Attorney
Tulsa, Oklahoma

Dear Mr. Deichman:

Replying to your letter of November 7, in connection with the estate of Alex Gibson, deceased, whose grandson, Willie Gibson, you state is in need of assistance, you are advised that the report of the Examiner of Inheritance was submitted to Washington February 24, 1919, covering the hearings held to determine the heirs to the estate of Willie Gibson.

Willie Gibson was an heir in the estate of Alex Gibson. Upon his death, Mary Gibson, widow of Willie Gibson and Willie Gibson, the son were heirs to Willie Gibson's share of Alex Gibson, deceased. However, no formal determination of the estate has been made by the Department as yet.

Very truly yours

J. L. Suffecool
Superintendent

JJ/JC

Sac & Fox – Shawnee Estates
1920-1924   Volume VIII

Shawnee Indian Agency
Shawnee, Oklahoma
November 10, 1921

Cicison[sic] National Bank
Emporia, Kansas

Gentlemen:

With reference to your letter of November 4, concerning the interest of Leonard Coon of your city, in an Indian allotment under this jurisdiction, you are advised that he is the som of Margaret Bedell according to the records of this office. He has been declared by the Secretary of the Interior to be one of the heirs to this estate. Benjamin Coon, his brother and W. R. Bedell, step brother are the other heirs to this Indian allotment.

The land they fall heir to is described as the E/2 of the NE/4 and the W/2 of the NW/4 of Section 24, Township 8 N, Range 4.

Benjamin Coon and W R. Bedell attempted to deed this land away and placed mortgages on the land and otherwise badly involved it.

It was necessary then for the Indian Department to bring suit in the U. S. Court for the Western district of Oklahoma, to quiet[sic] title. The title to this land has been cleared by the Court order.

It is not known to this office just how competent Leonard Coon is, however, from the reports we have received it would appear that his is not very bright. No reason is known to this office why the disposition of this land should be hastened, until after a thorough investigation has been made as to the competency of the heirs. Benjamin Coon, brother of Leonard Coon is not satisfied as to Leonard Coon being his brother, however, the matter will be handled under the jurisdiction of the United States, through this office.

Very truly yours

J. L. Suffecool
Superintendent

JJ/JC

Shawnee Indian Agency
Shawnee, Oklahoma,
Nov. 12, 1921.

Mr. John McKinney,
Rosedale, Okla.

Sac & Fox – Shawnee Estates
1920-1924 Volume VIII

Dear Sir:

Replying to your letter of the 30th of Oct., concerning certain affidavit you were requested to sign, as follows:-

You are advised that the matter in connection with the affidavit you were requested to sign was in charge of the Examiner of Inheritance. Therefore, this office does not know the nature of the paper.

You are further advised that you may be able to to[sic] procure such information as you desire from the Examiner of Inheritance, S.Y. Tutwiler, Kiowa Agency, Anadarko, Okla.

Very trul[sic] yours,

11 od 12

J. L. Suffecool
Supt. & S.D.A.

Shawnee Indian Agency
Shawnee, Oklahoma
November 15, 1921

Commissioner of Indian Affairs
Washington D.C.

Dear Mr. Commissioner:

Thomas C. Miles of Shawnee, Oklahoma Route #2, a Sac & Fox Indian of this jurisdiction, desires to take a Civil Service examination to enter the Indian Service.

It is presumed, that he being an Indian, a non-competitive examination could be given him. He attended school at Carlisle Indian School, Carlisle, Pa. He is married and has two children, I believe. He worked in the Ship Yards in Philadelphia, Pa. for two or three years but later he was laid off along with others. He states that several thousand work men were laid off from this Ship Yards[sic]. He is a carpenter by trade and the work he would like to do in the Indian Service, would be along the line of a general mechanic. It is presumed that an examination covering his qualifications of this character can be given him.

Very truly yours

J. L. Suffecool
Superintendent

JJ/JC

Sac & Fox – Shawnee Estates
1920-1924 Volume VIII

215008-1

In re: L-C
102057-20
LL

Shawnee Indian Agency
Shawnee, Oklahoma
November 15, 1921

The Honorable
The Commissioner of Indian Affairs
Washington D.C.

My dear Mr. Commissioner:

I have the honor to [illegible] reference, which is the caption of a letter under date of March 26, 1921 addressed to the Honorable Secretary of the Interior the Interior by the Assistant Attorney General, relative to the delinquency of Daniel L. Poole, under the terms of lease number 3882, covering Sac & Fox allotment number 52, to Josephine Brown, deceased.

In this letter it has been noted that the U. S. Attorney for the western district of Oklahoma, has been instructed to investigate the matter and to help appropriate action. It would appear that no action whatever, has been taken in this matter, and it is earnestly requested that the necessary steps be taken to see that this matter is immediately adjusted. The heirs of the deceased Allottee are constantly making inquiry at this office with reference to this delinquent [illegible].

Very respectfully,

J. L. Suffecool
Superintendent

JLS/JC

Shawnee Indian Agency
Shawnee, Oklahoma
November 15, 1921

Miss Anna Kahdot
Mayetta, Kansas
c/o Fred Croch

Dear Madam:

Replying to your letter about the rentals from the allotment of Ho no ko kat, in which you have a 1/4 interest, you are advised that, as stated before, Mary Rhodd, the other heir in the estate, I understand has been using this

Sac & Fox – Shawnee Estates
1920-1924 Volume VIII

allotment but that she was unable to raise the money with which to pay the rent. Her failure to complete the lease has also been caused by her inability to secure proper bondsmen on her lease. I am taking this matter up with the Farmer, Mr. Edmister, in this district to see what can be done about collecting money from Mary Rhodd.

You are hereby assured that if it is possible at all to get the money from this allotment, we will get it and send you your share. Hereafter, this allotment will be leased regularly through this office and lease completed in order that we may have some basis from which proper collection of rentals can be made.

Very truly yours

J. L. Suffecool
Superintendent

JJ/JC

C.C. to Mr. Edmister.

Shawnee Indian Agency
Shawnee, Oklahoma,
Nov. 16, 1921.

Lincoln County Abstract Co.,
Chandler, Oklahoma.

Gentlemen:

Complying with your request over the telephone the other day for a certified copy of the declaration of heirship by the Department of the Interior to the estate of Mollie Guthrie, Sac & Fox allottee No. 299, it is herewith transmitted.

You are advised that there is no charge for this portioning instance but that similar service in the future will be charged and a bill submitted.

Very truly yours,

11 od 16

J. S[sic]. Suffecool,
Supt. & S.D.A.

Sac & Fox – Shawnee Estates
1920-1924 Volume VIII

Shawnee Indian Agency
Shawnee, Oklahoma
November 17, 1921

Mr. Chas. W. Edmister
U. S. Indian Farmer
Shawnee, Oklahoma

Dear Mr. Edmister:

The enclosed carbon copy of my letter to Josephine Zugg, nee Dimbler, who is an heir in the Elizabeth Dimbler allotment is self explanatory.

I wish, that at your earliest opportunity, you would investigate the allotment of Elizabeth Dimbler and ascertain who is using the land and attempt to collect reasonable trespass fees.

I am advised that this land has never been regularly leased through this office but that we have been able to collect trespass fees each year until now. There has been no trespass fees collected for the past season.

It is very much desired that you look after this matter as soon as you can, for the heirs appear to be non-residents and are asking for the rents.

Very truly yours

J. L. Suffecool
Superintendent

JJ/JC

Shawnee Indian Agency
Shawnee, Oklahoma
November 17, 1921

Mr. Wm. G. Foster
Cushing, Oklahoma
Route #4

Dear Sir:

This refers to your letter of November 9, in which you made several inquiries.

Sac & Fox – Shawnee Estates
1920-1924 Volume VIII

In connection with your son, Roy Foster wanting to purchase furniture belonging to the estate of Theresa Smith, you are advised that Edward Rice has purchased and paid for this furniture before any action was taken on your son's request.

The Isaac Struble estate you refer to has been settled, and if the heirs want to find out the exact amount of money they have on the books, they should go to the Farmer to ascertain for themselves, or from this office direct. We do not care to give such information to other than themselves, and it is against the Department regulations to do so.

With regard to the Matilda Givens matter, I have to advise that she should take the matter of the purchase of chickens and the building of a chicken house, up with the Farmer, Mr. Collins, and he will see about these matters for her.

Very truly yours

J. L. Suffecool
Superintendent

JJ/JC

Shawnee Indian Agency
Shawnee, Oklahoma
November 17, 1921

Pah-nah-ketho
c/o W. A. Bonnet
Co. Judge Maverick Co.,
Eagle Pace, Texas

My friend:

This office has your letter of November 14, asking for money to be sent to you.

In this connection, you are advised that the lessee on your allotment has not paid the rentals. This is the reason that you did not get any money from John E. Snake, who was down there with the money for the Kickapoos.

The money belonging to your late husband, Ah kis kuk can not be paid to any one until a hearing has been held and his heirs determined legally by the Secretary of the Interior.

Sac & Fox – Shawnee Estates
1920-1924 Volume VIII

                                    Very truly yours

                                    J. L. Suffecool
                                    Superintendent

JJ/JC

                    Shawnee Indian Agency
                    Shawnee, Oklahoma
                    Nov. 19, 1921.

Mr. A. B. Collins,

Cushing, Oklahoma

Dear Mr. Collins:

      There is enclosed herewith a list of names of Indians left here by one Harris, I think, and request-[sic] that dates of death of three of them as checked on the lisft[sic] be found and shown. The Indians are Sarah Turner Harris, and her heirs, and the dates are shown in figurse[sic] on the list.

      It is requested that you deliver the list to Harris, his first name was not given me.

                    Very truly yours,

                                    J. L. Suffecool
                                    Superintendent
                      By
                                    Charles Dushane
                                    Sac & Fox Lease Clerk.

                    Shawnee Indian Agency
                    Shawnee, Oklahoma
                    Nov. 21, 1921

Mr. Peter Pah mah mie
c/O Mashno
R #3. Mayetta. Kansas

Dear Sir:

Sac & Fox – Shawnee Estates
1920-1924 Volume VIII

With reference to your inquiry concerning the estate of Ketumwa, deceased, you are advised that the Examiner of Inheritance reported the case to Washington, some time ago.

We have not yet been advised as to action taken in the case. The Examiner reported, according to the testimony, that:

>Mah me ah
>Louis Zahn-qua
>John Zahn-qua
>Peter McCoonse
>Joseph McCoonse
>James McCoonse
>Francis McCoonse

would probably inherit the estate. However, until the Department finally declares the heirs legally, we will not be fully advised as to who the heirs will be.

Very truly yours

JJ

J. L. Suffecool
Superintendent

Shawnee Indian Agency
Shawnee, Oklahoma

Nov. 21, 1921

Mr. Walter Luthye
R #6, North Topeka, Kansas

Dear Sir:

In reply to your letter of Nov. 18, 1921 on the stationery of Citizens State Bank, of Topeka, Kansas, concerning the shortage which appears to you to have been made when the funds to the credit of the estate of Fred Luthye, deceased was transferred to your account and paid to you; you are advised that the $64.58 which we mailed to you and which you say you have received, is all that we had to your credit.

It is true that Fred Luthye's account showed $78.07 to his credit, however, under the act of congress[sic] which authorizes the Secretary of the Interior to determine the heirs of deceased Indian estates, hearing fee based on the value of the estate is deducted. Therefore $15.00 was deducted from the estate of Fred Luthye. This left $63.07, which amount was then

Sac & Fox – Shawnee Estates
1920-1924 Volume VIII

transferred to your credit, after you had been declared legally to be his heir. This then when added to the $1.51 which you had to your credit already made the amount of $64.58 which was sent to you.

The hearing fees charged all Indian estates when the heirs are determined goes toward paying a part of the expenses of conducting the hearings.

Very truly yours

J. L. Suffecool
Superintendent

JJ

Shawnee Indian Agency
Shawnee, Oklahoma

Nov. 21, 1921

Mr. Chas. K. Wells
Attorney and Counsellor at Law
Elks Building
Shawnee, Oklahoma

Dear Sir:

We have your letter of Nov. 16, relative to settlement of the Julia Shawnee matter covering the allotment of William Shawnee, Sr. We have been waiting to see what Julia was going to do about it.

She was in the office some time ago and she wanted time in which to consider the matter and to confer with the other heirs. She promised she would come back and advise us of her attitude toward the manner of settlement proposed and after a conference with the other heirs.

We also have, in connection with this matter, carbon copy of the Commissioner's letter to you dated Nov. 14, 1921. You will see that the Indian Office is willing to entertain the basis of settlement you proposed, provided; the heirs will execute the deeds as proposed and Mr. Reed to execute to the heirs including Julia Shawnee, the 4/143 interest.

Now, it appears to this office that, the matter is up to Julia Shawnee and the other heirs. It is going to be difficult to secure the execution of the deed for the heirs appear to be scattered all over the country. Julia also promised to bring to us the post office addresses of all the heirs. She has not come around yet to tell us what she has finally decided to do.

Sac & Fox – Shawnee Estates
1920-1924 Volume VIII

We will do what we can officially to bring about a settlement of this matter satisfactory to all concerned.

Very truly yours

J. L. Suffecool
Superintendent

JJ

Shawnee Indian Agency
Shawnee, Oklahoma
Nov. 21, 1921

The Commissioner of Indian Affairs
Washington, D. C.

Dear Mr. Commissioner:

Transmitted herewith is affidavit of Dollie Gokey, now Scott, setting forth the fact that Frank Gokey, who died at Camp Logan, Texas, was her husband; that at the time of his death she was his wife and that she has one daughter by him. The affidavit is also sworn to[sic] set for the correct facts by two disinterested parties, Lelia Big Walker and Esther B. Jefferson.

Frank Gokey, deceased, Acct. G-39, has to its credit $79.09, which is not likely to be augmented as the decedent has no inherited interests in any estate under the jurisdiction of this Agency. It would appear that the wife, Dollie Gokey and his daughter, Augustine Gokey, should inherit this estate in equal shares.

It is requested that I be authorized to pay from the estate in equal shares to Dollie Gokey and Augustine Gokey. The amount of funds to the credit of the estate does not exceed $250.00.

Very truly yours

J. L. Suffecool
Superintendent

JJ

Sac & Fox – Shawnee Estates
1920-1924 Volume VIII

Shawnee Indian Agency,
Shawnee, Oklahoma,
Nov. 21, 1921.

Mr. Thomas Lybarger,
524 So. Broadway,
Ft. Scott, Kansas.

Dear Mr. Lybarger:

In reply to your letter of no date received recently relative to you inherited interests yourare[sic] informed as follows:

An effort is being made to secure for the heir s[sic] of Helen Cook a patent in fee for her allotment. There is enclosed carbon copy of the letter to the Commissioner of Indian Affairs on this subject.

There is also enclosed herewith a receipt for a patent in fee for the allotment of Caroline Frayer, No. 303 which you will please sign and have as many as possible of the other heirs sign and return the same to this office with instruction to whom the patent should be mailed.

Very truly yours,

11 od 23. J. L. Suffecool
Supt. & S.D.A.

Shawnee Indian Agency
Shawnee, Oklahoma
November 23, 1921

Mr. Ira C. Deaver
Shawnee, Oklahoma

My dear Sir:

This is to advise that I have been to Cushing and made an investigation of the leasing of the land of Jennie Bigwalker, deceased, and as a result of that investigation, your lease prepared here last Saturday will not be approved, but that I have decided to advertise this land and will receive sealed bids for the leasing of the same, up until 2 P. M. Tuesday, December 6.

Your cashier's check number 60020 payable to your order in the sum of $1,275.00 is returned herewith.

Very respectfully

J. L. Suffecool
Superintendent

JLS/JC

Shawnee Indian Agency
Shawnee, Oklahoma
November 28, 1921

Mr. Benjamin F. Coon
Maud, Oklahoma
Route #2

Dear Sir:

Report has [illegible] this office that you are using the allotment of Margaret Bedell and there is no record in this office that you are paying any rents for this land into this office, for the benefit of the heirs.

It is also reported that you are leasing this land out and that you are cutting timber and selling it to sever school houses and collecting the money for your own benefit, that you now have a contract for 800 posts at $5.00 per hundred and 10 ricks of woods at $1.50 per rick, and that you intend to collect the agricultural rental lease moneys for the year 1922. It is also reported that you claim to own and have possession of the east [?]0 acres of this allotment and that W. R. Bedell is supposed to [sic] the west half. In this connection, you are advised that the whole allotment belongs to the heirs as determined by the Department, and has never been divided. Therefore, each heir has an undivided interest in the whole allotment.

With reference to you having possession and use of this allotment for your sole benefit, you are advised that it will be necessary for you to lease this land through this office regularly and under Departmental supervision, and pay the rentals into this office to be pro-rated among the heirs and that the proceeds of the timber and posts that you have sold off of this allotment, should be paid into this office also, to be pro-rated among the heirs entitled.

You should, therefore discontinue the cutting of the timber and posts and the use of the land for your sole benefit and take steps at once to lease this allotment through this office regularly and to pay into this office the

Sac & Fox – Shawnee Estates
1920-1924 Volume VIII

proceeds of the timber and posts you have already sold and secure a Government permit, if you wish to further cut and sell the timber off of this allotment.

Please look after this matter and report to this office at once as to your position in the matter.

Very truly yours

J. L. Suffecool
Superintendent

JJ/JC

C. C. to Mr. Edmister
" " " W. R. Bedell

****

Shawnee Indian Agency
Shawnee, Oklahoma
November 30, 1921

Mr. Chas. W. Edmister
U. S. Farmer
Shawnee, Oklahoma

Dear Mr. Edmister:

The enclosed carbon copies of letters to Benjamin F. Coon and W. R. Bedell, heirs to the allotment of Margaret Bedell, are self explanatory.

I want you, at your earliest convenience, to investigate the conditions stated concerning the use of the allotment referred to, by Benjamin F. Coon, and see that proper leases are executed whereby rentals should be paid into this office for the benefit of all the heirs.

Please attend to this as soon as you can and report the case to this office, iand[sic] what action is being taken to dispose of the matter to the satisfaction of all concerned.

Very truly yours

J. L. Suffecool
Superintendent

JJ/JC

****

Sac & Fox – Shawnee Estates
1920-1924 Volume VIII

Shawnee Indian Agency
Shawnee, Oklahoma
November 28, 1921

Mr. W. R. Bedell
1102 E. Eighth St.
Okmulgee, Oklahoma

Dear Sir:

For your information and in reply to our letter of November 22, I enclose herewith letter addressed to Benjamin F. Coon, concerning the complaint you have made to us, which is self explanatory and advises you of the action taken by this office.

Very truly yours

J. L. Suffecool
Superintendent

JJ/JC

C. C. to Mr. Edmister

Shawnee Indian Agency
Shawnee, Oklahoma
November 29, 1921

Stanard & Ennis
Attorneys for Emma Griffinstein
Shawnee, Oklahoma.

Gentlemen:

Mrs. Emma Griffinstein of Kansas, through her Attorneys, Stanard & Ennis, has filed a claim of $1450.00 with the Department of the Inferior, for the care of Catherine Griffinstein deceased, for consideration by the Indian Office as to allowing same out of the estate.

Sac & Fox – Shawnee Estates
1920-1924 Volume VIII

In support of her claim, she has filed several affidavits which are now on file in the Indian Office at Washington D.C.

The Commissioner of Indian Affairs has directed that a hearing be held, on due notice, to all interested parties, for the purpose of ascertaining the merits of the claim, in order that we may make the report to the Office as to the investigation.

You are, therefore, notified herein, that on Thursday afternoon at 2 o'clock December 29, 1921, testimony will be taken from all interested parties, concerning the claim of Mrs. Emma Griffinstein, and you are requested to be present to give such testimony as will bear upon the matter in hand.

The notice herein given, gives you practically 30 days.

Very truly yours

J. L. Suffecool
Superintendent

JJ/JC

****

Shawnee Indian Agency
Shawnee, Oklahoma
November 29, 1921

Mr. William T. Griffinstein
c/o Tulsa Shirt Co.,
Tulsa, Oklahoma

Dear Sir:

Mrs. Emma Griffinstein of Kansas, through her Attorneys, Stanard & Ennis, has filed a claim of $1450.00 with the Department of the Inferior, for the care of Catherine Griffinstein deceased, for consideration by the Indian Office as to allowing same out of the estate.

In support of her claim, she has filed several affidavits which are now on file in the Indian Office at Washington D.C.

The Commissioner of Indian Affairs has directed that a hearing be held, on due notice, to all interested parties, for the purpose of ascertaining the merits of the claim, in order that we may make the report to the Office as to the investigation.

Sac & Fox – Shawnee Estates
1920-1924   Volume VIII

You are, therefore, notified herein, that on Thursday afternoon at 2 o'clock December 29, 1921, testimony will be taken from all interested parties, concerning the claim of Mrs. Emma Griffinstein, and you are requested to be present to give such testimony as will bear upon the matter in hand.

The notice herein given, gives you practically 30 days.

          Very truly yours

          J. L. Suffecool
          Superintendent

JJ/JC

      ****

         Shawnee Indian Agency
         Shawnee, Oklahoma
         November 29, 1921

Mr. Chas. J. Griffinstein
c/o Deason & Moody
Shawnee, Oklahoma

Dear Sir:

Mrs. Emma Griffinstein of Kansas, through her Attorneys, Stanard & Ennis, has filed a claim of $1450.00 with the Department of the Inferior, for the care of Catherine Griffinstein deceased, for consideration by the Indian Office as to allowing same out of the estate.

In support of her claim, she has filed several affidavits which are now on file in the Indian Office at Washington D.C.

The Commissioner of Indian Affairs has directed that a hearing be held, on due notice, to all interested parties, for the purpose of ascertaining the merits of the claim, in order that we may make the report to the Office as to the investigation.

You are, therefore, notified herein, that on Thursday afternoon at 2 o'clock December 29, 1921, testimony will be taken from all interested parties, concerning the claim of Mrs. Emma Griffinstein, and you are requested to be present to give such testimony as will bear upon the matter in hand.

The notice herein given, gives you practically 30 days.

Sac & Fox – Shawnee Estates
1920-1924 Volume VIII

                                        Very truly yours

                                        J. L. Suffecool
JJ/JC   Superintendent

                           ****

                                  Shawnee Indian Agency
                                  Shawnee, Oklahoma
                                  November 29, 1921

Mr. Burton G. Raymond
c/o Tulsa Shirt Co.,
Tulsa, Oklahoma

Dear Sir:

Mrs. Emma Griffinstein of Kansas, through her Attorneys, Stanard & Ennis, has filed a claim of $1450.00 with the Department of the Inferior, for the care of Catherine Griffinstein deceased, for consideration by the Indian Office as to allowing same out of the estate.

In support of her claim, she has filed several affidavits which are now on file in the Indian Office at Washington D.C.

The Commissioner of Indian Affairs has directed that a hearing be held, on due notice, to all interested parties, for the purpose of ascertaining the merits of the claim, in order that we may make the report to the Office as to the investigation.

You are, therefore, notified herein, that on Thursday afternoon at 2 o'clock December 29, 1921, testimony will be taken from all interested parties, concerning the claim of Mrs. Emma Griffinstein, and you are requested to be present to give such testimony as will bear upon the matter in hand.

The notice herein given, gives you practically 30 days.

                                        Very truly yours

                                        J. L. Suffecool
JJ/JC   Superintendent

                           ****

Sac & Fox – Shawnee Estates
1920-1924 Volume VIII

Shawnee Indian Agency
Shawnee, Oklahoma
November 29, 1921

Mr. Chas. W. Raymond
c/o Tulsa Shirt Co.,
Tulsa, Oklahoma

Dear Sir:

Mrs. Emma Griffinstein of Kansas, through her Attorneys, Stanard & Ennis, has filed a claim of $1450.00 with the Department of the Inferior, for the care of Catherine Griffinstein deceased, for consideration by the Indian Office as to allowing same out of the estate.

In support of her claim, she has filed several affidavits which are now on file in the Indian Office at Washington D.C.

The Commissioner of Indian Affairs has directed that a hearing be held, on due notice, to all interested parties, for the purpose of ascertaining the merits of the claim, in order that we may make the report to the Office as to the investigation.

You are, therefore, notified herein, that on Thursday afternoon at 2 o'clock December 29, 1921, testimony will be taken from all interested parties, concerning the claim of Mrs. Emma Griffinstein, and you are requested to be present to give such testimony as will bear upon the matter in hand.

The notice herein given, gives you practically 30 days.

Very truly yours

J. L. Suffecool
Superintendent

JJ/JC

****

Shawnee Indian Agency
Shawnee, Oklahoma
November 29, 1921

Mrs. Emma Griffinstein
c/o Stanard & Ennis, Attorneys
Shawnee, Oklahoma

Sac & Fox – Shawnee Estates
1920-1924 Volume VIII

Dear Madam:

Mrs. Emma Griffinstein of Kansas, through her Attorneys, Stanard & Ennis, has filed a claim of $1450.00 with the Department of the Inferior, for the care of Catherine Griffinstein deceased, for consideration by the Indian Office as to allowing same out of the estate.

In support of her claim, she has filed several affidavits which are now on file in the Indian Office at Washington D.C.

The Commissioner of Indian Affairs has directed that a hearing be held, on due notice, to all interested parties, for the purpose of ascertaining the merits of the claim, in order that we may make the report to the Office as to the investigation.

You are, therefore, notified herein, that on Thursday afternoon at 2 o'clock December 29, 1921, testimony will be taken from all interested parties, concerning the claim of Mrs. Emma Griffinstein, and you are requested to be present to give such testimony as will bear upon the matter in hand.

The notice herein given, gives you practically 30 days.

Very truly yours

J. L. Suffecool
Superintendent

JJ/JC

Shawnee Indian Agency
Shawnee, Oklahoma
November 30, 1921

Mr. Chas. E. Wells
Attorney at Law
Elks Building
Shawnee, Oklahoma

Dear Sir:

Your letter of November 21, concerning the Julia Shawnee land matter involving the allotment of Wm. Shawnee, has lain unanswered, pending Julia Shawnee's decision as to what she wants in regard to the proposition of settlement of the F. B. Reed matter. Julia has not showed up to do anything about the matter.

Sac & Fox – Shawnee Estates
1920-1924 Volume VIII

From carbon copies of Indian Office correspondence on file in this office, which were addressed to you, you are undoubtedly aware of the position the Commissioner of Indian Affairs has taken in this matter. The Indian Office practically agrees to the proposition of settlement in that Julia Shawnee and the other heirs are to deed to F. E. Reed 20 acres of the land and F. E. Reed to deed to Julia Shawnee and others 4/145 interests. It is understood that there are no heirs who are minors in this case. Therefore, there will be no expense of the appointment of a guardian over minors.

As stated before, Julia Shawnee is the only one who lives around this section of the country and this office has no record as to the post office addresses of the other heirs, who should sign the deed to Mr. Reed, and that Julia Shawnee does not take very much interest in this settlement, evidently, as she has not been around to see about the matter.

Very truly yours

J. L. Suffecool
Superintendent

JJ/JC

Shawnee Indian Agency
Shawnee, Oklahoma
December 3, 1921

Mrs. Emma Griffinstein
c/o Stanard & Ennis, Attorneys
Shawnee, Oklahoma

Dear Madam:

On November 29, 1921, notice was given you that on Thursday afternoon at 2 o'clock December 29, 1921, testimony would be taken at the Shawnee Agency, from all interested parties, concerning the claim of Mrs. Emma Griffinstein and you were requested to be present to give an on testimony as would bear upon the matter in hand. The claim of Mrs. Emma Griffinstein was stated to be $1,450.00.

On account of the discrepancies in the engagement set for December 29, it has been deemed advisable now to give the supplementary notice herein that the hearing will be conducted beginning at 2 o'clock sharp, Tuesday afternoon, December 27, 1921 instead of December 29 as stated in the former notice. Please govern yourself accordingly.

Sac & Fox – Shawnee Estates
1920-1924 Volume VIII

Very truly yours

J. L. Suffecool
Superintendent

JJ/JC

****

Shawnee Indian Agency
Shawnee, Oklahoma
December 3, 1921

Mr. Chas. W. Raymond
c/o Tulsa Shirt Co.,
Tulsa, Oklahoma

Dear Sir:

On November 29, 1921, notice was given you that on Thursday afternoon at 2 o'clock December 29, 1911, testimony would be taken at the Shawnee Agency, from all interested parties, concerning the claim of Mrs. Emma Griffinstein and you were requested to be present to give an on testimony as would bear upon the matter in hand. The claim of Mrs. Emma Griffinstein was stated to be $1,450.00.

On account of the discrepancies in the engagement set for December 29, it has been deemed advisable now to give the supplementary notice herein that the hearing will be conducted beginning at 2 o'clock sharp, Tuesday afternoon, December 27, 1921 instead of December 29 as stated in the former notice. Please govern yourself accordingly.

Very truly yours

J. L. Suffecool
Superintendent

JJ/JC

****

Shawnee Indian Agency
Shawnee, Oklahoma
December 3, 1921

Sac & Fox – Shawnee Estates
1920-1924 Volume VIII

Mr. Burton C. Raymond
c/o Tulsa Shirt Co.,
Tulsa, Oklahoma

Dear Sir:

On November 29, 1921, notice was given you that on Thursday afternoon at 2 o'clock December 29, 1911, testimony would be taken at the Shawnee Agency, from all interested parties, concerning the claim of Mrs. Emma Griffinstein and you were requested to be present to give an on testimony as would bear upon the matter in hand. The claim of Mrs. Emma Griffinstein was stated to be $1,450.00.

On account of the discrepancies in the engagement set for December 29, it has been deemed advisable now to give the supplementary notice herein that the hearing will be conducted beginning at 2 o'clock sharp, Tuesday afternoon, December 27, 1921 instead of December 29 as stated in the former notice. Please govern yourself accordingly.

Very truly yours

J. L. Suffecool
Superintendent

JJ/JC

****

Shawnee Indian Agency
Shawnee, Oklahoma
December 3, 1921

Mr. William T. Griffinstein
c/o Tulsa Shirt Co.,
Tulsa, Oklahoma

Dear Sir:

On November 29, 1921, notice was given you that on Thursday afternoon at 2 o'clock December 29, 1911, testimony would be taken at the Shawnee Agency, from all interested parties, concerning the claim of Mrs. Emma Griffinstein and you were requested to be present to give an on testimony as would bear upon the matter in hand. The claim of Mrs. Emma Griffinstein was stated to be $1,450.00.

On account of the discrepancies in the engagement set for December 29, it has been deemed advisable now to give the supplementary notice herein that the hearing will be conducted beginning at 2 o'clock sharp, Tuesday afternoon, December 27, 1921 instead of December 29 as stated in the former notice. Please govern yourself accordingly.

         Very truly yours

         J. L. Suffecool
         Superintendent

JJ/JC

     ****
     Shawnee Indian Agency
     Shawnee, Oklahoma
     December 3, 1921

Mr. Chas. J. Griffinstein
c/o Deason & Moody
Shawnee, Oklahoma

Dear Sir:

On November 29, 1921, notice was given you that on Thursday afternoon at 2 o'clock December 29, 1911, testimony would be taken at the Shawnee Agency, from all interested parties, concerning the claim of Mrs. Emma Griffinstein and you were requested to be present to give an on testimony as would bear upon the matter in hand. The claim of Mrs. Emma Griffinstein was stated to be $1,450.00.

On account of the discrepancies in the engagement set for December 29, it has been deemed advisable now to give the supplementary notice herein that the hearing will be conducted beginning at 2 o'clock sharp, Tuesday afternoon, December 27, 1921 instead of December 29 as stated in the former notice. Please govern yourself accordingly.

         Very truly yours

         J. L. Suffecool
         Superintendent

JJ/JC

     ****
     Shawnee Indian Agency
     Shawnee, Oklahoma
     December 3, 1921

Stanard & Ennis
Attorneys for Emma Griffinstein
Shawnee, Oklahoma

Sac & Fox – Shawnee Estates
1920-1924 Volume VIII

Gentlemen:

On November 29, 1921, notice was given you that on Thursday afternoon at 2 o'clock December 29, 1911, testimony would be taken at the Shawnee Agency, from all interested parties, concerning the claim of Mrs. Emma Griffinstein and you were requested to be present to give an on testimony as would bear upon the matter in hand. The claim of Mrs. Emma Griffinstein was stated to be $1,450.00.

On account of the discrepancies in the engagement set for December 29, it has been deemed advisable now to give the supplementary notice herein that the hearing will be conducted beginning at 2 o'clock sharp, Tuesday afternoon, December 27, 1921 instead of December 29 as stated in the former notice. Please govern yourself accordingly.

Very truly yours

J. L. Suffecool
Superintendent

JJ/JC

Shawnee Indian Agency,
Shawnee, Oklahoma,
Dec. 3, 1921.

Supt. E. L. Swartzlander,
Umatilla Indian School,
Pendleton, Oregon.

Dear Sir:

This is in reply to your letter of the 28th instant relative to the estate of Billie Marhardy in which Oscar Marhardy has an interest.

There is enclosed herewith my official check No 9549, The Shawnee National Bank, Shawnee, Okla., which represents Oscar Mahardy's share, viz. $7.31, of the lease rentals of this estate.

Please inform Oscar that his interest in this estate is an undivided interest. It will require a joint petition of all the heirs. There is no sale of land contemplated here in the near future. However, should a sale of land be undertaken he will be offered an opportunity, together with the other heirs, to sign the necessary petition.

Sac & Fox – Shawnee Estates
1920-1924 Volume VIII

Very respectfully,

12 od 5,   J. L. Suffecool,
   Superintendent

Shawnee Indian Agency.
Shawnee, Oklahoma,
December 6, 1923.

Mr. John A. Buntin,
Anadarko, Oklahoma.

Dear Sir:

Enclosed herewith are my official checks which represent money due the payees from the Joe French estate. Please deliver these checks to the payees.

Check No. 17870 payable to Harry Harry[sic] for #3.04

Check No. 17869 payable to Jessie Guam Tussinger for $3.04.

Very truly yours,

_____
J. L. Suffecool
Superintendent.

AMS.

Shawnee Indian Agency
Shawnee, Oklahoma
December 5, 1921

Mrs. [?]. G. Brodie
c/o Mrs. D. Mackinnon
High Prairie
Alla, Canada

Dear Madam:

Replying to your letter of November 22, in which you stage that Mr. [?]old and Mrs. Ogee are going to sell certain land down here, you are advised that we are unable to ascertain from your letter what estate you

Sac & Fox – Shawnee Estates
1920-1924 Volume VIII

refer to and whether or not this estate is still held in trust by the United States.

If you will give us more complete information as to what estate you refer to, we will be glad to give you more [illegible] information.

Very truly yours,

J. L. Suffecool
Superintendent

JJ/JC

Shawnee Indian Agency,
Shawnee, Oklahoma,
Dec. 6, 1921.

Mr. John Bogle,
Mayetta, Kansas.

Dear Sir:

This is in reply to your letter of the 30th of November regarding your inherited interests under this jurisdiction, rentals, patent in fee, etc.

You are informed that your shares in these estates are as follows:-Helen Cook 1/12, and Caroline Frayer 1/6.

The annual agricultural rental in the Helen Cook allotment is $10 per year, and on the Caroline Frayer allotment is $20. The oil and gas rental and royalties amount to on the last year $141.05.

You are further informed that all money derived from these estates is usually transferred to Mayetta, Kansas (Potawatomi Agency) as soon as it is collected from the lessees. Receipt for patent in fee mailed to Thomas Lybarger, Ft. Scott, Kansas.

Very truly yours,

12 od 6.

J. L. Suffecool,
Superintendent.

Sac & Fox – Shawnee Estates
1920-1924 Volume VIII

Shawnee Indian Agency,
Shawnee, Oklahoma,
Dec. 7, 1921.

Mrs Malinda Harvey,
Talala, Oklahoma.

Dear Madam:

This will answer your letter of the 1st of last month einquiring[sic] as to the status of the estate of Flora Taylor, Abs. Shawnee No. 630.

In reply thereto you are advised that Flora Taylor was never allotted any land but that her husband received the entire allotment in accordance with the Act of February 6, 1998 (34 Stat. L., 388).

Records in this office show that there is due Flora Taylor in unpaid annuitants the sum of $103.00. There is an equal amount due John Taylor from the same source.

You are further informed that the Department determined the heirs in Law-Heirship 137315-1915. According to this finding there are 36 heirs, and none of those mentioned by you are included. Understand I am speaking of John Taylor estate. Your grandmother Flora Taylor's heirs have never been determined.

Very truly yours,

12 od 7

J.L. Suffecool,
Superintendent.
By

Sac & Fox Lease Clerk.

Shawnee Indian Agency
Shawnee, Oklahoma
December 8, 1921

Commissioner of Indian Affairs
Washington D.C.

Dear Sir:

Sac & Fox – Shawnee Estates
1920-1924 Volume VIII

This will refer the Office to department finding on June 17, 1913 of the heirs of Eugenie Tah-ho-ka-la-tha, deceased Absentee Shawnee Allottee 467, which bears the reference to file above indicated.

This Allottee, it appears, was also given an allotment as a Creek allottee under the name of [?]ancy Davy. This land, this office is informed, has been sold except the 40 acres home stead in the Creek Nation. Attorneys Conner & Hagan of Tulsa, Oklahoma, has requested that certified copy of the department findings be furnished to them in connection with an oil and gas lease Mr. J. W. Henry of Tulsa, Oklahoma, has filed with the Superintendent of the five[sic] civilized[sic] tribes[sic] as Muskogee, Oklahoma. The lessee if the allotment in the Creek County has been requested to file proof of heirship or the certified copy of the finding in connection with the Shawnee allotment as assistance in making the proof This certified copy should be mailed to this office with the amount of the charges indicated and before delivering the copy to the applicant, the amount will be collected and forwarded to the office.

Very respectfully

JJ/JC
J. L. Suffecool
Superintendent

Shawnee Indian Agency
Shawnee, Oklahoma
December 8, 1921

Mr. Horace H. Hagan
Attorney
Kennedy Bldg.
Tulsa, Oklahoma

Dear Mr. Hagan:

Your letter of December 1, to our Chief Clerk, Mr. Jones enclosing affidavit to be executed by our Chief of Police, John E. Snake and certificate to be signed by me in connection with the estate of Eugenie Tah-ho-ka-la-tha, has received attention. The certificate properly signed by me and the affidavit of Mr. Snake are enclosed herewith.

As to the certified copy of the determination of the heirs of this allottee by the department, you are advised this has been requested of the Commissioner of Indian Affairs in Washington, as we have not been given the authority to certify to the records as the certification is altogether within the province of the Indian Office in Washington. Upon receipt of the certificate from the Indian Office, same will be mailed to you immediately.

The proceeds of your $2.00 check will be held until we find out how much the certificate will be and if there be any difference, it will be mailed to you.

Very truly yours

J. L. Suffecool
Superintendent

JJ/JC

Supt. A. R. Snyder
Potawatomi Indian Agency
Mayetta, Kansas

Dear Mr. Snyder:

  Mrs. Louise Melot of Box 22c, Tecumseh, Oklahoma was in the office yesterday and requested that I write to you in behalf of the heirs of Black Wolf estate recently probated. She wants you to send her share of this estate if there be any to her, at Tecumseh.

Very truly yours

J. L. Suffecool
Superintendent

JJ/JC

Shawnee Indian Agency
Shawnee, Oklahoma
December 9, 1921

Mrs. Sally Panther
Tecumseh, Oklahoma
Route #2
c/o Billie Panther

Dear Madam:

Sac & Fox – Shawnee Estates
1920-1924 Volume VIII

Replying to your statement of December 2 concerning the estate of Ko-no-che-pea-ne or Annie Gibson, deceased wife of Scott Johnson that Ah-che-pea-se, the mother, was left out, you are advised that the hearing as approved by the Department, on file in this office show Scott Johnson and Ah-che-pea-se were given equal parts in the estate. Therefore, it is not believed necessary for a new hearing to be held, as the heirs determined appear to be according to the laws of the state of Oklahoma.

Very truly yours

J. L. Suffecool
Superintendent

JJ/JC

Shawnee Indian Agency
Shawnee, Oklahoma
December 10, 1921

Commissioner of Indian Affairs
Washington D.C.

Dear Sir:

Transmitted herewith is testimony adduced at the hearing conducted at Cushing, Oklahoma by the Examiner of Inheritance, Warner L. Wilmeth, and testimony taken by Examiner of Inheritance S. Y. Tutwiler, September 14, 1921 and Mr. Tutwiler's report thereon.

Mr. Tutwiler has submitted the report through me on account of the alleged will produced by Dollie Gokey and Esther and Lelia Bigwalker. The alleged will, with a copy of it are attached to the Examiner's report. The testimony of Dollie Bigwalker or Gokey, stated that the will was made out by Mrs. Mary Johnson, who is the wife of Mr. Horace J. Johnson, former Superintendent of the Sac & Fox Indian Agency and who is now Superintendent at the Espanola jurisdiction, New Mexico.

I agree with the Examiner in his statement to me, that no credence should be given the alleged will on account of the fact that it is not made out according to the laws of Oklahoma, in not having two witnesses to the signature, and the circumstances connected with it. My opinion is added to his statement that under Section 3 of the regulations adopted and approved on Sept. 13, 1915, relating to the determination of heirs and approval of wills, that the will is not valid, as it has not been approved by the Secretary of the Interior, as required by this regulation.

Sac & Fox – Shawnee Estates
1920-1924 Volume VIII

                                          Very truly yours

                                          J. L. Suffecool
JJ/JC   Superintendent

                                Shawnee Indian Agency
                                Shawnee, Oklahoma
                                December 10, 1921

Connor & Hagan
Attorneys at Law
Tulsa, Oklahoma

Gentlemen:

With reference to your letter of December 8 to our Mr. Jones in the office here, you are informed that the affidavit of Mr. Snake and the Certificate of the Superintendent were mailed to you with our letter of December 6, which was written December 5. No doubt you have received these papers by this time. This refers to the estate known under this Agency as Eugenie To-he-ke-la-tha[sic].

You will note, when you receive our letter referred to, that certified copy of the determination of the heirs has been requested from the Indian office. Upon receipt of it, we will immediately mail it to you.

                                        Very truly yours

                                        J. L. Suffecool
JJ/JC   Superintendent

Law-Heirship
65912-1914
 F W S
                              Shawnee Indian Agency
                              Shawnee, Oklahoma
                                Dec. 14, 1921.

The Honorable,
The Com. of Indian Affairs,
Washington, D. C.

Dear Mr. Commissioner:

Sac & Fox – Shawnee Estates
1920-1924 Volume VIII

Reference is made to the estate of Lizzie Crane, deceased Sac & Fox No. 468, the heirs to which were determined in Law-Heirship above.

The present status of this estate is becoming more complicated due to the fact that some of the heirs died and one of the probable heirs of the undetermined is about to die. Sarah Ellis, one of the heirs, placed upon this allotment improvements from her own private funds and later further improvements were made by the Superintendent, thereby approving the disbursements, from the funds in this office to the credit of Sarah Ellis, with the understanding that a transfer would be made to Sarah Ellis by the heirs. In support of this there is on file in this office Form of Affidavit of Vendee a copy of which is enclosed herewith. Moreover, there are four minors and the undetermined heirs of Edward L. Morris or Crane to be considered. (Under Ira C. Deaver's Admin.)

It is the desire of the heirs that some form of transfer of this allotment to Sarah Ellis from the other heirs be authorized and that the Superintnedent[sic] be authorized to act on behalf of the minors and the undetermined heirs of Edward L. Morris in order to properly take care of the rights of Sarah Ellis.

Very respectfully,

12 od 14.　　　　　　　　　　　　　　　　　　J. L. Suffecool
　　　　　　　　　　　　　　　　　　　　　　　　Supt. & S.D.A.

Shawnee Indian Agency,
Shawnee, Oklahoma,
Dec. 15, 1921.

Mrs. L.C. Bregonze,
P.O. Box 143,
Chitina, Alaska.

Dear Madam:

I have your letter dated Oct. 31, 1921 concerning your share in the estate of William Smith or McLane.

In connection with this matter you are informed that there are over twenty heirs to this estate. Among these are several nieces and that there is no way in which we can tell which one of these nieces you are. It is an easy matter for us to tell you that there is no one on our records by the name of Mrs. L.C. Bregonze. You can materially assist this office, if, when writing for information, you will write your name as it appears here, in this office.

Sac & Fox – Shawnee Estates
1920-1924 Volume VIII

    Enclosed herewith is a list of the heirs of William Smith showing their shares. It is presumed that you will be able to distinguish if you are included therein.

Very respectfully,

12 od 14.	J. L. Suffecool
Incl.	Supt. & S.D.A

Shawnee Indian Agency
Shawnee, Oklahoma
December 16, 1921

Mrs Eveh[sic] S. Lowe
C. A. & H. University
Langston, Oklahoma

Dear Madam:

In connection with your inquiry concerning the settlement of the Wm. Shawnee estate, which is being attempted, you are advised that the heirs who sold out to your mother, are Walter, Dudley and George Shawnee, they having had 2/39 interest in the said estate. Your mother, Julia Shawnee acquired 6/39 undivided and unrestricted interest in this land besides her own.

Since this 6/39 undivided, unrestricted interest that your mother has acquired is not restricted, shehas[sic] perfect right to sell it, to mortgage it or to otherwise encumber it and the Department of the Interior is without jurisdiction or authority to protect her from encumbering the unrestricted interest, consequently she has mortgaged it two or three times and on account of her inability to take up the mortgages, the people holding the mortgage on this interest, have secured the Decree of the court[sic], which must be admitted to be valid with the exception of the court's Order being for 2/11 undivided interest instead of 6/39, the proper share of your mothers. The court order covers a share of 4/143 in excess of the unrestricted interest in the land. Immediate attention of the Department was called to the Decree of the Court. This was discovered and an agreement has been reached whereby your mother should deed 20 acres of this allotment, set aside at the north end of the E. 80 acres, and that the people who have foreclosed on the mortgage should deed to your mother and the rest of the heirs the 4/143 excess interest they have acquired illegally.

Sac & Fox – Shawnee Estates
1920-1924 Volume VIII

Through the court order, now, the 6/39 interest of the 160 acres would amount to 24.6 acres, but these people are willing to take the 20 acres, as stated above. Of course, the land set aside, will be appraised by this office, and if your mother's indebtedness covers the 20 acres, there will be no consideration paid to her. If the appraisement of the 20 acres is in excess of her indebtedness, the difference will be paid to her.

The deed that she signs, setting aside her 6/39 interest, which is unrestricted, will be signed also by the other heirs, you included, not because you have any material interest in the 20 acres but that you would be interested in clearing the title to this land.

Under the conditions above stated, please advise us when the deed referred to, herein, is presented to you and if you will be willing to sign it in order to clear the cloud from the title to the allotment in which you are interested. The complaint involves only your mother's unrestricted share of 6/39.

Very truly yours

J. L. Suffecool
Superintendent

JJ/JC

****

Shawnee Indian Agency
Shawnee, Oklahoma
December 16, 1921

Mrs. Lydia Ragsdale
1140 N. Denver
Tulsa, Oklahoma
c/o Fredonia Owens

Dear Madam:

The following is an explanation as to the method being used to settle up your mother's undivided and unrestricted interest in the allotment of Wm. Shawnee, which does not affect your interest, only to clear the title to the land. With this understanding you will see more clearly as to the transactions that are being attempted to clear the title to your mother's interest in the land.

The heirs that sold out to your mother are Walter, Dudley and George Shawnee, they having had 2/39 interest in the said estate. Your mother,

Sac & Fox – Shawnee Estates
1920-1924 Volume VIII

Julia Shawnee acquired 6/39 undivided and unrestricted interest in this land besides her own.

Since this 6/39 undivided, unrestricted interest that your mother has acquired is not restricted, she has perfect right to sell it, to mortgage it or to otherwise encumber it and the Department of the Interior is withour[sic] jurisdiction or authority to protect her from encumbering the unrestricted interest, consequently she has mortgaged it two or three times and on account of her inability to take up the mortgages, the people holding the mortgage on this interest, have secured the Decree of the court, which must be admitted to be valid with the exception of the court's Order being for 2/11 undivided interest instead of 6/39, the proper share of your mothers. The court order covers a share of 4/143 in excess of the unrestricted interest in the land. Immediate attention of the Department was called to the Decree of the Court. This was discovered and an agreement has been reached whereby your mother should deed 20 acres of this allotment, set aside at the north end of the E. 80 acres, and that the people who have foreclosed on the mortgage should deed to your mother and the rest of the heirs the 4/143 excess interest they have acquired illegally.

Through the court order, now, the 6/39 interest of the 160 acres would amount to 24.6 acres, but these people are willing to take the 20 acres, as stated above. Of course, the land set aside, will be appraised by this office, and if your mother's indebtedness covers the 20 acres, there will be no consideration paid to her. If the appraisement of the 20 acres is in excess of her indebtedness, the difference will be paid to her.

The deed that she signs, setting aside her 6/39 interest, which is unrestricted, will be signed also by the other heirs, you included, not because you have any material interest in the 20 acres but that you would be interested in clearing the title to this land.

Under the conditions above stated, please advise us when the deed referred to, herein, is presented to you and if you will be willing to sign it in order to clear the cloud from the title to the allotment in which you are interested. The complaint involves only your mother's unrestricted share of 6/39.

                                  Very truly yours

                                  J. L. Suffecool
                                  Superintendent

JJ/JC

****

Sac & Fox – Shawnee Estates
1920-1924 Volume VIII

Shawnee Indian Agency
Shawnee, Oklahoma
December 16, 1921

Mrs. Julia DeRadcliff
554 S. Seventh St.
Muskogee, Oklahoma

Dear Madam:

The following is an explanation as to the method being used to settle up your mother's undivided and unrestricted interest in the allotment of Wm. Shawnee, which does not affect your interest, only to clear the title to the land. With this understanding you will see more clearly as to the transactions that are being attempted to clear the title to your mother's interest in the land.

The heirs that sold out to your mother are Walter, Dudley and George Shawnee, they having had 2/39 interest in the said estate. Your mother, Julia Shawnee acquired 6/39 undivided and unrestricted interest in this land besides her own.

Since this 6/39 undivided, unrestricted interest that your mother has acquired is not restricted, she has perfect right to sell it, to mortgage it or to otherwise encumber it and the Department of the Interior is withour[sic] jurisdiction or authority to protect her from encumbering the unrestricted interest, consequently she has mortgaged it two or three times and on account of her inability to take up the mortgages, the people holding the mortgage on this interest, have secured the Decree of the court, which must be admitted to be valid with the exception of the court's Order being for 2/11 undivided interest instead of 6/39, the proper share of your mothers. The court order covers a share of 4/143 in excess of the unrestricted interest in the land. Immediate attention of the Department was called to the Decree of the Court. This was discovered and an agreement has been reached whereby your mother should deed 20 acres of this allotment, set aside at the north end of the E. 80 acres, and that the people who have foreclosed on the mortgage should deed to your mother and the rest of the heirs the 4/143 excess interest they have acquired illegally.

Through the court order, now, the 6/39 interest of the 160 acres would amount to 24.6 acres, but these people are willing to take the 20 acres, as stated above. Of course, the land set aside, will be appraised by this office, and if your mother's indebtedness covers the 20 acres, there will be no consideration paid to her. If the appraisement of the 20 acres is in excess of her indebtedness, the difference will be paid to her.

Sac & Fox – Shawnee Estates
1920-1924 Volume VIII

The deed that she signs, setting aside her 6/39 interest, which is unrestricted, will be signed also by the other heirs, you included, not because you have any material interest in the 20 acres but that you would be interested in clearing the title to this land.

Under the conditions above stated, please advise us when the deed referred to, herein, is presented to you and if you will be willing to sign it in order to clear the cloud from the title to the allotment in which you are interested. The complaint involves only your mother's unrestricted share of 6/39.

        Very truly yours

        J. L. Suffecool
        Superintendent

JJ/JC

     ****

     Shawnee Indian Agency
     Shawnee, Oklahoma
     December 16, 1921

Mrs. Rebecca Walker
1140 N. Denver
Tulsa, Oklahoma
c/o Fredonia Owens

Dear Madam:

The following is an explanation as to the method being used to settle up your mother's undivided and unrestricted interest in the allotment of Wm. Shawnee, which does not affect your interest, only to clear the title to the land. With this understanding you will see more clearly as to the transactions that are being attempted to clear the title to your mother's interest in the land.

The heirs that sold out to your mother are Walter, Dudley and George Shawnee, they having had 2/39 interest in the said estate. Your mother, Julia Shawnee acquired 6/39 undivided and unrestricted interest in this land besides her own.

Since this 6/39 undivided, unrestricted interest that your mother has acquired is not restricted, she has perfect right to sell it, to mortgage it or

Sac & Fox – Shawnee Estates
1920-1924 Volume VIII

to otherwise encumber it and the Department of the Interior is without jurisdiction or authority to protect her from encumbering the unrestricted interest, consequently she has mortgaged it two or three times and on account of her inability to take up the mortgages, the people holding the mortgage on this interest, have secured the Decree of the court, which must be admitted to be valid with the exception of the court's Order being for 2/11 undivided interest instead of 6/39, the proper share of your mothers. The court order covers a share of 4/143 in excess of the unrestricted interest in the land. Immediate attention of the Department was called to the Decree of the Court. This was discovered and an agreement has been reached whereby your mother should deed 20 acres of this allotment, set aside at the north end of the E. 80 acres, and that the people who have foreclosed on the mortgage should deed to your mother and the rest of the heirs the 4/143 excess interest they have acquired illegally.

Through the court order, now, the 6/39 interest of the 160 acres would amount to 24.6 acres, but these people are willing to take the 20 acres, as stated above. Of course, the land set aside, will be appraised by this office, and if your mother's indebtedness covers the 20 acres, there will be no consideration paid to her. If the appraisement of the 20 acres is in excess of her indebtedness, the difference will be paid to her.

The deed that she signs, setting aside her 6/39 interest, which is unrestricted, will be signed also by the other heirs, you included, not because you have any material interest in the 20 acres but that you would be interested in clearing the title to this land.

Under the conditions above stated, please advise us when the deed referred to, herein, is presented to you and if you will be willing to sign it in order to clear the cloud from the title to the allotment in which you are interested. The complaint involves only your mother's unrestricted share of 6/39.

Very truly yours

J. L. Suffecool
Superintendent

JJ/JC

****

Sac & Fox – Shawnee Estates
1920-1924 Volume VIII

Shawnee Indian Agency
Shawnee, Oklahoma
December 16, 1921

Mrs. Emmaline Wafford
1140 N. Denver
Tulsa, Oklahoma
c/o Fredonia Owens

Dear Madam:

The following is an explanation as to the method being used to settle up your mother's undivided and unrestricted interest in the allotment of Wm. Shawnee, which does not affect your interest, only to clear the title to the land. With this understanding you will see more clearly as to the transactions that are being attempted to clear the title to your mother's interest in the land.

The heirs that sold out to your mother are Walter, Dudley and George Shawnee, they having had 2/39 interest in the said estate. Your mother, Julia Shawnee acquired 6/39 undivided and unrestricted interest in this land besides her own.

Since this 6/39 undivided, unrestricted interest that your mother has acquired is not restricted, she has perfect right to sell it, to mortgage it or to otherwise encumber it and the Department of the Interior is withour[sic] jurisdiction or authority to protect her from encumbering the unrestricted interest, consequently she has mortgaged it two or three times and on account of her inability to take up the mortgages, the people holding the mortgage on this interest, have secured the Decree of the court[sic], which must be admitted to be valid with the exception of the court's Order being for 2/11 undivided interest instead of 6/39, the proper share of your mothers. The court order covers a share of 4/143 in excess of the unrestricted interest in the land. Immediate attention of the Department was called to the Decree of the Court. This was discovered and an agreement has been reached whereby your mother should deed 20 acres of this allotment, set aside at the north end of the E. 80 acres, and that the people who have foreclosed on the mortgage should deed to your mother and the rest of the heirs the 4/143 excess interest they have acquired illegally.

Through the court order, now, the 6/39 interest of the 160 acres would amount to 24.6 acres, but these people are willing to take the 20 acres, as stated above. Of course, the land set aside, will be appraised by this office, and if your mother's indebtedness covers the 20 acres, there will be no consideration paid to her. If the appraisement of the 20 acres is in excess of her indebtedness, the difference will be paid to her.

Sac & Fox – Shawnee Estates
1920-1924 Volume VIII

The deed that she signs, setting aside her 6/39 interest, which is unrestricted, will be signed also by the other heirs, you included, not because you have any material interest in the 20 acres but that you would be interested in clearing the title to this land.

Under the conditions above stated, please advise us when the deed referred to, herein, is presented to you and if you will be willing to sign it in order to clear the cloud from the title to the allotment in which you are interested. The complaint involves only your mother's unrestricted share of 6/39.

Very truly yours

J. L. Suffecool
Superintendent

JJ/JC

****

Shawnee Indian Agency
Shawnee, Oklahoma
December 16, 1921

Mrs. Myrtle Shawnee
Route #6 Box 24
Shawnee, Oklahoma

Dear Madam:

The following is an explanation as to the method being used to settle up your mother's undivided and unrestricted interest in the allotment of Wm. Shawnee, which does not affect your interest, only to clear the title to the land. With this understanding you will see more clearly as to the transactions that are being attempted to clear the title to your mother's interest in the land.

The heirs that sold out to your mother are Walter, Dudley and George Shawnee, they having had 2/39 interest in the said estate. Your mother, Julia Shawnee acquired 6/39 undivided and unrestricted interest in this land besides her own.

Since this 6/39 undivided, unrestricted interest that your mother has acquired is not restricted, she has perfect right to sell it, to mortgage it or to otherwise encumber it and the Department of the Interior is withour[sic] jurisdiction or authority to protect her from encumbering the unrestricted interest, consequently she has mortgaged it two or three times and on account of her inability to take up the mortgages, the people holding the

Sac & Fox – Shawnee Estates
1920-1924 Volume VIII

mortgage on this interest, have secured the Decree of the court[sic], which must be admitted to be valid with the exception of the court's Order being for 2/11 undivided interest instead of 6/39, the proper share of your mothers. The court order covers a share of 4/143 in excess of the unrestricted interest in the land. Immediate attention of the Department was called to the Decree of the Court. This was discovered and an agreement has been reached whereby your mother should deed 20 acres of this allotment, set aside at the north end of the E. 80 acres, and that the people who have foreclosed on the mortgage should deed to your mother and the rest of the heirs the 4/143 excess interest they have acquired illegally.

Through the court order, now, the 6/39 interest of the 160 acres would amount to 24.6 acres, but these people are willing to take the 20 acres, as stated above. Of course, the land set aside, will be appraised by this office, and if your mother's indebtedness covers the 20 acres, there will be no consideration paid to her. If the appraisement of the 20 acres is in excess of her indebtedness, the difference will be paid to her.

The deed that she signs, setting aside her 6/39 interest, which is unrestricted, will be signed also by the other heirs, you included, not because you have any material interest in the 20 acres but that you would be interested in clearing the title to this land.

Under the conditions above stated, please advise us when the deed referred to, herein, is presented to you and if you will be willing to sign it in order to clear the cloud from the title to the allotment in which you are interested. The complaint involves only your mother's unrestricted share of 6/39.

Very truly yours

J. L. Suffecool
Superintendent

JJ/JC

****

Shawnee Indian Agency
Shawnee, Oklahoma
December 16, 1921

Mr. David Shawnee
Hampton Inst.
Hampton, Va.

Dear Sir:

Sac & Fox – Shawnee Estates
1920-1924 Volume VIII

The following is an explanation as to the method being used to settle up your mother's undivided and unrestricted interest in the allotment of Wm. Shawnee, which does not affect your interest, only to clear the title to the land. With this understanding you will see more clearly as to the transactions that are being attempted to clear the title to your mother's interest in the land.

The heirs that sold out to your mother are Walter, Dudley and George Shawnee, they having had 2/39 interest in the said estate. Your mother, Julia Shawnee acquired 6/39 undivided and unrestricted interest in this land besides her own.

Since this 6/39 undivided, unrestricted interest that your mother has acquired is not restricted, she has perfect right to sell it, to mortgage it or to otherwise encumber it and the Department of the Interior is without jurisdiction or authority to protect her from encumbering the unrestricted interest, consequently she has mortgaged it two or three times and on account of her inability to take up the mortgages, the people holding the mortgage on this interest, have secured the Decree of the court[sic], which must be admitted to be valid with the exception of the court's Order being for 2/11 undivided interest instead of 6/39, the proper share of your mothers. The court order covers a share of 4/143 in excess of the unrestricted interest in the land. Immediate attention of the Department was called to the Decree of the Court. This was discovered and an agreement has been reached whereby your mother should deed 20 acres of this allotment, set aside at the north end of the E. 80 acres, and that the people who have foreclosed on the mortgage should deed to your mother and the rest of the heirs the 4/143 excess interest they have acquired illegally.

Through the court order, now, the 6/39 interest of the 160 acres would amount to 24.6 acres, but these people are willing to take the 20 acres, as stated above. Of course, the land set aside, will be appraised by this office, and if your mother's indebtedness covers the 20 acres, there will be no consideration paid to her. If the appraisement of the 20 acres is in excess of her indebtedness, the difference will be paid to her.

The deed that she signs, setting aside her 6/39 interest, which is unrestricted, will be signed also by the other heirs, you included, not because you have any material interest in the 20 acres but that you would be interested in clearing the title to this land.

Under the conditions above stated, please advise us when the deed referred to, herein, is presented to you and if you will be willing to sign it in order to clear the cloud from the title to the allotment in which you are interested. The complaint involves only your mother's unrestricted share of 6/39.

Sac & Fox – Shawnee Estates
1920-1924 Volume VIII

                              Very truly yours

                              J. L. Suffecool
                              Superintendent
JJ/JC
                    ****

                            Shawnee Indian Agency
                            Shawnee, Oklahoma
                            December 16, 1921

Fredonia Owens
1140 N. Denver
Tulsa, Oklahoma

Dear Madam:

The following is an explanation as to the method being used to settle up your mother's undivided and unrestricted interest in the allotment of Wm. Shawnee, which does not affect your interest, only to clear the title to the land. With this understanding you will see more clearly as to the transactions that are being attempted to clear the title to your mother's interest in the land.

The heirs that sold out to your mother are Walter, Dudley and George Shawnee, they having had 2/39 interest in the said estate. Your mother, Julia Shawnee acquired 6/39 undivided and unrestricted interest in this land besides her own.

Since this 6/39 undivided, unrestricted interest that your mother has acquired is not restricted, she has perfect right to sell it, to mortgage it or to otherwise encumber it and the Department of the Interior is without jurisdiction or authority to protect her from encumbering the unrestricted interest, consequently she has mortgaged it two or three times and on account of her inability to take up the mortgages, the people holding the mortgage on this interest, have secured the Decree of the court[sic], which must be admitted to be valid with the exception of the court's Order being for 2/11 undivided interest instead of 6/39, the proper share of your mothers. The court order covers a share of 4/143 in excess of the unrestricted interest in the land. Immediate attention of the Department was called to the Decree of the Court. This was discovered and an agreement has been reached whereby your mother should deed 20 acres of this allotment, set aside at the north end of the E. 80 acres, and that the people who have foreclosed on the mortgage should deed to your mother and the rest of the heirs the 4/143 excess interest they have acquired illegally.

Sac & Fox – Shawnee Estates
1920-1924 Volume VIII

Through the court order, now, the 6/39 interest of the 160 acres would amount to 24.6 acres, but these people are willing to take the 20 acres, as stated above. Of course, the land set aside, will be appraised by this office, and if your mother's indebtedness covers the 20 acres, there will be no consideration paid to her. If the appraisement of the 20 acres is in excess of her indebtedness, the difference will be paid to her.

The deed that she signs, setting aside her 6/39 interest, which is unrestricted, will be signed also by the other heirs, you included, not because you have any material interest in the 20 acres but that you would be interested in clearing the title to this land.

Under the conditions above stated, please advise us when the deed referred to, herein, is presented to you and if you will be willing to sign it in order to clear the cloud from the title to the allotment in which you are interested. The complaint involves only your mother's unrestricted share of 6/39.

                                                Very truly yours

                                                J. L. Suffecool
                                                Superintendent
JJ/JC

****

                                    Shawnee Indian Agency
                                    Shawnee, Oklahoma
                                    December 17, 1921

Attorney Chas. E. Wells
Elks Bldg.
Shawnee, Oklahoma

Dear Sir:

With reference to your letter of December 14, concerning the Wm. Shawnee allotment and the names and addresses of the heirs which you sent us recently, I am enclosing carbon copy of letter to Lafayette Shawnee, for your information in connection with this matter. A letter similar to that enclosed herewith, has been sent to all the heirs in order that some action may be started. The heirs as determined by the Department on June 25, 1913 are:

Julia Shawnee,	wife,	- 1/3
Walter " ,	son	,-2/39
Dudley " ,	"	,-2/39
George " ,	"	,-2/39

Sac & Fox – Shawnee Estates
1920-1924 Volume VIII

Evah	" ,	daughter,-2/39
Rebecca	" ,	" ,-2/39
Lydia	" ,	" ,-2/39
Lafayetta[sic]	" ,	son ,-2/39
Emeline	" ,	daughter,-2/39
Julia	" ,	" ,-2/39
Fredonia	" ,	" ,-2/39
Myrtle	" ,	" ,-2/39
David	" ,	"[sic],-2/39
Ethel Shawnee Bruner		
grand-daughter		,-2/39
(daughter of deceased son)		

Julia Shawnee acquired through purchase, 6/39 interest from Walter, Dudley and George Shawnee, each of whom had 6/39 interest in the estate.

    Very truly yours

        J. L. Suffecool
        Superintendent

JJ/JV[sic]

    ****

      Shawnee Indian Agency
      Shawnee, Oklahoma
      December 17, 1921

Mr. Lafayette Shawnee
Kingfisher, Oklahoma

Dear Sir:

The following is an explanation as to the method being used to settle up your mother's undivided and unrestricted interest in the allotment of Wm. Shawnee, which does not affect your interest, only to clear the title to the land. With this understanding you will see more clearly as to the transactions that are being attempted to clear the title to your mother's interest in the land.

The heirs that sold out to your mother are Walter, Dudley and George Shawnee, they having had 2/39 interest in the said estate. Your mother, Julia Shawnee acquired 6/39 undivided and unrestricted interest in this land besides her own.

Sac & Fox – Shawnee Estates
1920-1924 Volume VIII

Since this 6/39 undivided, unrestricted interest that your mother has acquired is not restricted, she has perfect right to sell it, to mortgage it or to otherwise encumber it and the Department of the Interior is without jurisdiction or authority to protect her from encumbering the unrestricted interest, consequently she has mortgaged it two or three times and on account of her inability to take up the mortgages, the people holding the mortgage on this interest, have secured the Decree of the court[sic], which must be admitted to be valid with the exception of the court's Order being for 2/11 undivided interest instead of 6/39, the proper share of your mothers. The court order covers a share of 4/143 in excess of the unrestricted interest in the land. Immediate attention of the Department was called to the Decree of the Court. This was discovered and an agreement has been reached whereby your mother should deed 20 acres of this allotment, set aside at the north end of the E. 80 acres, and that the people who have foreclosed on the mortgage should deed to your mother and the rest of the heirs the 4/143 excess interest they have acquired illegally.

Through the court order, now, the 6/39 interest of the 160 acres would amount to 24.6 acres, but these people are willing to take the 20 acres, as stated above. Of course, the land set aside, will be appraised by this office, and if your mother's indebtedness covers the 20 acres, there will be no consideration paid to her. If the appraisement of the 20 acres is in excess of her indebtedness, the difference will be paid to her.

The deed that she signs, setting aside her 6/39 interest, which is unrestricted, will be signed also by the other heirs, you included, not because you have any material interest in the 20 acres but that you would be interested in clearing the title to this land.

Under the conditions above stated, please advise us when the deed referred to, herein, is presented to you and if you will be willing to sign it in order to clear the cloud from the title to the allotment in which you are interested. The complaint involves only your mother's unrestricted share of 6/39.

            Very truly yours

            J. L. Suffecool
            Superintendent

JJ/JC

       ****

           Shawnee Indian Agency
           Shawnee, Oklahoma
           December 17, 1921

Sac & Fox – Shawnee Estates
1920-1924 Volume VIII

Mrs. Ethel Bruner
Wewoka, Oklahoma

Dear Madam:

The following is an explanation as to the method being used to settle up your grandmother's undivided and unrestricted interest in the allotment of Wm. Shawnee, which does not affect your interest, only to clear the title to the land. With this understanding you will see more clearly as to the transactions that are being attempted to clear the title to your grand-mother's interest in the land.

The heirs that sold out to your grand-mother are Walter, Dudley and George Shawnee, they having had 2/39 interest in the said estate. Your grandmother, Julia Shawnee acquired 6/39 undivided and unrestricted interest in this land besides her own.

Since this 6/39 undivided, unrestricted interest that your grand-mother has acquired is not restricted, she has perfect right to sell it, to mortgage it or to otherwise encumber it and the Department of the Interior is without jurisdiction or authority to protect her from encumbering the unrestricted interest, consequently she has mortgaged it two or three times and on account of her inability to take up the mortgages, the people holding the mortgage on this interest, have secured the Decree of the court[sic], which must be admitted to be valid with the exception of the court's Order being for 2/11 undivided interest instead of 6/39, the proper share of your grand-mothers. The court order covers a share of 4/143 in excess of the unrestricted interest in the land. Immediate attention of the Department was called to the Decree of the Court. This was discovered and an agreement has been reached whereby your grand-mother should deed 20 acres of this allotment, set aside at the north end of the E. 80 acres, and that the people who have foreclosed on the mortgage should deed to your grand-mother and the rest of the heirs the 4/143 excess interest they have acquired illegally.

Through the court order, now, the 6/39 interest of the 160 acres would amount to 24.6 acres, but these people are willing to take the 20 acres, as stated above. Of course, the land set aside, will be appraised by this office, and if your grand-mother's indebtedness covers the 20 acres, there will be no consideration paid to her. If the appraisement of the 20 acres is in excess of her indebtedness, the difference will be paid to her.

The deed that she signs, setting aside her 6/39 interest, which is unrestricted, will be signed also by the other heirs, you included, not because you have any material interest in the 20 acres but that you would be interested in clearing the title to this land.

Sac & Fox – Shawnee Estates
1920-1924 Volume VIII

Under the conditions above stated, please advise us when the deed referred to, herein, is presented to you and if you will be willing to sign it in order to clear the cloud from the title to the allotment in which you are interested. The complaint involves only your mother's unrestricted share of 6/39.

Very truly yours

J. L. Suffecool
Superintendent

JJ/JC

Shawnee Indian Agency
Shawnee, Oklahoma
December 21, 1921

Connor & Hagan
Attorneys at Law
Kennedy Building
Tulsa, Oklahoma

Gentlemen:

Referring to our correspondence on connection with the estate of Eugenie Tah ho ka la tha, deceased Absentee Shawnee Allottee number 467, you are informed that this office has just received a letter from Washington, stating that the Indian Office has furnished you with certified copies of papers showing the heirs in this estate. If you have received these papers the $2.00 which you sent us will be returned to you upon advice that you have secured the papers direct from Washington.

Very truly yours

J. L. Suffecool
Superintendent

JJ/JC

Shawnee Indian Agency
Shawnee, Oklahoma
December 21, 1921

W. L. Chapman
Attorney at Law
Shawnee, Oklahoma

Sac & Fox – Shawnee Estates
1920-1924 Volume VIII

Dear Sir:

Replying to your letter of December 19 concerning the Mark Charley estate, you are advised that when the Examiner of Inheritance is assigned to take testimony to determine his heirs, your letter and your request will be called to his attention for such action as he may deem necessary in the case.

Very truly yours

J. L. Suffecool
Superintendent

JJ/JC

Shawnee Indian Agency
Shawnee, Oklahoma
December 22, 1921

Mr. Henry Black
Redrock, Oklahoma

Dear Sir:

In answer to your letter of December 19, concerning the hearing that was held to determine the heirs of Phoebe Whitecloud estate, you are advised that the Department determined the heirs July 12, 1921 to be:

Henry Black	2/6
James Black	1/6
Earnest Black	1/6
Emanuel Black	1/6
Theodore Black	1/6

The records of this office show that the rentals which were to the credit of the estate of Phoeve[sic] Black has been transferred to the heirs, you receiving $14.08 and the other boys $7.04 each.

It was not know where the heirs to this estate were, hence the money was held here to their credit, until such time as we can secure that you are under the jurisdiction of Ponca Indian Agency. If you desire that we forward checks covering the amounts to the credit of the heirs, we will forward same to Mr. Hoyo, the Superintendent of Ponca Indian Agency.

Very truly yours

J. L. Suffecool
Superintendent

JJ/JC

Sac & Fox – Shawnee Estates
1920-1924 Volume VIII

Shawnee Indian Agency
Shawnee, Oklahoma
December 23, 1921

Mr. Michael Martin
1562 Broadway
c/o Vaudeville News
New York City, N. Y.

Dear Mr. Martin:

This refers to your letter of December 19, concerning the estate of Little Fish under this jurisdiction.

In this connection you are advised that this estate is in the same shape that it was when allotted, and no division of it has been made and no patent in fee issued to the heirs. It is not leased to any one the past season. Your father, Thomas Worcester has the same share in the estate that he had at the time of the determination of the heirs.

If your father, Thomas Worcester was enrolled and allotted under the Kiowa Agency jurisdiction, perhaps his heirs are determined under that Agency, and his heirs would take his share of the estate of Little Fish under this jurisdiction.

The allotment you refer to is located where there is no oil development at the present time and has only speculative oil value. It is true that they have brought in a small well down in the southern part of this county, but this will have little effect, if any, on the allotment in which you are interested.

Very truly yours

J. L. Suffecool
Superintendent

JJ/JC

****

Shawnee Indian Agency
Shawnee, Oklahoma
December 23, 1921

Supt. C. V. Stinchecun
Kiowa Indian Agency
Anadarko, Oklahoma

Sac & Fox – Shawnee Estates
1920-1924 Volume VIII

Dear Mr. Stinchecun:

Michael Martin writes from New York City and states that his father, Thomas Worcester has been dead for some time.

Michael Martin and his father, Thomas Worcester are shown to be heirs in the Little Fish estate under this jurisdiction. If Thomas Worcester is enrolled and allotted and has property under your jurisdiction, it is probably that his heirs have been determined covering that property under your Agency. If that be true, will you please furnish this office a copy of the Department finding in Thomas Worcester's estate?

Very truly yours,

J. L. Suffecool
Superintendent

JJ/JC

Shawnee Indian Agency
Shawnee, Oklahoma
December 27, 1921

Mr. Thomas K. Oliver
c/o Grant We we nas
R.F.D. No. 2
Whiting, Kansas

Dear Sir:

Replying to your letter of December 24, concerning the estate of Oliver Jackson, you are advised that check for $2,402.94 was mailed to Superintendent Snyder of Potawatomi Agency, Kansas at Mayetta on November 30, 1921.

No doubt, the Agency there has this money to your credit by this time.

Very truly yours

J. L. Suffecool
Superintendent

JJ/JC

Sac & Fox – Shawnee Estates
1920-1924 Volume VIII

Shawnee Indian Agency
Shawnee, Oklahoma
December 28, 1921

Mr. Wm. G. Foster
Cushing, Oklahoma
c/o Silas Grass

My friend:

On my return home from Cushing, I took up the matter of the heirship in the estate of Thurma Smith, and Mr. Snake tells me that he has already sent you a copy of the findings, but you say to me that it has not reached you, and I am directing that he furnish you with another copy, which he has promised to do and I think you will receive it in a few days.

Your friend,

J. L. Suffecool
Superintendent

JLS/JC

Shawnee Indian Agency
Shawnee, Oklahoma
Dec. 31, 1921

Mr. W. O. Roberts, Lawyer
Kress Building
Emporia, Kansas

Dear Sir:

Answering your letter of Dec. 28, 1921 concerning the interest of Leonard Coon, of your City, in the Margaret Bedell allotment which is under the supervision of the Department of the Interior, you are advised that the necessary protection of the rights of the heirs has been in the past and is now being extended.

No conveyance or encumbrance of the land can be legal without the consent and approval of the Secretary of the Interior. Hence, the heirs need entertain any alarm that the land might be sold or conveyed without their consent, illegally.

It is true that some of the land which was originally allotted to Margaret Bedell was sold with the consent and approval of the Secretary of the Interior some years ago. The remainder of 160 acres is still held in trust.

Sac & Fox – Shawnee Estates
1920-1924 Volume VIII

Certain deeds were executed by Benjamin F. Coon which clouded the title, but the Government in its protection of the land for the heirs brought suit in the United States district court and a decree entered clearing the title to the land and it is not likely to be encumbered again.

Very truly yours

J. L. Suffecool
Superintendent

JJ

Shawnee Indian Agency
Shawnee, Oklahoma
December 31, 1921

Mr. F. E. Brandon, Special Supervisor
Potawatomi Indian Agency
Mayetta, Kansas

Dear Mr. Brandon:

The enclosed carbon copy of my report to Mr. Snyder covering the status of the Joe Whipple allotment under this jurisdiction, a part of whose heirs are under his Agency, is self explanatory and is in response to your letter of Dec. 30, 1921 concerning the matter.

Very truly yours

J. L. Suffecool
Superintendent

Incl. CC of letter to
Mr. Snyder.
JJ

****

Shawnee Indian Agency
Shawnee, Oklahoma
Dec. 31, 1921

Mr. A. R. Snyder, Superintendent
Potawatomi Indian Agency
Mayetta, Kansas

Dear Mr. Snyder:

Sac & Fox – Shawnee Estates
1920-1924 Volume VIII

Special Supervisor, F. E. Brandon, states in his letter of Dec. 30, that Louis Wabaunce complains about not having been able to get any information concerning the estate of Joe Whipple, deceased allottee under this Agency, and that you informed him of having made inquiry of this office several times in the past but were unable to get any information on the subject. Mr. Brandon has requested that I make a report to you for the information of the heirs who live under your Agency.

Luis Wabaunce is not shown to be an heir in the Joe Whipple estate, unless he is under one of the names given on the card on which are listed the heirs of James Thompson which you sent to this office Feb. 2, 1920. We do not find any inquiries on file in this office where any of the heirs ever made. Those on file are from your office for the heirs, to each of which, the records in this office show, we made replies promptly. Your files should show this.

Joe Whipple died. His heirs were legally declared to be:

Angeline Whipple,	1/3
Andrew Whipple,	1/3
Alice Whipple,	1/3

Angeline Whipple died. Her heir was declared to be James Thompson of your Agency. He then inherited, thru Angeline Whipple, the 1/3 interest in the Joe Whipple estate. Alice Whipple purchased the 1/3 interest of Andrew Whipple, making her the owner of 2/3 interest in the Joe Whipple estate, while James Thompson owned 1/3 interest in said estate.

James Thompson died. His heirs were declared under your Agency. They were found to be:

Peter Thompson,	1/4
Angeline Thompson,	1/4
Ellen Atkins,	1/4
Edward Shenreshquah	1/12
Edith "	1/12
Theresa "	1/12

James Thompson's share of the rentals derived from the Joe Whipple allotment were forwarded to your office each year while he was living.

Since his death there accumulated to his credit $161.67 as his share of the rentals derived from the Joe Whipple allotment. Check 3424 for this amount was transferred to your office Jan. 11, 1920 for which we have your official receipt No. 143760 dated Feb. 14, 1920.

Sac & Fox – Shawnee Estates
1920-1924 Volume VIII

We now enclose checks due the heirs who reside under Agency as follows:

    Check 9777, Peter Thompson, $11.10
    "   9778, Angeline Thompson,   11.10
    "   9779, Ellen Atkins,   11.10
    "   9780, Edward Shenreshquah,   3.69
    "   9781, Edith Shenreshquah,   3.69
    "   9782, Theresa Shenreshquah,   3.69

all made payable to your order to be receipted for and taken up to the credit of the payee's indicated and to be disbursed for them in your discretion. These amounts are their shares of the $133.12 we collected recently as trespass fee as there was no lease for 1921. This is all the funds we have derived from the Joe Whipple allotment.

Concerning the many inquiries; the first one came from this office on Sept. 2, 1928 addressed to Mr. J. A. Garber, then Supt. Potawatomi Agency. In this information is requested for a copy of the finding as to the heirs of James Thompson. Mr. Garber replied to the inquiry from this office on Sept. 4, 1918, stating that the heirs to the estate of James Thompson had not been determined. The accumulated rentals then was held pending advise from your office as to the determination of the heirs.

The next inquiry came from your office in letter dated Jan. 19, 1920 stating that the heirs of James Thompson had received no income from the Joe Whipple estate since his death. On Jan. 31, 1920 we asked for a copy of the finding of the heirs of James Thompson. You replied on Feb. 2, 1920 inclosing a card on which the heirs were listed. On Feb. 11, 1920 we wrote you advising that we decided to send a check covering the balance to the credit of James Thompson to be distributed by you. We enclosed in this letter the check 2434 for $161.67, for which we received your receipt 143760 dated Feb. 14, 1920.

The next inquiry from your office dated Aug. 16, 1920 was received, stating that Wabaunce tells you that the heirs have received no rentals from this office on the Joe Whipple allotment since the death of James Thompson and requesting that we transfer any funds that may be to his credit to your Agency. To this we replied on August 18, 1920 in which your office was advised that on January 11, 1920 we transferred to your Agency check 3424 for $161.67 for the heirs of James Thompson. No doubt, since you receipted for this, you took the money up to the credit of the heirs interested and they should have known that they had received money since the death of James Thompson. Your file should indicate this.

Again received inquiry from your office dated Dec. 8, 1920, in the second paragraph of which it is stated that the heirs of James Thompson have not received any benefits in the way of rentals for a long time as Jim

Sac & Fox – Shawnee Estates
1920-1924 Volume VIII

Thompson has been dead for about three years, no money have been forwarded to your office since that time. To this we replied on dec. 21, 1920 setting forth in detail just how much, and when funds to the credit of James Thompson, was transferred to your office. Your files should indicate the various inquiries and replies from this office.

I trust from this you will be able to advise the heirs of Joe Whipple, thru James Thompson, deceased, who live under your Agency the information they want. You might state to them that the allotment was not leased this year but collected trespass fee their share of which are represented in the checks enclosed herewith.

Very truly yours

J. L. Suffecool
Superintendent

CC to Special Supervisor
F. E. Brandon.
JJ

Shawnee Indian Agency
Shawnee, Oklahoma,
January 3, 1923.

The Honorable,
  The Commissioner
    of Indian Affairs,
      Washington, D. C.

My dear Mr. Commissioner:-

    There is inclosed herewith for consideration of the Office and for decision two leases on the NW/4 of Section 28-9-1 containing 160 acres, for one year from the first day of January, 1923 and ended on the 31st of December, 1923, for a consideration of $325.00 per annum, on the allotment of Big Jim, or Wah-pah-seap-to, deceased Absentee Shawnee allottee No. 500. The heirs of which, as determined by the Department, reference "Law-heirship 42859-19049-12 J B K" being Little Jim, Charley Bob, and Sally Bob.

    One of the leases was prepared on the 19th day of December, 1922 in favor of Ed Brannon. The other was prepared under date of December 22, 1922 in favor of William M. Willingham.

    The lease prepared on the 19th of December, 1922 for Mr. Ed. Brannon was at his request, as sealed bids had been received he being

Sac & Fox – Shawnee Estates
1920-1924 Volume VIII

present on the day that the bids were opened. After Mr. Brannon's lease had been prepared he was requested to bring in the heirs and have them complete the same. This he has failed to do, probably due to the fact that he was unable to get the heirs to accompany him to this office for that purpose.

On the 22nd day of December, 1922, Wm. M. Willingham came to the office with the heirs and at their request lease was prepared in his favor and all of the heirs signed it which is indicative of the fact that they wished Mr. Willingham to have the lease.

The subject of leasing this particular tract of land has been the source of a great deal of annoyance and trouble to this office. Both sides representing their claims by influence brought from the outside. Mr Brannon has had the lease for the last three years and to the best of my knowledge has been satisfactory having met his obligations and the conditions set forth in his lease without annoyance to this office, and it has been the policy of this office to lease the land to the present lessee and to give them the preference, and Mr. Brannon was so advised. The matter was put to sealed bids which were opened on the 19th day of December. Mr. Willingham made an offer of $325.00 cash. Mr. Brannon made a bid of $285.00, cash--said bids are inclosed herewith for the information of the Office. Mr. Brannon stated at this time that he would meet the other man's bid; hence, his lease was prepared with the request as noted above that he should get the heirs to sign the same, and as will be noted on the lease in this he has failed. Mr. Willingham came in afterwards with the heirs and the lease was properly executed.

In view of the above circumstances and of the conditions it is believed by this office that the lease rightfully belongs to Mr. Brannon, and the heirs should have been willing to sign for him but for some reason unknown to this office they preferred Mr. Willingham and showed that preference by having signed his lease. However, they were given an opportunity to sign Mr. Brannon's lease.

I would respectfully request that the Office make a decision in this matter and instruct this office which lease to accept. I would also request that the entire file which is inclosed herewith for the information of the Office be returned.

There is a letter inclosed in this file addressed to this office under date of December 20th, 1922 by Mark Goode, Attorney at Law, who is representing Mr. E. T. Carson, his client, who according to a recent decision of the Court of Appeals was awarded an undivided one-fourth interest in the tract of land in question. The matter of this decision has been the subject of two communications to the Office under date of December 22, 1922 and December 28, 1922.

Sac & Fox – Shawnee Estates
1920-1924 Volume VIII

Very respectfully,

J. L. Suffecool
Superintendent

JBS:EV.
ENCLS. file.

Land-Sales
124446-13
12342 -21

Shawnee Indian Agency,
Shawnee, Oklahoma,
Jan. 3, 1922.

The Honorable
Commissioner of Indian Affairs,
Washington, D. C.

Dear Mr. Commissioner:

Reference is made to Office Letter replying to our letter of the above caption concerning the sale of the allotment of Joe Vetter, deceased, Iowa allottee No. 16. The letter contained authority to sell the two-thirds (2/3) interest of the other heirs to R. A Brooks, the owner of the one-third interest by purchase from Clarence Z. Spurlock and his wife Lizzie Spurlock, devisees of Nesojame Vetter, for 2/3 of the value of the appraisement, and to accept a deposit of 2/3 of the apprisement[sic] in return for a deed from the heirs to R. A. Brooks.

There are enclosed herewith Certificate of Appraisement, form 5-110a, and an Indian Deed Inherited Lands, form 5-183. In view of the fact that Mr. R.A. Brooks had considerable difficulty in making this settlement of the estate of Joe Vetter it was considered that the approval of the Department to be most appropriate. There has been deposited in the Shawnee National Bank, Shawnee, Okla., to the official credit of the Superintendent of the Shawnee Indian Agency, $2,333.33, 2/3 of the appraised value of the allotment, which will be placed to the credit of the heirs upon approval of the deed.

The Letter authorizing the sale of this allotment was misplaced. A copy is desired for the files in this office.

Very respectfully,

1 cd 3,
Incls.

J. L. Suffecool
Supt. & S.D.A.

Probate:
29985-14
28106-21
J E P

Shawnee Indian Agency
Shawnee, Oklahoma
Jan. 5, 1922

The Commissioner of Indian Affairs
Washington, D. C.

Sir:

The Department authorized a modification of the determination of the heirs of Kasson, deceased Absentee Shawnee Allottee No. 395 on October 19, 1921, for the reason that the last determination was based on the laws of Arkansas, whereas the land was located in Pottawatomie County, Oklahoma, that portion of Oklahoma that was included in the Territory of Oklahoma.

As directed, due notice was served on all of the interested parties, by mail, on November 2, 1921. In this notice, each interested party was given thirty days from the receipt of this notice to cause why, if any there be, why the said proposed amendment should not be made.

The heirs in prospect have all expressed themselves as being satisfied for the Department to make the amendment to the finding as proposed.

Very truly yours

J. L. Suffecool
Superintendent

JJ

Shawnee Indian Agency,
Shawnee, Oklahoma,
January 9, 1922.

Mr. A. R. Snyder,
Supt. Potawatomie Indian Agency,
Mayetta, Kansas.

Sac & Fox – Shawnee Estates
1920-1924   Volume VIII

Dear Mr. Snyder:

We have received your letter of January 3rd, 1922, concerning the funds which are on deposit with you to the estates of Penathoquah in which one, Wahthouquah is interested. The information contained in your letter will be given to Wahthouquah.
Very truly yours,

J. L. Suffecool
SUPERINTENDENT

JJ:E7

Shawnee Indian School,
Shawnee, Okla.,
Jan. 11, 1922.

Mr. A. R. Snyder,
   Supt. Potawatomi Indian Agency,
     Mayetta, Kansas.

Dear Mr Snyder:

    This is in reply to your letter of Jan. 3, concerning the interest of some of your Indians in the Joe Whipple estate, through James Thompson, you are advised that the accumulated rentals due the heirs of James Thompson from this estate during the years 1918-1919 was $70.00; that the rentals for 1920 as James Thompson's share was $91.67, making a total of $161.67; check covering which was mailed to you as stated in my letter of December 31, 1920, and for which you receipted Feb. 14, 1920.

    During the year 1921 this land was used without a regularly executed lease but that we were able to collect $133.12, 1/3 of which amounted to $44.37, checks covering it were mailed to you with my letter of December 31, all made payable to the heirs of James Thompson. A lease, however, was made up in this office covering the Joe Whipple allotment for the year 1921, but the price of things began to come down, bondsmen were hard to get and the lease was never completed by the man who used the allotment, hence the collection of the trespass fee.

    I trust that the heirs to this estate on your reservation will see clearly just how the matter has been handled from the information give-in herein.

Sac & Fox – Shawnee Estates
1920-1924 Volume VIII

Very truly yours,

J. L. Suffecool
SUPERINTENDENT

JJ:EV

Shawnee Indian Agency
Shawnee, Oklahoma,
Jan. 13, 1922

Mr. A. R. Snyder,
  Supt. Indian School,
    Mayetta, Kansas.

My Dear Mr. Snyder:

Joseph Springer of Perkins, Oklahoma, Iowa Indian under the supervision of this unit, was in the office yesterday afternoon and brought to my attention his request that I write you concerning the heirs of old lady Roubidoux.

It would appear from the information secured from him that this old lady was alloted[sic] on the Great [Illegible] reservation in Southeastern Nebraska, and that she died and left at the time of her death 3 living children, Felix, Charlie, and [Illegible] Roubidoux, and the issue of a deceased daughter Katherine Dorian. It would appear that the issue of Katherine Dorian, from what he tells me, was not included. This issue consisted of 2 daughters, Josie Springer now living and the wife of Joseph Springer the man referred to above, and Dupuis, who is now dead, and being survived by one Osie Dupuis, who is now attending school at Chilocco.

From the information gathered from him in talking it seems that his wife Josie Springer is entitled to share in Mrs. Roubidoux estate.

I would be pleased to have you make a very careful investigation of this estate and report the status as it now exists and send a carbon of the report to J. Springer, Perkins, Okla.

I am somewhat familiar with the names mentioned as the heirs of Mrs. Roubidoux, as I was in charge of that reservation for several years and I had an opportunity to become acquainted with the parties mentioned.

Thank you for any consideration that you might give this matter.

Very respectfully,

J. L. Suffecool
SUPERINTENDENT

JBS:EV

Shawnee Indian Agency,
Shawnee, Oklahoma, Jan. 13, 1922.

Mr. Arza B. Collins,

  U. S. Indian Farmer,

    Cushing, Oklahoma.

Dear Mr. Collins:

      I am returning you herewith two lease upon the allotments of Hester Pennock and William Pennock, deceased. I have secure[sic] the signature of David Pennock at your request. I have to advise you that the Heirs of Inez Bass have been determined by the Department and the heirs are as follows: Andre Conger, Lee Bass and Ione C. Bass.

      I am also enclosing you herewith a lease upon the allotment of Rhoda Mansur, in favor of Edward McClellan, consideration be $125.00 on the approval of this lease.

Very respectfully,

J.L. Suffecool
Superintendent

TBA

Shawnee Indian Agency,
Shawnee, Oklahoma,
Jan. 16, 1922.

Mr. S. A. Doyle,
1817 West 10th St.,
Oklahoma City, Okla.

Dear Mr. Doyle:

Sac & Fox – Shawnee Estates
1920-1924 Volume VIII

Replying to your letter of the 14th instant in regard to the estate of Sidney Smith in which Renal Richardson has an interest, you are advised as follows:- In as much as you seem to feel aggrieved by the simplest method advanced by this office to settle the difference of the heirs every effort will be made by me to accomplish the same by the method you have chosen, viz. to secure a patent in fee for the heirs.

Enclosed herewith are partially filled blanks for an application for patent in fee, to be completed by Mrs. Richardson. It should be signed, acknowledged before a notary public, and returned to this office. The application will be transmitted to the Indian Office, Washington, with my full report and approval. I have chosen this course in order that you may have no reason to charge this office with unfairness. However, it is suggested now that you must be satisfied with the result. A copy of my letter to the Indian Office will be mailed you.

In the matter of rentals Mrs Richardson was mailed recently. prior to your visit here, $23.14. Furthe[sic] collections are being looked after and you will be fully advised within the near future.

> Very truly yours,

1.cd 18.   J. L. Suffecool,
                                                            Superintendent.

[Illegible]
  [Illegible]-21
  103[???]-21
  C D C
  Heirship
  fees, etc.

Shawnee Indian Agency,
Shawnee, Okla.,
Jan. 19, 1922.

Mr. W. C. Willahan,
   Superintendent Sisseton Agency,
      Sisseton, S. Dakota.

My Dear Mr; Willahan:

There is inclosed herewith Office letter of above reference under date of Jan. 16, 1922 with reference in the collection of certain heirship fees at the Sisseton School.

Sac & Fox – Shawnee Estates
1920-1924 Volume VIII

Will you kindly take this matter up with the Office giving the information desired and furnish me with a copy of your report.

Sincerely yours,

JLS:EV

J. L. Suffecool
SUPERINTENDENT

CC to Indian Office,
Washington, D. C.

Shawnee Indian Agency,
Shawnee, Oklahoma,
Jan. 23, 1922.

Mr. Patrick Matchie,
R. #3, Box 37, Mayetta, Kan.

My Friend:

In reply to your letter of Jan. 18th, in which you state that you understood that a hearing was to be held to determine the heirs to the estate of Kitch-kum-me-qua deceased, you are advised that the records of this office do not show such an estate which is pending under the name you state.

If you can give me any further information concerning the estate, I would be glad to advise you further in the premises.

Very truly yours,

J. L. Suffecool
SUPERINTENDENT

JJ:EV

Shawnee Indian Agency,
Shawnee, Oklahoma,
Jan. 23, 1922

Mr. Geo. A. Hoyo,
Supt. Ponca Agency,
Whiteagle, Oklahoma.

Dear Mr. Hoyo:

Sac & Fox – Shawnee Estates
1920-1924 Volume VIII

There has been received in this office a deed, inherited lands for 5-183, by the heirs of Charles Murray, in favor of Alice Murray wife of Kirwin Murray.

In connection with this matter it is the wish of these heirs that you be informed of the transmittal of this deed to the Indian Office, in order that you may be able to advise these heirs concerning the use of the funds belonging to Alice Murray under your supervision. The deed is being forwarded this day.

Very respectfully,

1 cd 23.   J. L. Suffecool,
                                          Superintendent.

****

Law-Heirship
65540-13
JBK

Shawnee Indian Agency
Shawnee, Oklahoma,
Jan. 24, 1922.

The Honorable
   The Com. of Indian Affairs;
      Washington, D. C.

Dear Mr. Commissioner:

Transmitted herewith is an Indian Deed Inherited Lands covering the allotment of Charles C. Murray, Iowa Allottee No. 68, reference as above, from the heirs to Alice Murray wife of Kerwin[sic] Murray one of the heirs.

The heirs in this estate are all one family and all live together on this allotment. Recently Kirwin Murray married an Otoe Indian girl belonging under Whiteagle Agency and brought his bride home where they all live. It is the desire of all these heirs these young people have a home of their own as evidenced by their signatures to the deed mentioned above. Kirwin Murray's share of the allotment amounts to about 8 or 9 acres. In order that he may be able to use funds belonging to his wife, Alice Murray, to be disbursed under supervision of the Supt. Whiteagle Agency, Whiteagle, Okla, and to protect her interest in the home the deed above mentioned was made in her name.

The action of the heirs in this matter appears to be fair, and I respectfully request the approval of the deed.

Sac & Fox – Shawnee Estates
1920-1924 Volume VIII

1 cd 24.

Very respectfully,
J. L. Suffecool,
Supt. & S.D.A.

Shawnee Indian Agency,
Shawnee, Oklahoma,
Jan. 28, 1922.

Mr. S.Y. Tutwiler,
Kiowa Indian Agency,
Anadarko, Oklahoma.

Dear Mr. Tutwiler:

    Inclosed herewith is the appraisement of the Little Fish allotment as requested by you for your use in connection with the hearing in the case of Nancy Longhat, an Indian of the Kiowa Agency. Since we had no appraisement on this allotment an appraisement had to be made.

Very truly yours,

1 cd 28.
Incls.

J.L. Suffecool,
Superintendent.

Shawnee Indian Agency,
Shawnee, Oklahoma,
Jan. 28, 1922.

Mrs. Louisa Bregange,
P.O. Box 148,
Chitina, Alaska.

Dear Madam:

    I have your letter of December 30 regarding the estate of William McLane.

    In connection with this matter you are informed that the allotment of William McLane consists of 130 acres of land most of which is all under water due to its location being at the lower end of Little River Drainage Ditch. This allotment is not bringing in any revenue at present.

Sac & Fox – Shawnee Estates
1920-1924 Volume VIII

The Government has a drainage tax against the land on account of the construction of the ditch.

The heirs of Rachel Catick in accordance with the Departmental Finding are Louisa Catick and Blanche Catick, each entitled to 1/2 of the estate. Therefore your share of the William McLane is 1/2 each of 504/4032, or 252/4032. You see Rachel Catick's share of the William McLane estate is 504/4032, and one half of which amounts 252/4032 which you and your sister could each get.

The final settlement in this would take place whenever the heirs make a sale of the allotment and a division made of the proceeds of the sale.

Very truly yours,

1 cd 28

J. L. Suffecool,
Superintendent.

Shawnee Indian Agency,
Shawnee, Oklahoma,
Jan. 30, 1922.

Mr. A. R. Snyder,
   Supt. Potawatomie Agency,
   Mayetta, Kansas.

My dear Sir:

Tecumzee, an Indian, under the supervision of this unit, came into this office this afternoon and requested that I write you concerning his lease money, due on the allotment of O-ketch-e-show-o-now, which he claims is now past due.

In view of the fact that he is indebted to this office, it is requested that if there is any money due this Indian from this estate on[sic] any other estate in Kansas, that the same be transferred to this unit, in order that his indebtedness to the Government may be liquidated.

Respectfully yours,

JLS:EV

<u>J. L. Suffecool</u>
SUPERINTENDENT

Sac & Fox – Shawnee Estates
1920-1924 Volume VIII

Probate
91654-21
W H C

Shawnee Indian Agency,
Shawnee, Oklahoma,
Jan. 30, 1922.

The Commissioner of Indian Affairs,
Washington, D. C.

Sir:

This will refer to Office letter of Jan. 27, 1922, bearing the above caption, concerning the claim of Emma Griffinstein against the estate of Catherine Griffinstein.

In connection with this, I have to advise that on Dec. 27th, and 28th, a hearing was held in this office concerning the claim. This hearing was attended by the claimant, Emma Griffinstein, represented by her attorney, C. F. Ennis of the Stanard, Ennis Firm, of Shawnee, Oklahoma, and the heirs of Catherine Griffinstein, represented by W. L. Chapman, an attorney of Shawnee, Oklahoma.

Quite a lengthy testimony was taken from each of the heirs and the claimant and[sic] are still on file in this office subject to inspection and agreement between the attorney who represented the heirs and claimant at this hearing. They had requested that the testimony as taken be held in this office until they called for inspection[sic]. This is the reason that the report has been held up, however, the attorneys are being notified today to attend to the matter, in order that we may make the report necessary.

Very truly yours,

JJ:EV

<u>J. L. Suffecool</u>
Superintendent.

Sac & Fox – Shawnee Estates
1920-1924 Volume VIII

Shawnee Indian Agency,
Shawnee, Oklahoma, Jan. 21, 1922.

Mrs. Minnie Varner,
Cushing, Oklahoma, R# 4

Dear Madam:

Referrence[sic] is made to your letter of the 29th instant, relative to the allotment of Harry Hall, deceased, Sac & Fox allottee No. 287, Lots 1 and 2 & S/2 of NE1/4 of section 4, township 17 north, range 4 east.

I have to advise you that the above lease was subbmitted[sic] to the Department for approval and approved December 15, 1921.

You also stated if you should come to Shawnee that you will like to go over the business of Rachel Hall Pate with me. I shall be glad at anytime to see you.

Very respectfully,

J. L. Suffecool,
Superintendent.

TBA.

Shawnee Indian Agency,
Shawnee, Oklahoma,
Jan. 31, 1922.

Mr. C. H. Ennis,
  Attorney at Law
    Shawnee Okla.

My dear Sir:

The inclosed carbon copy of our letter to the Indian Office in answer to it inquiry as to the hearing that was to be conducted in the matter of the claim of Emma Griffinstein against the estate of Catherine Griffinstein is self-explanatory.

Sac & Fox – Shawnee Estates
1920-1924 Volume VIII

As you know the hearing was conducted before this office on December 27th, and 28th and the hearing has been written up and it is awaiting on file in this office subject to your inspection. We have taken no action in connection with reporting it to the Office in Washington until you shall have had an opportunity to go over the issues with Mr. W. L. Chapman, attorney for the heirs.

Will you go over this matter and return the papers, in order that we may make the report to Washington.

Very truly yours,

JJ:EV
J. L. Suffecool
SUPERINTENDENT

CC to Indian Office,
Washington, D. C.

****

Shawnee Indian Agency,
Shawnee, Oklahoma,
Jan. 31. 1922.

Mr. W. L. Chapman,
Attorney at Law,
Shawnee, Okla.

My dear Sir:

The inclosed copy of our letter to the Indian Office is self-explanatory.

As you know the testimony was taken at this office on December the 27th and 28th, and is awaiting on file in this office subject to your inspection.

Very truly yours,

JJ:EV
J. L. Suffecool
SUPERINTENDENT

Sac & Fox – Shawnee Estates
1920-1924 Volume VIII

Shawnee Indian Agency,
Shawnee, Oklahoma,
Jan. 31, 1922.

Mr. S. Y. Tutwiler,
  Examiner of Inheritance,
    Kiowa Indian Agency,
      Anadarko, Okla.

My dear Mr. Tutwiler:

    We have just received a letter from the Indian Office stating that we did not submit the original papers in the matter of a hearing to determine the heirs of Emily Johnson, Sac and Fox allottee, No. 235.

    You remember you submitted the papers with your letter of December 6, 1921 for us to make a report in connection with the will and to submit the papers. We did so on December 10, but at the time we could find no original papers with your letter and submitted the copies.

    We have looked high and low in this office for the original papers and we are unable to locate them, nor the original folder which should be with the files. It is thought perhaps you have them among your papers.

    Please look through your papers and see if you cannot find the folder and the original papers on the hearing. If you do, please forward them, in order that we may make a further report in the case.

Very truly yours,

JJ:EV

J. L. Suffecool
SUPERINTENDENT

****

Shawnee Indian Agency,
Shawnee, Okla.,
Jan. 31, 1911.

Mrs. Horace J. Johnson,
  c/o Indian Agency,
    Espanola, New Mexico.

My dear Mrs. Johnson:

Examiner of Inheritance, Mr. Tutwiler, and Mr. Wilmeth, took testimony to determine the heirs of Emily Johnson deceased Sac and Fox allottee, No. 236.

At the hearing Dolly Gokey, Esther Bigwalker, and Lelia Bigwalker produced a paper alleged to be the last will and testament of this Sac and Fox Indian woman, Emily Johnson deceased, in which they are shown to be the beneficiaries. They claim that you made up this will in the office at Sac and Fox for Mrs. Emily Johnson. The Examiner of Inheritance has not given it much credence on account of the fact that certain Attorneys of Oklahoma City are representing Dolly Gokey, Esther Bigwalker and Lelia Bigwalker, in connection with this will and that it is not made according to the laws of the State of Okla. However, we made a report on the will to the Indian Office.

Now we want an affidavit from you as to circumstances connected with the making of this will, if you remember. I will be pleased to have you submit an affidavit in connection with this will setting for ~~to~~ the circumstances under which you were requested to make out this will, by whom, who were present, and if Emily Johnson, at the time was present and was of a sound and disposing mind.

We shall appreciate a reply at your earliest convenience.

Very truly yours,

J. L. Suffecool
SUPERINTENDENT

JJ:EV

****

Probate
101697-21
W W G

Shawnee Indian Agency,
Shawnee, Oklahoma,
Jan. 31, 1922.

The Commissioner of Indian Affairs,
Washington, D. C.

Sir:

This is to acknowledge receipt of Office letter, dated Jan. 27, 1911, bearing the above reference, concerning the heirship papers and will of Emily Johnson deceased Sac & Fox allottee #236.

Sac & Fox – Shawnee Estates
1920-1924 Volume VIII

The Office states that we submitted copies of the papers instead of the originals of these papers. These papers or the originals of these papers are not on file in this office, neither can we find the folder for Emily Johnson in this office, except the folder which the Examiner of Inheritance forwarded to us from Kiowa Agency Anadarko, Okla. We are writing to him today to see if he still has some of these papers with his files.

In the mean time[sic], we are taking the matter of the will up with Mrs. Horace J. Johnson of Espanola, New Mexico, to ascertain from her what she remembers about the making of this will.

When the evidence and the original papers are assembled a full report will be made in this connection.

Very truly yours,

J. L. Suffecool
JJ:EV   SUPERINTENDENT

5995-22
ACH

Shawnee Indian Agency,
Shawnee, Oklahoma,
Feb. 1st, 1922.

The Honorable
  The Com. of Indian Affairs,
    Washington, D. C.

Dear Mr. Commissioner:

Reference is made to a letter written by James E. Smith dated Jan. 18-22, attached to slip bearing above caption, requesting for a report concerning the children of John B. McKee, Citizen Pottawatomie allottee No. 821.

Our records indicate that the following are the children of John B. McKee, above mentioned, together with the dates of their birth, all unallotted, and degree of Indian blood:-

Edward McKee,	born	1896	1/8
Gertrude McKee	"	1894	1/8
John T. McKee	"	1892	1/8
Ruby McKee	"	1900	1/8
Bessie McKee	"	1902	1/8

Sac & Fox – Shawnee Estates
1920-1924 Volume VIII

What was said to Eddie McKee in Office Letter Land-Allotments, 116941-1914 HVC dated Nov. 6, 1914 may be applicable to all the heirs of John B. McKee.

Copy of this letter, and copy of letter referred to in paragraph above are now being mailed to James E. Smith, 32 W D Ave., Oklahoma City, Okla.

Very truly yours,

2 od 1   J. L. Suffecool
Incl.   Supt. & S.D.A.

Shawnee Indian Agency,
Shawnee, Okla.,
Feb. 2, 1922.

Mr. Joseph Springer,
    Perkins, Okla.

My dear Mr. Springer:

You will re-call that sometime ago you came to my office and requested that I write to the Supt. of the Indian Agency of the Potawatomie Indians, Mayetta, Kansas and ascertain if the heirs of Mrs. Roubidoux had been determined.

This matter was attended to at once and I am in receipt of a letter from the Supt, which is inclosed for your information.

Very respectfully,

J. L. Suffecool
SUPERINTENDENT

JLS:EV

Shawnee Indian Agency,
Shawnee, Oklahoma,
February 3, 1922.

Mr. A. R. Snyder,
    Supt. Indian Agency,
        Mayetta, Kansas.

Sac & Fox – Shawnee Estates
1920-1924 Volume VIII

My dear Mr. Snyder:

Lily Neal, now Gokey, of this reservation, came into the office this afternoon and requested that I write you concerning lease money due her on the estate of Wah-they-the-quah. Should there be any lease money due this woman from that estate, I would be pleased to have it transferred to this Agency for her, if the amount is small, it would probably be best to have a check written in her name and we can hand the same to her.

Your immediate attention to this matter will be appreciated for the reason that the lady wishes to use the money for use in the purchase of seeds and etc., for the spring work.

       Very respectfully,

JLS:EV   J. L. SUFFECOOL
             SUPERINTENDENT

           Shawnee Indian Agency,
           Shawnee, Oklahoma,
           February 4, 1924.

Mr. S. Y. Tutwiler,
 Examiner of Inheritance.
  Indian Agency
   Concho, Oklahoma.

Dear Mr. Tutwiler:

Referring to my letter of the 28th ultimo transmitting list of deceased Indians and probable heirs, I have received from Supt. Hoyo the names and addresses as follows of the probable heirs of Mary Vetter McGlaslin, Iowa:

  Elizabeth McGlaslin, daughter, born 5-12-09
  Robert McGlaslin, Jr., son   " 4-22-18
  Charles McGlaslin, divorced husband, all of
    Red Rock, Oklahoma.

       Very truly yours,

        J. L. Suffecool,
Mc--   Superintendent.

Sac & Fox – Shawnee Estates
1920-1924 Volume VIII

Land-Sales.
35671-13

545-22
NR

Shawnee Indian Agency,
Shawnee, Oklahoma,
Feb. 7, 1922.

The Commissioner of Indian Affairs,
Washington, D. C.

Sir:

This refers to Office letter dated Feb. 1, 1922, with reference to correspondence, concerning the allotment of Clarisse Tescier deceased, stating that as soon as the heirs of Rosalie Goyer, a deceased heir, are determined or if all are competent adults, a patent in fee to the heirs jointly will be issued.

In this connection, I have to advise that all of the heirs are competnent[sic] adults; that the husband of the deceased heir Rosalie Goyer is a white man, and Lula Tescier, the wife of Robert Tescier, who is one of the heirs, is a white woman. It is believed that a patent in fee issued to the heirs jointly will facilitate matters greatly.

Anthony Tescier and the other heirs live as white people and are practically white to all intents and purposes, and they should be given a patent in fee for this allotment, as well as that of Robert Tescier.

Anthony Tescier and Lula Goyer are heirs and equal shares to the Robert Tescier allotment.

The matter in which Anthony Tescier desires the allotment to be partitioned would hardly meet the approval of the Office, as the descriptions in most cases are not of legal divisions.

If a patent in fee was to be issued to the heirs and if they wish a division to be made of the allotment, they could do so through the State courts.

Sac & Fox – Shawnee Estates
1920-1924 Volume VIII

Very truly yours,

John Jones
Clerk in Charge

JJ:EV

Land-Sales
60885-13
72029-15
87983-21
F I P

Shawnee Indian Agency,
Shawnee, Oklahoma,
Feb. 7, 1922.

The Commissioner of Indian Affairs,
Washington, D. C.

Sir:

This will refer the Office to correspondence had in connection with the settlement of William Shawnee, Sr, allotment under this jurisdiction. We especially refer to Office letter, dated Nov. 14, 1911, bearing the above caption, in which a sale of 20 acres of this allotment is authorized, in order that the 6/39ths unrestricted interest of Julia Shawnee may be set aside to satisfy judgment rendered ~~info~~ in favor of one, F. B. Reed.

In this connection, I inclose, herewith, a letter from the attorney in the case, Charles E. Wells, dated Feb. 4, 1922, in answer to our letter of Jan. 31, in which we went into the matter of settlement of this case with him after making several attempts to get into communication by correspondence with the heirs, all of which brought no result, altho Julia Shawnee states that she has heard from most of the heirs and they are all willing to execute papers to settle the case in the manner proposed.

Mr. Wells is under the impression that this 20 acres referred to should be deeded by the heirs to satisfy the judgment against Julia Shawnee covering the 6/39ths interest she has in the land which is not restricted.

In our letter to him of Jan. 31, we advised him that the proposition made by the Office was to make a sale of the 20 acres to F. B. Reed, or to the highest bidder and if it should bring the appraised value (appraisal to be made by this office) and if the proceeds exceeded the amount of her indebtedness the excess to be paid to Julia Shawnee, or if the indebtedness

Sac & Fox – Shawnee Estates
1920-1924 Volume VIII

equals the amount of the sale, proceeds of the 20 acres then she would received nothing.

It is noted that Mr. Wells states that Mr. Reed will be willing to take the loss, if the appraised value put on the 20 acres is less than the indebtedness he has purchased of other parties on the 6/39ths interest, but if it should bring more than the appraised value, Mr. Reed will not be willing to pay out more any more than he is out already.

This matter is referred to the Office again for its information as to the attitude of the attorney and Mr. Reed in the matter.

This case is a very difficult one to settle for the reason that the other heirs to this allotment are scattered all over Oklahoma, and some of the letters which we have addressed to each of the heirs have been returned unclaimed and no answer received from those letters that have not been returned to us. This is one reason for the delay in consummating this matter, and another reason is that we do not wish to consummate several transactions all under separate correspondence with each of the heirs; we are making provisions in consummating the transactions up to a state where all the papers necessary to or signed by the heirs may be inclosed with one communication. The matter will be, under these conditions, handled as expeditiously as possible.

Very truly yours,

JOHN JONES
JJ:EV CLERK IN CHARGE

Shawnee Indian Agency,
Shawnee, Oklahoma,
Feb. 9th, 1922.

Supt. George A. Hoyo,
Ponca Indian Agency,
Whiteagle, Okla.

Dear Mr. Hoyo:

In reply to your letter of the 6th instant you are advised that the heirs of Jefferson Kihega have not been determined. The heirs of Phoebe Black have been determined and a copy of the Secretary's finding is herewith inclosed.

Sac & Fox – Shawnee Estates
1920-1924 Volume VIII

Upon receipt of the approval of the sale of five acres of the allotment of Charles Murray to Alice Murray by deed you will be immediately informed of the date thereof.

Very truly yours,

2 od 9.
Incl.

John Jones,
Clerk in charge.

Shawnee Indian Agency,
Shawnee, Oklahoma,
Feb. 10, 1922.

Dr. Jacob Breid,
Sac & Fox Sanatorium,
Toledo, Iowa.

My dear Doctor Breid:

In reply to your letter of the 8th instant regarding the interests, inherited and otherwise, under this Agency of Thomas Chuck and Alice Lincoln, heirs of Jim Scott, and Sa-ke-na-we-qua:

Inform Thomas Chuck and Alice Lincoln that Jim Scott was never allotted here but that he is an heir in the following estates,

Susie Grant Scott,	share,	1/2
Gertrude Givens,	"	64/1080[sic]
Charlotte Pattequa,	"	448/5400
Lucy Thurman,	"	64/180
Mary Thurman, unallot.	"	All.

Of these only the allotment of Lucy Thurman was sold. From the proceeds of this sale, etc., they have to their credit, Thomas Chuck $517.23, Alice Lincoln $421.04

The oil lease which Sa-ke-na-we-qua signed recently is still incomplete. It will be hastened as rapidly as possible. This party has to her credit in this office $513.85.

Supt. J. L. Suffecool has gone to Mexico to pay Indians belonging under this Agency located there and will return next week. Upon his return the funds mentioned abov[sic] will be transferred to you for disbursement in accordance with your instruction governing such matters.

Sac & Fox – Shawnee Estates
1920-1924 Volume VIII

Very sincerely,

2 od 10.
John Jones,
Clerk in charge.

****

DR. JACOB BREID
SUPERINTENDENT AND PHYSICIAN

DEPARTMENT OF THE INTERIOR

UNITED STATES INDIAN SERVICE

SAC & FOX SANATORIUM
TOLEDO, IOWA

RECEIVED
FEB 10 1922
SHAWNEE INDIAN AGENCY

Feb. 8, 1922.

Supt. J. L. Suffecool,
Shawnee Indian Agency,
Shawnee, Okla.

My dear Mr. Suffecool:

  The heirs of Jim Scott, who live on this reservation have asked me to write you regarding their share of this allotment which, they understand, has been sold. The heirs are Thomas Chuck, Alice Lincoln.

  Sa-ke-na-we-qua also inquires regarding funds which she may have in your office. She signed an oil and gas lease recently.

Very respectfully,

Jacob Breid
Jb/EA   Superintendent.

refer to
  Dushane:- about sale
   Judge:- " Lease – incomplete
   MPG:- " Money
        JHJ

****

Sac & Fox – Shawnee Estates
1920-1924 Volume VIII

Shawnee Indian Agency,
Shawnee, Oklahoma,
Feb. 10, 1922.

Dr. Jacob Breid,
Sac & Fox Sanatorium,
Toledo, Iowa.

My dear Doctor Breid:

In reply to your letter of the 8th instant regarding the interests, inherited and otherwise, under this Agency of Thomas Chuck and Alice Lincoln, heirs of Jim Scott, and Sa-ke-na-we-qua:

Inform Thomas Chuck and Alice Lincoln that Jim Scott was never allotted here but that he is an heir in the following estates,

Susie Grant Scott,	share,	1/2
Gertrude Givens,	"	64/1080[sic]
Charlotte Pattequa,	"	448/5400
Lucy Thurman,	"	64/180
Mary Thurman, unallot.	"	All.

Of these only the allotment of Lucy Thurman was sold. From the proceeds of this sale, etc., they have to their credit, Thomas Chuck $517.23, Alice Lincoln $421.04

The oil lease which Sa-ke-na-we-qua signed recently is still incomplete. It will be hastened as rapidly as possible. This party has to her credit in this office $513.85.

Supt. J. L. Suffecool has gone to Mexico to pay Indians belonging under this Agency located there and will return next week. Upon his return the funds mentioned abov[sic] will be transferred to you for disbursement in accordance with your instruction governing such matters.

Very sincerely,

2 od 10.
John Jones,
Clerk in charge.

Sac & Fox – Shawnee Estates
1920-1924 Volume VIII

Land Heirship
91743-1912
4806 -1013
  F. E.

Shawnee Indian Agency,
Shawnee, Oklahoma,
Feb. 11, 1922.

The Honorable,
    The Com. of Ind. Affairs.
      Washington, D.C.

Dear Mr. Commissioner:

    Walter Washington, one of the heirs of Stella Washington, above reference, wishes to purchase the shares of the other heirs to the allotment of this estate described as NE/4 of the SW/4 of Section 31, Township 11 north of Range 5 east of the Indian Meridian in Oklahoma.

    The heirs have requested the sale of this allotment. At appraisement of $1100.00 has recently been made. Walter Washington will pay $1,200.00 for the land which is above appraisement.

    Two of the heirs, as declared above, are dead, viz. Nannie Washington, or Quah-qua-che-qua, and Mary Washington, and their heirs were determined in Law-Heirship 74360-14 F W S, and Probate 8162-19 W H G, respectively. One of the heirs of Nannie Washington, viz. Hah-wah-che-se-mo, also died, and his sole heir was first determined to be Willie Gibson, father, Jan. 5, 1915 (112258-14) then by Modification Feb. 13, 1921 (71675-21) Minnie Chisholm, half sister, was declared to be his sole heir. This gave Minnie Chisholm two thirds interest of the one eleventh interest of Nannie Washington in the estate of Stella Washington. Minnie Chisholm is the only minor heir.

    I wish to be advised of such transaction the Office will approve.

        Very respectfully,

2 od 11.
        John Jones,
        Clerk in charge

Sac & Fox – Shawnee Estates
1920-1924 Volume VIII

Shawnee Indian Agency,
Shawnee, Oklahoma,
Feb. 11, 1922.

Mr. James Shopwetuck,
Konowa[sic], Oklahoma.

Dear Sir:

This in reply to your letter of the 4th instant, concerning the estate of So-sah.

You are informed that there [sic] no forms of affidavit in regular use in connection with such cases you mentioned. Also it would be necessary for me to have full knowledge of the matter which you wish embodied in an affidavit before I could make you one that would in any way meet your requirements.

I would advise you that it may be the best for you to come to this office in order that we may obtain from you the facts necessary. In that way we will be able to help you to better advantage.

Very truly yours,

2 od 11.

John Jones,
Clk. in charge.

Shawnee Indian Agency,
Shawnee, Oklahoma,
Feb. 14, 1922.

Miss Edith Johnson,
911 College Ave.,
Topeka, Kansas.

Dear Miss Johnson:

This is in reply to your letter of the 12 instant regarding to the Madeline Denton estate.

You are kindly informed that on account the present abnormal conditions, and to the fact that this allotment is not a desirable tract of land agriculturally that we have not been able to get a lessee. Further there are

Sac & Fox – Shawnee Estates
1920-1924 Volume VIII

no funds to the credit Oscar Johnson, George Johnson, Silas Johnson and Edith Johnson for the reason as set forth above.

At your request I am submitting you the name and address of a bonded abstracter, as follows:- J. Harmon Lewis, Tecumseh, Oklahoma. This man should be able to give you all information if you will give him the description of the land or the name of the owner of the allotment you have in mind.

Very truly yours,

2 od 14.   J. L. Suffecool,
                                                   Superintendent.

Shawnee Indian Agency,
Shawnee, Oklahoma,
February 17, 1922.

Mr. A. R. Snyder,
   Potawatomie Indian Agency,
   Mayetta, Kansas.

My dear Mr. Snyder:

With reference to your letter of February 13th, in which you informed us as to the determination of the heirs of Ke-ah-tah-be-ah, I have to advise that Wah-pah-nah-pe-ah, who is declared to be sole heir, is the wife of the decedent, who we have on our rolls here as Wah-pah-nah-pe-quah.

On behalf of this heir, who lives in this jurisdiction, I will be pleased to have you transfer the funds, to the decedents[sic] credit in your office, to this Agency and at the same time furnish us with a copy of the Department's finding in this case, in order that we may complete our records.

Ke-ah-tah-be-ah had certain inherited interests under this jurisdiction which would fall to his surviving wife, Wah-pah-nah-pe-ah, hence the request for the copy of Department finding.

Very truly yours,

JJ:EV   J. L. Suffecool
                                                   Superintendent

Sac & Fox – Shawnee Estates
1920-1924   Volume VIII

Shawnee Indian Agency,
Shawnee, Oklahoma,
February 17, 1922.

Mr. Walter D. Sullins,
Red Rock, Oklahoma.

My dear Mr. Sullins:

This has reference to your letter written at the bottom of a letter which was written to you by Supt. George A. Hoyo, Ponca Indian Agency, which has reference to a claim of $415.20 against the estate if Mary O. Grant.

We have made a thorough examination of the records and we are unable to find any claim filed against this estate; that the determination by the Department of the heirs of this deceased Indian, has no reference to any claim which has been filed.

That the funds which were in this office to the decedent's credit in this office have long since been transferred to Supt. Hoyo of the Ponca Indian Agency. Further receipt of funds derived from this estate will be transferred to the Supt. at Ponca Indian Agency from time to time.

We regret that we are unable to give you any further light on this matter than we have.

Very truly yours,

J. L. Suffecool
Superintendent

JJ:EV

Shawnee Indian Agency
Shawnee, Oklahoma
Feb/ 2-. 1022

Dr. Jacob Breid, Supt.
Sac & Fox Sanatorium
Toledo, Iowa

Dear Mr[sic]. Breid:

With reference to your letter concerning the James, John and Jane Wolfe estates under this jurisdiction in which you state there are more claimants, I have to advise that this will be called to the attention of the Examiner of Inheritance when he is assigned to this Agency again.

future. It looks as though the Office will assign one her with the near

Very truly yours

J. L. Suffecool
Superintendent

JJ

Shawnee Indian Agency
Shawnee, Oklahoma
Feb. 20, 1922

Mr. S. Y. Tutwiler
Examiner of Inheritance
Kiowa Indian Agency
Anadarko, Oklahoma

Dear Mr. Tutwiler:

      In compliance with your request in your letter of February 17, 1922 for retained filed in the matter of the hearing conducted to determine the heirs of John Nix (Mah mah qua cho), I herewith inclose the file in the case.

      If there is anything else you need in this connection, just say the word and we will be glad to comply.

Very truly yours

J. L. Suffecool
Superintendent

Incls.

Shawnee Indian Agency
Shawnee, Oklahoma
Feb. 21, 1922

Mr. A. E. Crane
Attorney at Law
516 New England Building
Topeka, Kansas

Sac & Fox – Shawnee Estates
1920-1924 Volume VIII

Dear Sir:

In reply to your letter of Feb. 17 in which you state that the Indian Office has held Peter Soldier to be the heir of Ke-tum-wa, deceased Pottawatomie allottee under this Agency; that the Department is waiting to receive the appraisement certificate to close the case and ask that we attend to this matter, you are advised that the heirs of Ke-tum-wa, deceased are not yet legally and officially determined by the Department.

In connection with the appraisement of the allotment, you are advised that the land was appraised and the appraisement certificate was forwarded to the Indian Office on July 27, 1921. Information of this action was [illegible] you, perhaps for reason that there is no record on file in this office showing that you have any interest in the case as an heir or any information that you are entitled to this information the property being solely under the jurisdiction of the Department.

Very truly yours

J. L. Suffecool
Superintendent

JJ

Shawnee Indian Agency,
Shawnee, Oklahoma,
Feb. 21, 1922.

Dr. Jacob Breid,
Sac & Fox sanatorium[sic],
Toledo, Iowa.

My dear Dr. Breid:

I have your letter of the 18th instant regarding the John McKuk allotment in which William Davenport has a 1/2 interest.

That due to the fact that some [sic] the heirs have died and their heirs have not been determined nothing can be done at the present.

If all of the heirs are determined in the near future please call our attention to this matter and your wishes and advice will be followed.

Sac & Fox – Shawnee Estates
1920-1924 Volume VIII

Sincerely yours,

J. L. Suffecool
Superintendent.

2 od 21.

Shawnee Indian Agency,
Shawnee, Oklahoma, Feb. 11, 1922.

Mr. John A. Neal,
    Wanette, Oklahoma.
Dear Sir:

    Referrence[sic] is made to your letter of the 18th instant, relative to Indian land in section 15-6N-2 East, I have to advise you that this Office has only one tract of Indian land in the above section, belonging to Mabel G. Quintard, deceased, Cit. Pottawatomie allottee No. 1096, described as the E/2 of the NE1/4 of section 15, Township 6 north, range 2 East.

    The sole heir in the above estate is Walter L. Luthie, of R# 6, North Topeka, Kansas.

    I am enclosing you herewith Regulations Governing[sic] leasing restricted allotted Indians land for mining purposes, which will give you all the information you desire.

Very respectfully,

J. L. Suffecool,
Superintendent

TBA

Probate
L L

Shawnee Indian Agency
Shawnee, Oklahoma
Feb. 21, 1922

Sac & Fox – Shawnee Estates
1920-1924 Volume VIII

The Commissioner of Indian Affairs
Washington, D. C.

Dear Mr. Commissioner:

Complying with the request in Office letter of Feb. 13, 1922 for information concerning the conditions of heirship work at this Agency and what accomodation[sic] can be furnished the Examiner of Inheritance and his official force, I have to advise that there are 10 new cases at this time, besides a number of requests for re-opening of cases, and some where rehearing has been authorized and there are those wherein hearing had been held but not completed [illegible] such lack of evidence or [illegible] other reasons. The cases, both new and old ones which require work of the Examiner of Inheritance will not, at this time, exceed twenty.

We have sufficient office space and quarters for the Examiner of Inheritance and his official force, therefore we will be able to take care of them.

Very truly yours

J. L. Suffecool
Superintendent

JJ

Shawnee Indian Agency,
Shawnee, Oklahoma,
Feb. 23, 1922.

Mr. Thomas Oliver,
Whiting, Kansas.

Dear Sir:

This is in answer to your letter of Feb. 13, last in regard to your rental in the Oliver Jackson estate, and the heirship matter in the John, James and Jane Wolf Estates.

There has recently been paid inon[sic] the Oliver Jackson lease $50, which is being place to your credit and will at once be transfered[sic] to Supt. A. R. Snyder, Mayetta, Kansas for disdursement[sic].

Sac & Fox – Shawnee Estates
1920-1924 Volume VIII

In the heirship matter of the Wolfe you are informed that there has been held several hearings at various places and that a supplemental hearing may yet be required before the case is determined.

Very truly yours,

2 od 23.

J. L. Suffecool,
Superintendent.

Shawnee Indian Agency,
Shawnee, Oklahoma,
February 23, 1922.

Mr. Wm. G. Foster,
R. #4, Cushing, Okla.

My dear Sir:

Replying to your letter of February 15, 1922, concerning the inquiry of Minnie Barker about the Samuel L. Brown estate, you are advised, that the Department decreed Fryor Franklin Brown to be the sole heir.

In [illegible] you and your daughter being entitled to get your lease money, you are advised that if there is any money on the books which is due you, it will be paid to you the 1st Thursday of March, as the 1st Thursday of each month is Sac & Fox day, and we plan to draw the checks and have them ready for delivery on that day. Usually we send the checks for money, that is to the credit of every Indian who lives in and around Cushing, to Mr. A. B. Collins in Cushing, the following Saturday after the 1st Thursday in each month.

Very truly yours,

JJ:EV

J. L. Suffecool
Superintendent

Sac & Fox – Shawnee Estates
1920-1924 Volume VIII

Shawnee Indian Agency,
Shawnee, Oklahoma,
February 23, 1922.

Mr. Pete Pah mah mie,
  c/o James F. McKeown,
  R. #5, Mayetta, Kan.

My dear Sir:

    This is to again acknowledge receipt of your letter of February 20, 1922, in which you go into the matter of your desire to acclaim in the estate of Ke tum wah.

    In this connection, you are advised, that the hearing in this case was forwarded to the Indian Office a long time ago, but no final determination has been made by the Department, however, your contention as contained in your letter will be brought to the attention of the Examiner of Inheritance when he is assigned to this Agency for heirship work, in order that he may look into the merits of your claim.

    Very truly yours,

    J. L. Suffecool
JJ:EV   Superintendent

Id-Ind
11896-22
E88

Shawnee Indian Agency,
Shawnee, Oklahoma,
February 24, 1922.

The Commissioner of Indian Affairs,
  Washington, D. C.

Sir:

    Replying to Office letter, dated February 18, 1922, in reply to mine of February 6th, concerning an account of L. J. Hampton against Samuel Houston, a deceased Sac & Fox Indian, I have to advise, that the prospective heirs are his children, Lee Cuppawhe, a son, and Madeline Houston Carter, a daughter.

Sac & Fox – Shawnee Estates
1920-1924 Volume VIII

Upon investigation we find that both of these prospective heirs are in fair circumstances especially the husband of Madeline Houston Carter, Joe Carter, the husband, is as well to do as the average white man in the community in which he lives. Lee Cuppawhe, the son, and his wife both receive rentals through this office and are fairly well to do financially.

The amount to the credit of Samuel Houston, deceased, is $147.22. Rentals will be accumulating to this account pending the determination of the heirs.

Very truly yours,

J. L. Suffecool
JJ:EV   Superintendent

Probate
101697-21
W H G

Shawnee Indian Agency,
Shawnee, Oklahoma,
February 24, 1922.

The Commissioner of Indian Affairs
  Washington, D. C.

Sir:

This will refer the Office to its letter of January 27, bearing the above reference to files, concerning the heirship papers and will of Emily Johnson, deceased Sac and Fox allottee, No. 235. The Office requested that the original papers be transmitted in addition to the carbon copies which were transmitted heretofore; and that we take such testimony as can be given by Mrs. Johnson now of Espanola, New Mexico.

At the time the papers were transmitted by this office, it was noted that the original papers were not with the file when it reached this office. Examiner of the Inheritance, Mr. Tutwiler, forwarded the file from the Kiowa Agency, Anadarko, Oklahoma.

Upon receiving request from the Office that originals of the papers be transmitted, we wrote to Mr. Tutwiler and asked him to search his records and files to ascertain whether he returned any of the original papers. He advises that he has searched among his papers carefully and he has been unable to find any papers connected with this case. He, also, states that the original was attached together in a separate bunch; and that the copies to be returned to this office were attached together in another bunch, but they were not found so when they reached this office.

We, also, addressed a letter to Mrs. Mary Johnson of Espanola, New Mexico, requesting her to submit an affidavit covering the circumstances connected with the making of the will by Emily Johnson in the office at Sac and Fox sub-agency, if she remembered anything in regard to the case. We received a reply on February 14th, from Mrs. Mary Johnson, stating that she doesnot[sic] remember of having prepared such a paper at the Sac and Fox Agency office.

We have searched thoroughly, the files in this office for the original papers in this heirship case and we are unable to furnish them for the reason that we do not have them, and we are also unable to furnish any further light in connection with the alleged last will and testament of Emily Johnson.

      Very truly yours,

      J. L. Suffecool
JJ:EV   Superintendent

      Shawnee Indian Agency,
      Shawnee, Oklahoma,
      Feb. 25, 1922.

Mr. Joseph Cooper,
Fort Thompson,
South Dakota.

Dear Sir:

Reference is mad[sic] to your letter of the 10th Instant regarding your claim in the estates of No-de-no-qua and Kon-ze-win.

You are informed that the heirs of No-de-no-qua were never determined for the reason that the alotment[sic] was sold Oct. 20, 1903 and that no reason exists for requiring such determination as there is no property to be considered. As to Kon-ze-win you are informed that there is no one on our rolls by that name.

Our records show fail to show any Departmental finding in the above estates have ever been made it is presumed for the reason above mentioned. If this office can assist you further your wishes in the matter are invited.

Very sincerely

2 od 25.
J. L. Suffecool,
Superintendent.

Shawnee Indian Agency,
Shawnee, Oklahoma,
March 3, 1922.

Burford, Miley, Hoffman & Burford,
　Lawyers,
906-912 State Nat'l Bank Bldg.,
　Oklahoma City, Oklahoma:

Gentlemen:

　　Replying to your letter of February 25, requesting information as to whether or not the Department has made a decision in the case of Emily Johnson, Sac and Fox allottee #235, you are advised, that we have received no official notice that the heirs to this estate have been determined. We recently submitted a supplementary report on this case, which will no doubt delay the decision further.

Very truly yours,

JJ:EV
J. L. Suffecool
Superintendent

Land-Sales
75351-12
1659-22
JTH

Shawnee Indian Agency,
Shawnee, Oklahoma,
March 4, 1922.

The Commissioner of Indian Affairs,
　Washington, D. C.

Sac & Fox – Shawnee Estates
1920-1924 Volume VIII

Sir:

This refers to Office letter of February 6, 1922, bearing the above caption, requesting that we consult the heirs of Samuel Cummings, concerning the deed that they should execute to J. R. Thorn, containing a clause reserving the oil and gas rights.

We have reviewed the file in this case, and submit the following report:

We have not consulted the heirs with regard to conveying the land to Mr. Thorn with the reservation clause.

Helen Cummings, one of the heirs to Samuel Cummings estate, is feeble minded, and is, therefore, incompetent to sign a deed. Andrew J. Cummings, her brother, with whom she lives, is understood to be her legal guardian.

In reviewing the case, we find that the Pottawatomie County Court refused to issue an order confirming the sale, which at one time stated that it had no further jurisdiction, as the land involved was sold through said court.

Attention is called to this fact, for the reason, that should a deed be executed by the heirs, containing a clause reserving the oil and gas rights, it will be necessary for the guardian to execute a deed in behalf of the feeble minded heir, which will require confirmation of sale by the Pottawatomie County Court. This will be one difficulty encountered when we attempt the sale to Mr. Thorne[sic] by a deed.

In a letter from this office, dated May 29, 1916, to the Office, the letter from Mr. J. R. Thorne was quoted, in which he made objections to the reservation of oil and gas rights to the heirs, stating that if the land is drilled full of holes, it would impair the value of the land for agricultural purposes. He probably would still object to the reservation, preferring to pay a reasonable prospective oil value to the heirs in addition to the consideration paid through the courts on August 26, 1912.

It would be remembered, that Assistant Oil Inspector Kent was assigned to appraise the prospective oil and gas value on this land. He reported that several dry holes had been drilled near this land; that a well is being drilled within 4 1/2 miles from this land, and he advised that the sale of the land be withheld until such time as the well which was being drilled was proved dry, or brought in with oil in paying quantities. As

Sac & Fox – Shawnee Estates
1920-1924 Volume VIII

reported to the Office, on Jan. 3rd, this well was brought in, but it has created no great amount of excitement, nor activities in the leasing of land for oil and gas purposes near this well.

Mr. Thorn, upon request by the Office, through this Agency, deposited $954.50 to protect the interests of the then minor heirs, and was placed to the credit of the following:

    Helen Cummings (incompetent) $419.39
    Clarence Shives(the then minor) $138.79
    Florence Shives- - - - - - - - - - - $139.80
    [Illegible] Shives- - - - - - - - - - $139.80
    [Name Illegible] - - - - - - - - - - $104.82

The money, which is now to the credit of Helen Cummings, incompetent, is $543.39, having grown to that amount from the original deposit of J. R. Thorn; and that the amount of $419.39, which was deposited for benefit of the Shives children had grown to $450.00 when it appears to have been withdrawn by my predecessor, during one of the Liberty Loan campaigns, for the purpose of purchasing bonds; but he later withdrew the proposition, and this amount was placed on Special Deposits, and it is still there. The amount of $104.82, the original deposit made by Mr. Thorn to the credit of Andy Albright, has grown to $134.80. Correspondence in the case shows that $943.50, original deposit made by Mr. Thorn, was to be paid back to him when title to land, which he attempted to purchase, was perfected in him; provided that the consideration he paid was found to be adequate; if not, the difference between what he did pay the heirs, and the value ascertained by this office, to be deducted from the amount he had deposited for the interests of the minor heirs and the incompetent one. However, some of the heirs contend that, as soon as the title was preferred in the alleged purchased, Mr. Thorn, this money was to be distributed to the minor heirs, and the incompetent, Helen Cummings.

Another difficulty, that will be encountered in the execution of a deed to Mr. Thorn, will be to find some of the heirs. Some of these heirs live in Colorado; some in Texas; and some of the others addresses are unknown at this time. It is believed, however, that we can find all of them through some of the heirs who still reside in this vicinity. However, these heirs have already received their portion of the consideration derived from the sale through the court of this land, and are not very much interested in executing papers to perfect the title in the

Sac & Fox – Shawnee Estates
1920-1924 Volume VIII

alleged purchaser[sic]; and we have found it, heretofore, a very difficult matter to get the papers executed without undue delay.

The correspondence shows, that during the Superintendency of Mr. O. J. Green, all the papers necessary in the case for the issuance of a patent in fee were submitted to the Office. These papers were all properly and duly executed by the heirs.

In view of the above facts, and the contemplated difficulties to be encountered in the execution of a deed by the heirs, it would be the better plan, it appears to me, to have an oil inspector to appraise the prospective oil and gas value contained in the allotment involved, and request Mr. Thorn to deposit this value in this office to be distributed to the heirs of Samuel Cummings; and when this is done, the land Office can be requested to issue a patent in fee to Mr. Thorne[sic].

It is possible, however, that Mr. Thorn well not be very willing to pay what he might consider to be an excessive valuation of the oil prospects in the land.

We will await further advices from the Office, in view of the above report, before proceeding to prepare the deed for execution by the heirs, especially in connection with the requirement of the Office to have a court order issued confirming the sale of the interests of the incompetent heir, Helen Cummings; and also of having the oil and gas value appraised; and requesting Mr. Thorn to deposit the amount in this office.

The Office will see the difficulties to be encountered by reviewing the correspondence in the case.

Very truly yours,

J. L. Suffecool
Superintendent

JJ:EV

Sac & Fox – Shawnee Estates
1920-1924 Volume VIII

Land-
Sales.
35671-13
11895-22
E R

Shawnee Indian Agency,
Shawnee, Oklahoma,
March 8, 1922.

The Commissioner of
Indian Affairs,
Washington, D. C.

Sir:-

    Referring to Office letter with above caption, dated March 3, with regard to partition of lands of the Tescier family, I have to advise, that Rosalie Goyer, a deceased heir of Clarisse Tescier, I understand left children and her husband, who is a white man. However, we have not[sic] information as to how old these children are. If they are of age, patent cannot be issued, however, it would appear that no action can be taken, whether for partition, or the issuance of a patent, until the heirs of Rosalie Goyer have been determined.

    It is noted, that the Office will take action in the case of Robert Anthony Tescier.

                Very truly yours,

                          J. L. Suffecool
                          Superintendent

JJ:EV

Shawnee Indian Agency
Shawnee, Oklahoma
March 11, 1922

Higgins & Barton, Attorneys
Rooms 23, 24, 26, Lutz Building
Cushing, Oklahoma

Gentlemen:

Sac & Fox – Shawnee Estates
1920-1924 Volume VIII

This is in answer to your letter of Mar. 10, 1923 in behalf of Mr. O. A. Corliss or A. G. Corliss. For his information I am inclosing herewith carbon copy of our letter to Supt. Hoyo of Ponca Indian Agency which shows the action taken with respect to securing reimbursement to him of money paid to heirs to which he was entitled as purchaser of the land.

You will note that not all the oil and ga lease rentals are due him. The rentals accrued up to Feb. 18, 1921, when his purchase of the land was approved, were due the heirs. The accruals of rentals subsequent to Feb. 18 is due the purchaser, Mr. Corliss, which is $7.67. Collection of this has been started as you see from our letter to Mr. Hoyo. You will also note that we are endeavoring to get back for him the $35.00 agricultural rental which was paid to the heirs, these rents having been received and accrued after the approval of the sale to him. The Department holds that all rents accrued up to and including the date of the approval of the sale are due the heirs or allottee.

Several communications have gone out from this office in connection with the collection of the rents paid to heirs which they received erroneously; also explanation of the matter to Mr. Corliss.

I trust that there is sufficient information in this an in the carbon copy of our letter to Mr. Hoyo in order that Mr. Corliss will understand the matter thoroughly.

      Very truly yours

         J. L. Suffecool
         Superintendent
Incl. CC to Mr. Hoyo
JJ

     ****

    Shawnee Indian Agency, Shawnee, Oklahoma
       March 11, 1922

Mr. George A. Hoyo, Supt.
Ponca Indian Agency
Whiteagle, Oklahoma

Dear Mr. Hoyo:

  This refers to John C. Falk's heirs having to reimburse Mr. A. G. Corliss for rent paid in after the approval of the sale of this

Sac & Fox – Shawnee Estates
1920-1924 Volume VIII

allotment. The agricultural rent paid in by the Lessee accrued subsequent to the approval date. It is due the purchaser of the land, Mr. Corliss.

The amount was $35.00 as stated in our letter of November 26, 1921 to you. The heirs were to reimburse in amounts set opposite their names as follows:

Maggie Ely,	$17.49
Margaret Bassett	5.84
Hoke S. Blackhawk	5.84
Nellie Pickering	5.83
	35.00

In your letter of Nov. 29, 1921 you advised us that you would see that checks in amounts indicated were drawn and sent to us for Mr. Corliss as money comes in to the credit of the Indians.

On December 22, 1921 we mentioned this matter again. On Feb. 21, 1922 you mailed check for $5.83 from Nellie Pickering. You stated that as soon as the others received funds to their credit you would mail us checks. The check from the Nellie Pickering account, $5.83, was mailed to Mr. Corliss with our letter to him of Feb. 24, 1922. You again state in your letter of Feb. 27, 1922 in answer to ours of Feb. 24, that you will see to this matter for us for which we thank you.

There was an oil and gas lease on the allotment of John C. Falk, deceased. This lease was approved by the Department on March 22, 1920. This made the annual rental due March 22, 1921. This rent was paid in Jan. 25, 1921. The rentals accrued up to and including Feb. 18, 1921 were due the heirs. From Feb. 18 to Mar. 22, 1921 the rental would become due the purchaser. $92.00 was paid in. This would entitle the purchased to $7.67. Now, we ask your cooperation in getting the little sum reimbursed to Mr. Corliss the purchaser. The amount due from each heir then would be:

Maggie Ely,	$3.83
Margaret Bassett,	1.28
Hoke S. Blackhawk,	1.28
Nellie Pickering.	1.28

I shall be glad if you will hypothecate the additional sum against the accounts of these Indians and include same in the checks when drawing them to transmit to us for Mr. Corliss.

Carbon copy of our letter to Higgins & Barton, Attorneys at Cushing, Oklahoma for information of Mr. Corliss is herewith for your

Sac & Fox – Shawnee Estates
1920-1924 Volume VIII

information. I am sending a carbon copy of this letter to these Attorneys also.

                      Very truly yours

                                  J. L. Suffecool
                                    Superintendent

Incl.
JJ
CC to Higgins & Barton, Cushing, Okla.

Probate-
131781-15
2713-21
48311-19
L A P
Heirship, Shawnee Agency.   Shawnee Indian Agency,
                                                    Shawnee, Oklahoma,
                                                      March 13, 1922.

        The Honorable,
           The Commissioner
             of Indian Affairs,
                Washington, D. C.

        Sir:

                Replying to Office letter, dated March 8, 1922, bearing the above caption, regarding the request for appraisement of the estate of Ke tum wa, No. 1070, I have to advise that appraisement of this allotment was made on July 23, 1921 by the Farmer, Mr. Charles W. Edmister. On July 27, 1921, this appraisement was transmitted to the Office with a letter from this Agency under that date. The original appraisement perhaps was misplaced in the Office; hence, a copy is being transmitted herewith for use of the Office.

                In connection with this estate, attention is called to several parties who are claiming to be heirs, and the correspondence in the case is being held open for attention of the Examiner of Inheritance when he is assigned to this Agency.

Sac & Fox – Shawnee Estates
1920-1924 Volume VIII

Very truly yours,

J. L. Suffecool
Superintendent

JJ:EV

Land-Sales
14298-22
J T H

Shawnee Indian Agency,
Shawnee, Oklahoma,
March 13, 1922.

The Honorable,
The Commissioner
of Indian Affairs,
Washington, D. C.

My dear Mr. Commissioner:-

    I have the honor to acknowledge the receipt of carbon copy of Office letter of above reference, under date of March 9, 1922, addressed to Ma ka se ah, in care of Mr. J. F. Daniels, Shawnee, Oklahoma, with reference to the sale of the allotment of his deceased father, Pa-kota.

    The following report is submitted herewith:

    On account of the extreme shortage of funds, and the seemingly impossibility to secure money from the various banks, it would be next to impossible to effect a sale of land at this time, unless it was appraised much below its actual value. This piece of land in question is a very valuable one, and it would not be advisable to attempt a sale.

    I would also call attention of the Office to the fact that it is the opinion of this office, that it is not the desire particularly of the Indian in question to sell this land, as it is that of J. W. Daniels.

    Mr. Daniels is a man who has in someway, I understand, gotten in debt to practically all of the Kickapoo Indians. It has been necessary, since I have

Sac & Fox – Shawnee Estates
1920-1924 Volume VIII

been in charge of this office to call his attention to the fact that the collection of accounts and bills unauthorized by this office could not be given consideration. Yet he has persisted in bringing them here with their accounts and has upon various occasions been present on pay day.

I have talked with Mr. Daniels in my office and have tried to explain to him in detail just how the Office feels toward indebtedness of the Indians incurred without the authority of this office. Yet he seems to think that if an Indian has the money and desires to pay that I should issue a check.

As noted above, it is my candid opinion, that the Indian in question is being influenced to a more or less extent by Mr. Daniels.

THe[sic] letter inclosed is returned herewith for your files.

Very respectfully,

J. L. Suffecool
Superintendent

JLS:EV

Ed-Inds.
14990-22

Shawnee Indian Agency,
Shawnee, Oklahoma,
Mar. 13, 1923.

The Honorable
The Com. of Indian Affairs,
Washington, D. C.

Dear Mr. Commissioner:

This has reference to a letter dated 2/18/22, regarding the allotment of Lizzie Hardin, Citizen Pottawatomie allottee No. 39, described as the SW/4 of Sec. 15, T. 10 E., R. 3 E. I.M. in Oklahoma, from Zoa H. Haney,

Sac & Fox – Shawnee Estates
1920-1924 Volume VIII

Pawhuska, Okla. to the Commissioner with slip attached, above reference, requesting for report and return of papers.

The Office is respectfully informed that full explanation of the disposition of this allotment will be found in Land-Heirship 131090-1912 STT. It appears there that Thomas Hardin, husband of Lizzie Hardin, transferred his undivided interest in the W/2 and NE/4 of SW/4 of Sec. 15, T10N, R3E. to the other heirs of Lizzie Hardin (his children) and in return Davis Hardin, legal guardian for the children, transferred to Thomas Hardin the SE/4 of the SW/4, Sec. 15, T10N. R3E. their undivided share of this tract of land.

Very respectfully,

3 od 13.   J. L. Suffecool
Incl. Ret.   Supt. & S. D. A.
CC to Zoa H. Haney
Pawhuska, Oklahoma.

Probate.
9255-21
WHG

Shawnee Indian Agency,
Shawnee, Oklahoma,
March 14, 1922.

The Honorable,
  The Commissioner of
  Indian Affairs,
    Washington, D. C.

My dear Mr. Commissioner:-

This will refer the Office to its letter dated November 16, 1921, in connection with the claim of Emma Griffinstein against the estate of Catherine Griffinstein, deceased.

The Office authorized and directed that a hearing be held on due notice to all interested parties, for the purpose of ascertaining the merits of this claim. Pursuant to the instructions of the Office, notices were sent out to all the heirs of Catherine Griffinstein and the Attorneys in the case on November 29, 1921, informing them that the hearing would be held at 2 o'clock on December 29, 1921. However, on account of the conflicting dates with assignments for

Sac & Fox – Shawnee Estates
1920-1924 Volume VIII

that day, a subsequent notice was sent out to all interested parties, saying that the hearing would be held at 2 o'clock, Tuesday afternoon, December 27, 1921. Copies of these notices are inclosed herewith.

Responsive to the notices sent out, the claimant, Emma Griffinstein, represented by her Attorney, C. H. Ennis and her sister as her witness appeared on the day and hour set; also, all of the heirs, represented by W. L. Chapman, their Attorney, appeared at the hearing.

The taking of the testimony was not completed until the evening of December 29th, 1921. The testimony taken at that time is inclosed herewith in duplicate for information of the Office. Attached to the testimony is Stipulation between the claimant through her Attorney, and the heirs through their Attorney, waiving the signatures of the witnesses, the certificate of the stenographer and Notary Public.

The Attorney for the claimant introduced depositions of several people in Kansas together with the proof of the receipt of notices. These are also inclosed.

During the hearing, Attorney for the claimant introduced copies of Application for Letters of Administration, Bond of Administrator, Oath of Administrator, Letters of Administration, Order of Appointment of Administrator, Demand of Emma Griffinstein, Order fixing date of hearing claim and appointment of Special Administrator, Order of continuance, Order allowing claim of Emma Griffinstein in the matter of the estate of Catherine Griffinstein, deceased. These papers are certified to from the Court records in Sedgwick County, Kansas. The Attorney for the claimant, also introduced certified copies of the divorce proceedings against Charles J. Griffinstein, one of the heirs to the estate, by Emma Griffinstein, the claimant. All of these papers are inclosed for the information of the Office.

It appears that during the controversy between Charles J. Griffinstein and his wife, Emma Griffinstein, they agreed to a division of property which they are supposed to have owned. Among which was his 1/3 interest in the allotment of Catherine Griffinstein which is held in trust. Subsequently, Charles J. Griffinstein appears to have deeded 1/2 of the undivided 1/3 interest in his allotment, which of course is of no effect only to cloud the title to the land. Attention of Mrs. Griffinstein was called to the fact that it was a violation of Section 5 of the Act of June 25, 1910, to take a deed of this character without the consent of the Secretary of

Sac & Fox – Shawnee Estates
1920-1924 Volume VIII

the Interior. Therefore, she has executed a deed to Charles J. Griffinstein which when recorded will clear that part of the cloud on the title to the allotment. Mr. Ennis, the Attorney, for the claimant in submitting this deed states that the deed is given to clear the title to the land without waiving in any way the claim of Emma Griffinstein to re-imbursement from the estate of Catherine Griffinstein on account of services rendered during the illness of Catherine Griffinstein.

The testimony taken at the hearing appears voluminous. It would appear, however, that Mrs. Emma Griffinstein should have some compensation for the services given by her to the deceased; and for the further fact that during the latter part of the illness of Catherine Griffinstein and while Mrs. Emma Griffinstein was caring for her, her husband, Charles J. Griffinstein, was at that time appearst[sic] to have been in intimate relations with another woman. This also was the cause of their separation and the demand of Emma Griffinstein, it seems, was then brought up for the services rendered; otherwise, it is not believed that she would have claimed anything for the services, for the home of herself and her husband would have been happy and he would have supported her and there would have been no need for any further compensation. From what we can learn Mrs. Emma Griffinstein has no visible means of support. During her marriage state with Charles J. Griffinstein, she was entirely dependent for her livelihood upon the resources of her husband.

The testimony shows that Charles J. Griffinstein turned over their home in Wichita, Kansas, one-half of their other articles of personal property, but the testimony further shows that all of this property was incumbered[sic] with mortgage or payments yet due.

From outside sources, we gained information that Mrs. Catherine Griffinstien[sic] stein was a very hard woman to please and to take care of, especially during her last illness when she was absolutely helpless.

In view of the testimony and all of the other papers submitted and of the comments set forth in my report herein, the case is referred to the Office for such disposition as it may deem proper to make of it.

Very truly yours,

J. L. Suffecool
Superintendent

JJ:EV

Sac & Fox – Shawnee Estates
1920-1924 Volume VIII

Shawnee Indian Agency,
Shawnee, Oklahoma,
Mar. 14, 1922.

Mr. S. A. Doyle,
1817 West 10th St.,
Oklahoma City, Okla.

Dear Mr. Doyle:

This has reference to your letter of Jan. 21/22 referring to the allotment of Sidney Smith, the father of Rena Smith Richardson.

In connection with this land you are informed that sufficient time has been allowed the other two heirs, Mrs. May Lewis and Bertie Smith, to take some action looking toward a settlement of some kind but to date they have not offered anything. Therefore, it is the purpose of this office to take immediate action so that Mrs. Richardson's interests may have due consideration. Inclosed herewith are partially filled applications for patent in fee for the use of Mrs. Richardson. Please have her attend to this at once and return them to this office and a report will at once go forward.

Sincerely yours,

3 od 14
Incl.

J. L. Suffecool
Supt. & S.D.A.

Shawnee Indian Agency,
Shawnee, Oklahoma,
Mar. 15, 1922.

Mr. Corbett White,
616 1/2 North Laird St.,
Oklahoma City, Okla.

Dear Mr. White:

In the matter of the sale of the Joe Vetter allotment by the heirs, among whom your wife is one, the funds derived from the sale were all transferred to Supt. Geo. A. Hoyo, Whiteagle, Okla., for disbursement.

Sac & Fox – Shawnee Estates
1920-1924 Volume VIII

However, inaaccoordance[sic] with the wish of your wife that her share be sent to her direct Supt. Hoyo is requested by letter carbon copy of which is inclosed herewith to mail her the check for her share.

Very sincerely yours,

3 od 15.   J. L. Suffecool
   Superintendent.

****

Shawnee Indian Agency,
Shawnee, Oklahoma,
Mar. 15, 1922.

Supt. Geo. A. Hoyo,
Ponca Indian Agency,
Whiteagle, Oklahoma.

Dear Mr. Hoyo:

Reference is made to the transfer of the funds derived from the sale of the Joe Vetter allotment No. 16, Iowa, for disbursement to the heirs who are living within your jurisdiction. There was inadvertently transfered[sic] to you the check for the share of Ruth Vetter White, wife of Corbett White of your Agency, who lives in Oklahoma City. It was our intention to forward to Ruth White her share direct. Therefore, you will please mail her a check for her share at 616 1/2 North Laird St., Oklahoma City, Okla.

Sincerely yours,

3 od 15.   J. L. Suffecool,
cc Corbett White   Superintendent

Sac & Fox – Shawnee Estates
1920-1924 Volume VIII

Shawnee Indian Agency,
Shawnee, Oklahoma,
March 15, 1922.

Mr. W. C. McIntosh,
Okemah, Oklahoma.

My dear Mr. McIntosh:-

Immediately upon receipt of your letter of March 9, 1922, in connection with the cashier's check for $164.00 made payable to the order of former Superintendent Ira C. Deaver in payment of annual rental and advance royalty under lease No. 10343 executed by the heirs of George Manatowa, we took the matter up with Mr. Deaver as to the disposition of the remaining $92.00 which has not been accounted for to you.

It was remembered by Mr. Alford, the Lease Clerk, that the cashier's check was handed to Mr. Deaver to cash and to bring back one-half of it to be accounted for officially, the other one-half was intended to be paid to the heirs or returned to you. The reason for this was that one-half of this allotment which you took the oil lease for was patented to the heirs and this office held no further jurisdiction covering that portion of the allotment.

Mr. Deaver called this office over the telephone this morning, after investigating the treposition[sic], and states that on the day that he purchased the cashier's check at the Shawnee Nat'l Bank for $92.00, Mrs. Carter and Bertha L. Dowd were with him; and that he is very certain that this money was turned over to them direct; and he also states that Mr. Ward, who is Assistant Cashier, at the Shawnee Nat'l Bank remembers paying this money to them.

If this is true, Mr. Deaver failed to take the precaution of obtaining a receipt from these people to be transmitted to you. He states that Mrs. Carter and the heirs will remember the transaction very clearly.

Therefore, this case will be held open and when these people come to the office, we will take the matter up with them and obtain receipts, if they received the money, and transmit it to you to complete your records of the payment of this rent and advance royalty direct. In the future, you will only be required by this office to remit for 1/2 or your lease.

Mr. Deaver retired from the Indian Service, September 30, 1921, and the undersigned assumed charge Oct. 1st, 1921, therefore, future remittances of any character, to this office, should be made payable to the undersigned.

Sac & Fox – Shawnee Estates
1920-1924 Volume VIII

We will advise you further as to the disposition of the other $92.00 of you remittance above referred to.

Very truly yours,

J. L. Suffecool
Superintendent

JJ:EV

Shawnee Indian Agency,
Shawnee, Oklahoma, March 16, 1922.

Hon. W. E. Wells,
Prague, Oklahoma.
Dear Sir:

Referrnce[sic] is made to your letter of the 15th instant, in which you state that you represent Mr. George Jepsen, who has been appointed as the administrator of the estate of James D. Davis, deceased. I have to advise you that James D. Davis, has two agricultural leases under this Agency, as follows:

Lease No. 3630, Mary Wilson, Sac & Fox allottee No. 246, to James D. Davis, for a term of one year from January 1, 1922, consideration being for crop rental. The lessee to plant the land to cotton and corn, giving the lessor 1/2 of the corn and cotton in the field. The land described as the SW 1/4 of NW 1/4 of section 23, township 11 N., range 5 east.

Lease No. 3631, Mary Wilson, Sac & Fox allottee #246, to James D. Davis, the SE1/4 of NE1/4 & NE1/4 of SE1/4, less the pasture in the SW corner of NE1/4 of SE1/4 and the house in the NW corner of the SE1/4 of the NE1/4 of section 22, township 11 north, range 5 east, for a term of one year from January 1, 1922, consideration being $300.00 per annum, to be paid in semi-annual payments to the Officer in charge of the Shawnee Indian Agency, Shawnee, Okla., for the use and benefit of the lessor on the first day of January 1922 and on the first day of July 1922.

Mr. Davis before his death paid the first-half payment amounting to $150.00 January 4, 1922.

Very respectfully,

J. L. Suffecool
Superintendent

TBA

Sac & Fox – Shawnee Estates
1920-1924 Volume VIII

Shawnee Indian Agency,
Shawnee, Oklahoma, March 17, 1922.

Mr. H. C. Rutledge,
McComb, Oklahoma, R# 2.

Dear Sir:

This is to advise you that John C. Motley has taken the lease at your offer upon the allotment of M at ma pa ka we, deceased, described as the SE1/4 of section 27, township 8 north, range 3 east of the Indian Meridian.

Very respectfully,

J. L. Suffecool,
Superintendent

TBA

Shawnee Indian Agency,
Shawnee, Oklahoma, March 17, 1922.

Mrs. Susie Jessepe,
Mayetta, Kansas.

Dear Madam:

Referring to your letter of the 6th instant, relative to the allotment of Alexander Rhodd, deceased, described as the 14.73 acres off the S/2 of lot 3 of NE1/4 and 10 acres off the S/2 of SW1/4 of NE1/4 of section 33, township 8 N., Range 5 east, containing 24.73 acres. This land is still in trust by the Government.

I have to advise you that this land has not been leased thru this Office since the year 1917 and have had no applicant to lease for the place since that time.

Sac & Fox – Shawnee Estates
1920-1924 Volume VIII

The following heirs and their shares in the above estate are as follows:

Zoa Rhodd	1/3
Susie Jessepe	10/105
Florence Copeland	2/105
Edward Copeland	2/105
Agnes Copeland	2/105
Eveline Copeland	2/105
Lizze Rhodd	10/105
Inez Rhodd	10/105
Enos Rhodd	10/105
Peter Rhodd	10/105
John Rhodd	10/105

Very respectfully,

J. L. Suffecool
Superintendent

TBA

Shawnee Indian Agency,
Shawnee, Oklahoma, March 20, 1922.

Allottee No. 343.

Mr. William W. Melott,

Meeker, Oklahoma, R# 2.

Dear Sir:

Referring to your lease upon the allotment of Edith Rice, deceased, the SW1/4 of section 2, township 11 north, range 4 east, for a term of one year from January 1, 1922, consideration being $200.00 per annum.

I have to advise you that this lease was executed by you on the 16th day of February 1922 and you were advise[sic] that[sic] that time not to go to work on the place unless you have a completed lease. There is one more bondsmen[sic] needed in your lease and if this lease is not completed by the last of this month it will be subject to cancellation.

If you want this land it is your duty to see to see[sic] to it.

Sac & Fox – Shawnee Estates
1920-1924 Volume VIII

Very respectfully,

J. L. Suffecool
Superintendent

TBA

Shawnee Indian Agency,
Shawnee, Oklahoma,
March 20, 1922.

Mr. A. O. Corliss,
 Cushing, Oklahoma.

My dear Sir:-

    With reference to the heirs of John C. Falk, deceased, reimbursing you with rents that were erroneously paid to them, I have to advise that Superintendent Hoyo of Ponca Indian Agency, has sent us 4 checks, as follows:

Check No.	Account	Amount
3998	Margaret Bassett	$5.84
3999	Margaret Bassett	1.28
4173	Nellie Pickering	1.28
4228	Maggie Whitehorn	21.32

    This completes the reimbursement to you with the exception of the one owed by Hoke S. Blackhawk. Mr. Hoyo states that as soon as he has sufficient funds to his credit, that a check will be drawn and sent to you. When this is done this matter will be closed.

Please acknowledge the receipt of these checks.

Very truly yours,

J. L. Suffecool
Superintendent

JJ:EV
INCL'S. 4 cks.

  C. C. to Higgins & Berton[sic],
    Cushing, Okla.

Sac & Fox – Shawnee Estates
1920-1924 Volume VIII

Shawnee Indian Agency,
Shawnee, Oklahoma,
March 20, 1922.

Mrs. Nellie Frances Schmidlkofer,
R#2, Shawnee, Oklahoma.

My dear Madam:-

In the matter of the hearing to determine the heirs of Rosalie Goyer, deceased, there is inclosed herewith 2 copies of notice of hearing. Keep one copy and sign the acknowledgment of the receipt of the original on the copy and return it to this office in the self-addressed envelope.

Please date the receipt of the one that you return to us.

Very truly yours,

J. L. Suffecool
Superintendent

JJ:EV
INCL. 2

Shawnee Indian Agency,
Shawnee, Oklahoma,
March 22, 1922.

Mr. S. Y. Tutwiler,
 Examiner of Inheritance,
 Kiowa Indian Agency,
 Anadarko, Oklahoma.

Dear Mr. Tutwiler;-

This is to acknowledge receipt of your letter of March 20, 1922, stating that you have been instructed to hold a supplemental hearing in the case of Mah mah qua che (John Mine), deceased Mexican-Kickapoo allottee, No. 75, in order to give Nan-I-toke an opportunity to make objections that she may have to the approval of the will made by the decedent; and asking where this party lives; and also of the whereabouts of

Sac & Fox – Shawnee Estates
1920-1924 Volume VIII

Bessie Hale, Jesse Murdock and Narcisse Pensoneau, Steve Pensoneau, and Wah nah be quah.

In this connection, you are advised that Nan-I-toke lives with the Kickapoos around Mc Loud or Harrah. Bessie Hale at Mc Loud. Jesse Murdock is also at Mc Loud, and Narcisse Pensoneau is working for some Oil Co., at Bigheart, Oklahoma. Steve Pensoneau lives near Jones, Oklahoma under this jurisdiction. We have not seen any of the Kickapoos in the office since the receipt of your letter, but John Snake does not know who Wah nah be quah is, unless the spelling of the name is a little different from what this woman is known by.

I trust that the information given you herein will serve the purpose.

Several deaths have occurred among the Indians under this jurisdiction, and you will probably have a number of cases when you arrive to conduct the hearing. We have now a special case set for April 21, to determine the heirs of a Pottawatomie estate, in order that the estate may be settled up properly.

Very truly yours,

J. L. Suffecool
Superintendent

JJ:EV

Shawnee Indian Agency,
Shawnee, Oklahoma,
Mar. 25, 1922.

Mr. S. Y. Tutwiler,
Examiner of Inheritance,
Anadarko, Oklahoma.

Dear Mr. Tutwiler:

Complying with your request you will find inclosed herewith the entire file relative to your report in the heirship case of George F. Pambogo, dec. unallotted Pottawatomie Indian of this Agency.

The finding in this case has not been declared, although the record shows on the folder, as you stated, this was submitted to the Indian Office 10/11/21.

Sac & Fox – Shawnee Estates
1920-1924 Volume VIII

Cordially yours,

J. L. Suffecool
Superintendent.

3 od 25.
Incl. file.

Land-Sales
17841-22
BDS

Shawnee Indian Agency,
Shawnee, Oklahoma,
Mar. 26, 1922.

The Honorable
The Com. of Indian Affairs,
Washington, D. C.

Dear Mr. Commissioner;

Transmitted herewith are the papers in the sale of 40 acres of the allotment of Sadie Carter, Sac & Fox allottee No. 319, deceased, authorized by Office telegram, above reference, dated March 7, 1922.

Very respectfully,

J. L. Suffecool
Supt. & S. D. Agt.

3 od 25.
Incls.

Shawnee Indian Agency,
Shawnee, Oklahoma,
March 27, 1922.

Mr. Emmett Tayiah,
Pawhuska, Okla.

Sir:-

In your letter of March 25, it is presumed that you refer to the timber cut from the Lizette Bertrand allotment, to which you are an heir, by J. H. Lansdowne.

Sac & Fox – Shawnee Estates
1920-1924 Volume VIII

A representative of this office made a thorough investigation and we reported all the facts to the Indian Office from this investigation. We find that the heirs should have coming to them $788.00. The Pottawatomie County has more than $1400.00 on deposit for purchase of the lumber on this allotment. We recently had a letter from the Indian Office, stating that the Office had requested the Department of Justice to take such steps as will be necessary to secure this money from the Pottawatomie County, for the benefit of the heirs. It is presumed from this that some action will be taken by the Department of Justice looking to the collection of the money for the heirs.

      Very respectfully,

          J. L. Suffecool
          Superintendent

JJ:EV

Petition
for
Part ition[sic]   Shawnee Indian Agency
Josephine Brown   Shawnee, Oklahoma,
allotment No. 63   Mar. 27, 1922.
Sac & Fox.

The Honorable
The Com. of Indian Affairs,
Washington, D. C.

Dear Mr. Commissioner:

  Transmitted herewith is a petition for partition of t he[sic] allotment of Josephine Brown, deceased Sac & Fox allottee No. 62, and the applications for patent in fee for t he[sic] shares of two of the heirs and the Superintendent's reports thereon.

  It will be noticed that the appraisements of the two tracts of land are equal but that the share of the father of the allotee is greater than the other two heirs' share. The Office is respectfully informed that the portion taken by the father, John Brown, has his home thereon, and that no other division is practicable, and the further fact that the three heirs signify this to be satisfactory and according to their wish I recommend the approval as petitioned.

Sac & Fox – Shawnee Estates
1920-1924 Volume VIII

Very respectfully,

3 od 27.　　　　　　　　　　　　　　　　J. L. Suffecool,
Incls.　　　　　　　　　　　　　　　　　Supt. & Sp. D. Agt.

Shawnee Indian Agency,
Shawnee, Oklahoma,
March 28, 1922.

Mr. A. R. Snyder,
　Supt. Potawatomi Indian Agency,
　Mayetta, Kansas.

My dear Mr. Snyder:-

　　The inclosed carbon copy of my letter to the Indian Office is self-explanatory. I am sending it to you, as in it is indicated the part where you are to furnish this office with the Departmental finding in the case of Ke-ah-tah-be-ah, in order that we may be able to transfer the funds to the credit of the estate, to his wife Wah-ah-nah-pe-quah.

　　Will you please send us copies of the finding, as we can use it in adjusting the different estates under this jurisdiction, in which Ke-ah-tah-be-ah was interested.

Very truly yours,

J. L. Suffecool
Superintendent

JJ:EV
INCL. 1

****

Ed-Ind
22885-22
E S S

Shawnee Indian Agency,
Shawnee, Oklahoma,
March 28, 1922.

Sac & Fox – Shawnee Estates
1920-1924 Volume VIII

The Commissioner
of Indian Affairs,
Washington, D. C.

Sir:-

The letter of Mr. E. D. Reasor, lawyer in Shawnee, Oklahoma, is returned herewith. This letter was sent to us with a carbon copy of Office letter to Mr. Reasor, dated March 25, 1922, bearing the above caption, for report and return of Mr. Reasor's letter.

In this connection, I have to advise tha Ke-ah-tah-be-ah is dead. He was allotted in Kansas under the jurisdiction of the Potawatomie Indian Agency. Mr. Reasor has reference to this allottee's wife, Wah-pah-nah-pe-quah, who lives under this jurisdiction. This woman has been in the office, a number of times with the other Kickapoo Indians, who live under this jurisdiction. As Kah-ah-tah-be-ah had an allotment under the jurisdiction of Supt. Snyder, the heirs to the estate would be determined under that Agency.

Superintendent Snyder on February 13, 1922 stated that the heirs of Ke-ah-tah-be-ah were determined on September[sic] 29, 1921; and that Wah-pah-nah-pe-quah was decreed to be sole heir. On Sept. 17th, we suggested to Mr. Snyder in our letter of that date, to forward to us funds to this estate; and also to furnish us with a copy of the Department findings, in order that we might have our records complete and transfer funds accordingly.

Ke-ah-tah-be-ah at the time of his death had certain inherited interests under this jurisdiction, all of which his wife, having been decreed the sole heir, would inherit. Supt. Snyder has transferred the funds to this jurisdiction and we have taken the same up to the credit of the estate, but until the office at Mayetta, Kansas, furnishes us with a copy of the Departmental findings, we cannot transfer the funds to the credit of the sole heir. This is the reason that Wah-pah-nah-pe-quah has not received any of the funds now to the credit of the estate of Ke-ah-tah-be-ah. This Indian woman takes care of a child belonging to another family and receives a monthly allowance for the child. She also received funds from other sources under this jurisdiction.

As soon as Mr. Snyder furnishes us the Departmental finding in the case of the estate to whose credit we now hold the money, we will be able to transfer it to the credit of this woman, and can then proceed to take care of her needs, although it has never come to the notice of this office that she is in very urgent need of funds to provide for her at this time.

Sac & Fox – Shawnee Estates
1920-1924 Volume VIII

  The matter in question would have been and will be handled as expeditiously as the circumstances will permit and the needs of this woman will be looked after very carefully. It is not believed that it is necessary for Mr. Reasor to attempt to make suggestions as to how matters within the province of the Office shall be handled, for he is not in a position to be informed sufficiently to attempt any adjustments between the Government and its Indian wards. However, it has been reported to me and I have observed that he attempts, at every opportunity, to transact business for the Indians which should be handled properly through this office.

Very truly yours,

J. L. Suffecool
Superintendent

JLS:EV
INCL. 1

  C. C. to Supt. Snyder,
    Mayetta, Kan.

Law-Heirship
39912-15
57936-15
FWS

Shawnee Indian Agency,
Shawnee, Oklahoma,
Mar. 28, 1922.

The Honorable
The Com. of Indian Affairs,
Washington, D. C.

Dear Mr. Commissioner:

  Transmitted herewith is an application for patent in fee for the allotment of Sidney Smith, Pottawatomie allotment No. 763, for the heirs of Sidney Smith, reference as above.

  It will be noted that Rena Richardson alone submits an application for the reason that the other two heirs refuse to sign an application. Mrs May Smith Lewis and Bertie Smith, the other two heirs, offer no reason

Sac & Fox – Shawnee Estates
1920-1924 Volume VIII

for this action. They are in possession of the allotment by crop rental lease. The revenue from this land has not been satisfactory to Mrs. Richardson for the reason that she receives a small amount for her share.

It will also be noted that these heirs are the heirs in the estates mentioned in letter of transmittal of application for patent in fee for the allotment of Josephine Bourassa, Pottawatomie No. 802, under date of March 23, 1911. As stated in that letter these heirs are fully competent and the further fact that Mrs. May Lewis is full blood white, the other heirs have practically no Indian blood they should be relieved of all restrictions. It is therefore recommended a patent in fee issue to the heirs for this allotment.

Very respectfully,

3 od 28.
Incls

J. L. Suffecool
Supt. & S. D. Agt.

Land-Sales
98963-14
7800-22
JTH

Shawnee Indian Agency,
Shawnee, Oklahoma,
March 28, 1922.

The Honorable
The Com. of Indian Affairs,
Washington, D. C.

Dear Mr. Commissioner

Reference is made to Land-Sales, above reference, wherein the heirs of Charles C. Murray transfer by deed to Alice Murray, wife of one of the heirs, five acres of the allottees[sic] land in order that Alice Murray may use her private funds to build a home for herself and husband, Kirwin Murray, thereon.

As required by Office letter above refered[sic] to the heirs have resources as follows:- Cash, Emily Roubidoux $833.98, Kirwin Murray $295.47, Franklin Murray 295.48, Pearl Murray $293.47, Vestina Murray, $295.48, Kate Murray $295.48, Velinda Murray $295.47;
Inherited estates and their shares,

Sac & Fox – Shawnee Estates
1920-1924 Volume VIII

Estate	Heir	Share
Charles C. Murray,	Emily Roubidoux	3/9
	Kirwin Murray	1/9
	Franklin Murray	1/9
	Pearl Murray	1/9
	Vestina Murray	1/9
	Kate Murray	1/9
	Velinda Murray	1/9
Kirwin Murray	Emily Roubidoux	1/6
	Kirwin Murray, Jr.	1/18
	Franklin Murray	1/18
	Pearl Murray	1/18
	Vestina Murray	1/18
	Kate Murray	1/18
	Velinda Murray	1/18.

Emily Roubidoux in addition to the above has her own allotment of 80 acres still held in trust.

Very respectfully,

3 od 28.
J. L. Suffecool
Supt. & S. D. Agt.

Shawnee Indian Agency,
Shawnee, Oklahoma,
Mar. 29, 1922.

Dr. Jacob Breid,
Sac & Fox Sanatorium,
Toledo, Iowa.

Dear Dr. Breid:

    Referring to your inquiry regarding the relationship of We-sho-ke-qua, an old Indian of your reservation, with Oliver Jackson, in connection with inherited interests, you are advised that the heirship to the estate of Oliver Jackson has been determined, and that Thomas K. Oliver, son, sole heir, according to finding Porbate[sic] 70181-21, declared Sept. 14, 1921.

Very cordially yours,

3 od 29.
J. L. Suffecool,
Superintendent.

Sac & Fox – Shawnee Estates
1920-1924 Volume VIII

Land-Sales
38206-17
3862 -22
JTH

Shawnee Indian Agency,
Shawnee, Oklahoma,
Mar. 30, 1922.

The Honorable
The Com. of Indian Affairs,
Washington, D. C.

Dear Mr. Commissioner:

Reference is made to Land-Sales, above caption, in which Mr. J. H. Martin desires to purchase the allotment of Mrs Charles Lewis, deceased Shawnee allottee No. 45.

The Office is respectfully informed that Mr. Martin submitted a bid of one thousand dollars ($1000) which was rejected by the heirs.

Very respectfully,

3 od 30.

J. L. Suffecool,
Superintendent.

Shawnee Indian Agency,

Shawnee, Oklahoma, March 30, 1922.

Mr. A. B. Collins,
    U. S. Indian Farmer,
        Cushing, Oklahoma.

Dear Mr. Collins:

I am enclosing you herewith a letter from Earle T. Miller, of Tulsa, Oklahoma, relative to bonuses paid to the heirs of Jerome Wolfe, deceased.

Mr. Miller states that the entire bonus consideration is for $376.00 and one-half of this amount should go to the five heirs

Sac & Fox – Shawnee Estates
1920-1924   Volume VIII

which is $188.00. But each of them was paid $10.00 at the time the lease was executed, which would leave $138.00 to be divided amon[sic] the five heirs when the lease is approved, which would be $27.60.

It appears that the bonus affidavit signed by the heirs, does not correspond with the above. Will you p lease see the heirs and get their statement as to their understanding in this matter. The five bonus affidavits are herewith enclosed. Please return them with your report.

Very respectfully,

Superintendent

TBA

Shawnee Indian Agency,
Shawnee, Oklahoma,
March 31, 1922.

Mr. A. B. Pambogo,
  R#3, Box 56,
    Bartlesville, Okla.

Dear Sir:-

In reply to your letter of March 30, concerning the heirship case of your brother, George F. Pambogo, and stating that Mr. Tutwiler, the Examiner of Inheritance, is somewhat negligent; you are advised that Mr. Tutwiler not very long after he conducted the hearing mailed his report to the Indian Office, which was on October 11, 1921.

From the records in the case it appears that his report has been lost in the mail, at least the Indian Office has never received the papers. On March 23, 1922 Mr. Tutwiler advised this office that the Indian Office had written for the report in this case; and that he has called for the papers; and on March 25, 1922 we mailed to him, copies of all the papers in the case, in order that he might make copies of the report and mail same to the Indian Office to take the place of those which it appears were lost.

In this connection, I wish to state that according to the correspondence on file in this office, Mr. Tutwiler is not at fault in the Indian Office not having received their report; but as stated herein the papers have been lost somewhere between here and Washington. Mr. Tutwiler in all probability has sent in his second report at this time and a

Sac & Fox – Shawnee Estates
1920-1924 Volume VIII

determination of the heirs to this estate will soon be made by the Department.

Very truly yours,

J. L. Suffecool
Superintendent

JJ:EV

Shawnee Indian Agency,
Shawnee, Oklahoma,
April 3, 1922.

Mr. Thomas S. Dodson,
McLoud, Okla.

My dear Sir:-

    I have before me this morning, lease No. 3304 on Shawnee allotment No. 187, the same being a part of the allotment of John King, deceased, and described as the SW of the NE of 22-11-2; in your favor, said lease expiring the 31 at[sic] of December 1922.

    In this connection, I desire to report that there appears to be some litigation with reference to a certain modification of the lease terms; and that the papers in question containing this notification were sent to you some time in December, or the 1st part of January; or rather you came and got them at that time for execution. These papers have not been returned, nor has this deal been consummated. In this respect, you are advised that you are delinquent and the time has long since passed for the return of the papers. The regulations provide that in event that lease papers are not completed within 30 days from the time that they are started, they automatically cancel themselves.

    You are, therefore, advised that if you do not come to this office immediately upon receipt of this letter and complete, to the satisfaction of the heirs of this land, the papers in question therewith, that the necessary papers will be taken out to have you ejected from the premises. You are negligent in this matter and it seems to me that there is no reasonable excuse for such negligence in keeping the rightful owners from having the satisfaction of knowing that this deal has been properly consummated.

    The records of this office would also indicate that you have the lease on the NW/4 of the NE/4 of 23-11-2, on the allotment of John King, deceased; and the lease is No. 3789. These papers were given to Etta

Sac & Fox – Shawnee Estates
1920-1924 Volume VIII

King, one of the heirs, on the 17th of January 1922; said papers were then delivered to you. These papers have not been returned properly completed. They, therefore, have the same status as the others and automatically cancel themselves. You are given the same time to come to this office and make explanation as to the delay in this matter and see that this matter is properly taken care of.

Very respectfully,

J. L. Suffecool
Superintendent.

JLS:EV
CC to Etta King,
    Shawnee, Okla.
    R#6, Box 119.

Shawnee Indian Agency,
Shawnee, Oklahoma,
April 4, 1922.

The Commissioner of
    Indian Affairs,
        Washington, D. C.

Sir:-

    The files of Hiram Weld, Citizen Pottawatomie allottee No. 833; and Joseph Weld, Citizen Pottawatomie allottee No. 1315; have been temporarily misplaced in this office, and we are at the present time unable to locate these files, however, it is remembered very distinctly by the office force here that these two allottees disappeared from this part of the country and have not been heard of for many years; and that the time of their death has not definitely been established.

    It is further remembered that a great deal of correspondence was had between various parties in various locations in an attempt to locate these allottees; and that hearings were held to determine the heirs to these estates, if they were to be legally declared dead.

    This letter is written to ascertain from the Office, the present status in the case above referred to.

Sac & Fox – Shawnee Estates
1920-1924 Volume VIII

Very truly yours,

J. L. Suffecool
Superintendent.

JJ:EV

Land-Sales
13623-22
W C

Shawnee Indian Agency,
Shawnee, Oklahoma,
April 5th, 1922.

The Honorable
The Com. of Indian Affairs,
Washington, D.C.

Dear Mr. Commissioner:

Reference is made to the application of Mr. Orlando Johnson for patent in fee, covering the allotment of Harry Johnson, deceased Sac & Fox allottee No. 375, requesting for further information by Office letter, above caption.

Inclosed herewith are the formal appraisement, and, as a separate item, a statement of the speculative value for oil and gas, of the foregoing mentioned allotment, made by Mr. A. B. Collins, U. S. Farmer located at Cushing, Oklahoma, an employee of this Agency.

Very respectfully,

4 od 5.
Incls. 2

J. L. Suffecool,
Superintendent.

Shawnee Indian Agency
Shawnee, Oklahoma
April 7, 1922

Dr. Jacob Breid,
Supt. Sac & Fox Sanatorium
Toledo, Iowa.

Sac & Fox – Shawnee Estates
1920-1924 Volume VIII

Dear Doctor:

This refers to your letter of April 4, 1922 concerning funds of Thomas Chuck and Alice Lincoln, heirs of Jim Scott. The funds in each case are as follows:

Thomas Chuck:

	Bal. for'd. from old ledger,	$95.20
	Land Sale,	406.75
	Lease money	11.60
	Lease Money	2.68
	Interest	.14

Total transferred to you..........................$516.37

Alice Lincoln:

	Land Sale,	$406.76
	Lease money,	11.60
	Lease Money,	2.68
	Interest,	.14

Total sent to you....................... $421.18

You will note that Thomas Chuck had $95.20 on hand when the land sale and lease money and interest was added to his balance. The land sale coming to each of these people amounted to $406.75 and $406.76 respectively, the extra cent going to Alice Lincoln.

Previous to the land sale, Alice Lincoln had $94.94 to her credit which was disposed of as follows:

Check for $52.72 was mailed to you for her Feb. 20, 1922. It had been drawn long before.
Check for $17.48 and one for $24.74 were mailed to you for her March 29, 1921.

I trust that this will clarify the situation and you will be able to explain it to Thomas Chuck and Alice Lincoln.

Very truly yours

JJ   Superintendent

Sac & Fox – Shawnee Estates
1920-1924 Volume VIII

Shawnee Indian Agency
Shawnee, Oklahoma
April 7, 1922

Wa se nah
Montour, Iowa

My friend:

This is to acknowledge receipt of your letter of April 5, 1922, in which you state that you have been informed that Emily Johnson died recently; that she has relatives in you part of the country.

The Examiner of Inheritance who was assigned to this Agency conducted a hearing in the case Sept. 14, 1921. His report and all the papers pertinent to the case are now on file in the Indian Office for consideration.

According to the testimony adduced at the hearing Frank B. Davis and Harry Davis would be entitled to the estate under the Oklahoma law. Dollie Gokey, Esther and Delia Bigwalker, produced what was alleged to be the will of Emily Johnson. This will is also before the Department for consideration.

Sif there are more relatives, as you state, in your part of the country who have not been included, and who by such relationship should inherit, an affidavit setting forth such relationship should be executed and submitted to this office with a request for a re-opening. If such relationship, upon investigation, appear to be entitled to something, a proper request for a re-opening of the case can then be made.

Very truly yours

J.L. Suffecool
Superintendent

JJ

Shawnee Indian Agency
Shawnee, Oklahoma
April 10, 1922

Mr. J. R. Thorn
Maud, Oklahoma

Dear Sir:

Sac & Fox – Shawnee Estates
1920-1924 Volume VIII

Since Maud Oil well No. 2 has been brought in we have been in correspondence with the Commissioner of Indian Affairs concerning the approval of a title to you covering the allotment of Samuel Cummings, deceased, which you, at one time, attempted to purchase through the Probate Court of Pottawatomie County, which had no jurisdiction.

The result of this correspondence the Commissioner has offered to assist you in securing full title to the land in the following two propositions:

1. That a patent in fee from the Government direct to you will be recommended, provided you deed all mineral rights to the heirs of Samuel Cummings.

2. That an effort will be made by this office to have a deed with a mineral reservation clause in it signed by all the heirs except Helen Cummings, who is incompetent. The Government requires that a Court order be entered for the sale of this incompetent's interest by the legal Guardian. This cannot be done in this case for the reason that the Probate Court at one time refused to do this stating that it had no further jurisdiction since the land was sold thru it and the case disposed of. The Commissioner of Indian Affairs states that for this reason it will be impossible to convey full title to you by the deed method as the deed cannot be executed by the legal Guardian of the incompetent without confirmation of the sale of her interest by the proper court.

We have been asked to advise you fully of the circumstances and to inform you that in case the land is conveyed to you by deed, all mineral rights will be reserved to the heirs; that if a patent in fee is issued you should deed to the heirs all the mineral rights in the land.

The deed method, you understand, is contingent on Helen Cummings, the incompetent heir, not being able to convey her interest in the deed.

Both methods outlined above results in the reservation by the heirs the mineral rights in the land. The patent in fee method outlined appear to be the best for it gives you absolute title to the land, except the mineral rights.

We have also been asked to obtain from you a written statement as to your wished in this case. Therefore, submit to this office a written statement in connection with the propositions contemplated to clear up this matter and give you title to the surface rights in the land.

We shall take no further action until we hear from you. Advise us soon.

Sac & Fox – Shawnee Estates
1920-1924   Volume VIII

Very truly yours

J. L. Suffecool
Superintendent

Carbon copy furnished
Harry Johnson, 123 North
Beard, Shawnee, Oklahoma.

JJ

Shawnee Indian Agency,
Shawnee, Oklahoma,
April 10, 1922.

Mr. Arza B. Collins,
United States Farmer,
Cushing, Oklahoma.

Dear Mr. Collins:

There is inclosed herewith a letter from Dr. Jacob Breid of Sac & Fox Sanatorium, Toledo, Iowa, returning deed for Robert Hunter allotment which the heirs refused to consider. The letter is self explanatory.

Please take the matter up with Henry Hunter and advise further.

Very truly yours,

4 od 10.   J. L. Suffecool,
Incls. deed & letter.   Supt. & Spl. Disb. Agt.

Shawnee Indian Agency
Shawnee, Oklahoma
April 11, 1922

Supt. A. R. Snyder
Potawatomi Indian Agency
Mayetta, Kansas

Dear Mr. Snyder:

Sac & Fox – Shawnee Estates
1920-1924 Volume VIII

Kish-kah-nah-kah-kah, one of the apparent heirs to to[sic] the estate of Me-ah-me-no-skuk, deceased, under your jurisdiction, brought Peck-ke-ah-peah, one of our Kickapoo Indian women in to make an affidavit for him concerning the relationship of the said Me-ah-me-no-skuk, deceased.

After securing the data from her knowledge of the relationship, we prepared for her an affidavit which she states is about what she knows. She has subscribed and sworn to it and it is herewith inclosed in triplicate.

Kish-kah-nah-kah-kah advises us that a hearing is to be held at your Agency by the Examiner of Inheritance soon and desired that this affidavit be forwarded to you for such use as you may deem proper to make of it.

Very truly yours,

J. L. Suffecool
Superintendent

Incl.
JJ

****

[The above letter given again]

****

State of Oklahoma   (
County of Pottawatomie   (SS

Affidavit in the matter of the estate of Me-ah-me-no-skuk, deceased Kansas Kickapoo Allottee under Pottawatomie Indian Agency, Mayetta, Kansas jurisdiction:

I, Peck-ke-ah-peah, a Mexican Kickapoo allottee, under the Shawnee Indian Agency, Oklahoma jurisdiction, of lawful age, and upon being first duly sworn upon oath states that, I was well acquainted with Me-ah-me-no-skuk during his life time; that he died in January, 1904; that he was about 75 years old at the time of his death.

I further state that he was married to Ah-yah-tah, who died long prior to his death; that they had no children; that the said Me-ah-me-no-skuk had no brothers and no sisters.

I further state that Me-ah-me-no-skuk's father was Tah-com-e, who died long prior to his death; that Tah-com-e had four sisters, Viz: Pah-pah-me-to-tha-quah, Me-thah-quah, Ke-wah-yah-ka-quah and Ko-ta-nah; that all of these died prior to the death of Me-ah-me-no-skuk; that the mother of the decedent is not known to me.

Sac & Fox – Shawnee Estates
1920-1924 Volume VIII

I further state that of the sisters of Tah-com-e, the father of Me-ah-me-no-skuk, Pah-pah-me-to-thah-quah had one child, Viz: Ah-ske-pah-kah; that Me-thah-quah had two children viz: Kah-e-shah, son, and Ah-the-pah-the quah, daughter; that Ke-wah-yah-ka-quah had two children, Viz: Wah-pah-ke-ah-she-ka, son, and Nah-kah-e-quah, daughter; that Ke-tah-nah had no children.

I further state that of the children of the sisters of Tah-com-e, the father of Me-ah-me-no-skuk, Ah-ske-pah-kah had two children, viz: Pe-tun-wah, son, who is dead, and We-we-nath, son, living; that Kah-e-shah had no children; that We-we-nath, son, living; that Kah-e-shah had no children; that Ah-the-pah-kah-the-quah, had four children: Viz: Mi-ah-ke-pe-ah, daughter, dead, Ahn-wah-na-ka, daughter, dead, Me-she-ka-ta-no-quah, daughter, dead, Ah-ske-pah-she-no-quah, daughter, dead; that Wah-pah-ke-ah-she-ka had five children, Viz: Mah-tash-kuk, son, dead, Pah-ah-the-quah, daughter, dead, Ko-che-shin-wah, son, dead, Ma-tha-ah-qua-twa, son, dead, Shi-ahn-wah, daughter, dead; that Nah-kah-e-quah had two children: Viz: Pe-ah-tah-tah-no-quah, living son, and Kiah-kah-nah-kah-kah, living son.

I further state that of the grand-children of the sisters of Tah-com-e, the father of the said Me-ah-me-no-skuk, deceased, who are dead, Pe-tun-wah had one child, who died, whose name is unknown to me; that Mi-ah-ke-pe-ah had several children, whose names I do not know, but all are dead; that Ahn-wah-na-ka had no children; that Ma-she-ka-ta-no-quah had one child, Viz: Charley Spear, who is dead; that Ah-she-pah-kah-she-no-quah had no children; that Mah-tash-kuk had no children; that Pah-ah-the-quah had one child, a girl, who is dead, do not know the name; that Ko-che-shin-quah had one child, a son, who is dead, whose name is unknown to me; that Na-tha-ah-qua-twa had no children; that Shi-ahn-wah had no children.

The above is all that I know of the relationship of Me-ah-me-no skuk, deceased, to the best of my knowledge and belief, so help me God.

Witnesses: Peck-ke-ah-peah   Her thumb Mark
JH Jones
Shawnee, Oklahoma

Charles Dushane
Shawnee, Oklahoma

Subscribed and sworn to before me this the 11th day of April, 1922.

J. L. Suffecool
Superintendent, Shawnee Indian
Agency, Shawnee, Oklahoma

JJ

Sac & Fox – Shawnee Estates
1920-1924 Volume VIII

I Certify that I interpreted and translated to the affiant from English into Kickapoo language of the affidavit to which she subscribed.

Chief of Police.

JJ

Shawnee Indian Agency,
Shawnee, Oklahoma, April 13, 1922.

The Pure Oil Company,
   Tulsa, Oklahoma.

Gentleman[sic]:

    Referring to your oil and gas lease No. 10043a upon the allotment of Watt Grayson, deceased, Sac & Fox allottee No. 502, described as the W/2 of the SE 1/4 of section 27, township 18 north, range 6 east of the Indian Meridian.

    It is requested that you drill an offset well within 10 days from date, or pay the market value of the 1/8 royalty of the oil production for the use and benefit of the heirs of this allotment in lieu of drilling from well #1, located 250 ft. south of the north line and 250 feet east of the west line of E/2 of the SE 1/4 of section 27, township 18 north, range 6 east.

Very respectfully,

J. L. Suffecool
Superintendent

TBA
C. C. to Collins

Shawnee Indian Agency
Shawnee, Oklahoma
April 14, 1922

Mr. W. R. Bedell
904 So. Alabama
Okmulgee, Oklahoma

Sac & Fox – Shawnee Estates
1920-1924 Volume VIII

Dear Sir:

   This has reference to your letter of April 10, 1922 concerning matters affecting the Margaret Bedell allotment in which you are interested as one of the heirs. You remember you wrote to us on November 22, 1921 stating that Benjamin F. Coon was reported to you to be cutting timber off of the land and selling it and collecting rentals, etc. You will also recall that we took steps to stop him, if reports were true, from cutting any more timber. Carbon copies of our letters were furnished you.

   We placed the matter in the hands of our district Farmer in that district for investigation and report on Nov. 22, 1921. On February 25, 1922, after reaching the point where he could give it proper attention, he submitted a report as a result of his investigation. His report in full is quoted below for your information.

> "Answering your request for a report on the timber, use of, present condition, and general relation to of Ben Coon, of the allotment of Margaret Bedell, I wish to submit:-
>
> "That up to 1917 the two eighties of this allotment which lay one half mile apart were "outlland[sic]," that is nothing had been done with them since the allotment in the way of improvement. As to the west eighty, in that your Joseph W. Bradburn made a lease through the Office, agreeing for the use of the pasture to put a two wire fence on the north and west lines. During the year 1918 this eighty does not seem to have been used. In 1919 the same lessee made a legal lease in which he paid $41 in money, put one more wire on the north and west fences, and repaired the South fence. In the year 1920 he again occupied this land, putting 5 acres in cultivation, a 3 wire division fence, and 3 wires on the east half of the south line. In 1921 he put on a boxed house 13x15 and 8' walls, and a side room 8x10, three windows and three doors, native material. During this time another six acres have been put in cultivation. In this period of five years the improvements are as much as we ordinarily get for that kind of land, and I feel that it has been well paid for.
>
> "On the east eighty Ben Coon cleared up some land in the year 1917, getting it all ready to plow. In 1918 Ernest Pratt put this same 20 acres which Ben had cleared the year before, in cultivation. In 1919 Bee Hanan[sic] put 15 acres in cultivation, and a three wire fence on the north and east and some posts on the south line, and some ditches. In 1920 the same man built a house 42x26 of hewn logs, including an alley 8' wide and a side room 10x24; a log crib 10x12, and put 6 spools of wire on the division fence. In 1921 he put in a well at a cost of $39, 180 posts and some wire, and $32 worth of work on the house.

Sac & Fox – Shawnee Estates
1920-1924 Volume VIII

"During the five years that this has been occupied I find much more in cultivation, a great deal better improvements than on the other eighty. It is the better eighty. However while the west eighty has been in the hands of one man practically all the time, this one has used by three, and the great bulk of the costly improvements have been made by Mr. Hanon during his three years, two of which have hardly paid him back anything. He claims that he has been out over $100 more than the third and fourth amounted to. There is no doubt about this, and the heirs have been overpaid in the way of improvements by this man. He asks that the use of the place for this year be given to him to reimburse him in part for what he has been out. It has already been leased for this year for $90 and I recommend some way be found whereby that money can be turned over to him, as having already been spent on the place.

"These men have not always had a legal lease on this land but through no fault of theirs, or anybody elses[sic] for that matter as it was a case of having too many irons in the fire, and some few of them had be skimped. So far as the east eighty is concerned I feel that it is in good shape, and the heirs interests are in good tack, and the same applies on the west eighty except that some timber has been cut off of the land which should not be put in cultivation.

"It seems that Ben Coon has no team but has been making some arrangements with these other men, wherein he has done the clearing, and they have done the team work. He has done well by both of these places, except that on the west one I feel that he has cut some trees where he ought not to have cut them, and should be restrained from cutting any more, except where it can and ought to be put in cultivation, which is very little, now left."

"Very truly yours,

(Signed) Chas. W. Edmister
F a r m e r."

Benjamin Coon, replying to our notice to stop cutting the timber, and to lease the land regularly through this office, under date of December 6, 1921 stated:

"Your letter of the 28th at hand concerning the Margaret Bedell allotment and as to your information concerning the cutting of this timber, and selling wood & posts, my friend Mr. B. Hanon written W. R. Bedell that I was slaying this timber, and was holding all rents, and wanted Bedell t put me off of this land. Now Mr. Suffecool, I am the only one that has tried to put this land in shape for cultivation and trying to take care of the land to make it bring something for the benefit of the heirs, it is a sad mistake about

Sac & Fox – Shawnee Estates
1920-1924 Volume VIII

claiming any part of this land till it is divided, only trying to make the land valuable, and as far as the rent on the east eighty, I got the proceeds of one crop, and that was 1919 and they should be rent paid this year, 1921, but B. Hanon is the man that is going to keep the heirs out of it in 1922 for he claims a debt against it, he started to move down and has moved a load back on the place and is going to stay on the place next year, he got mad at me and this the spite he is taking, I written Bedell since, concerning the letter Hanon written to him and advised him to come here by brother's man did and this is the remark he made to me, the land should be cleared before it would be worth anything and I am willing if you say so to make a lease and while I am selling this wood on the ground for one dollar a rick I want pay by the acre for clearing this land for the plow and I would like for some reliable man to be sent down by you and look at this timber, will you Mr. Suffecool as scarce as money is believe I am getting rich selling wood and posts, know you folks up there have been told that Bee Hanon was not entitled to nothing for I, Benjamin Coon, has never signed a lease contract or Bee Hanon made any bond since he has had the place so I have taken this matter up with the Secretary of the Interior Department wanting something done, I claim a hundred fifty dollars damages against the place for the protection of the heirs against Bee Hanon. Well, Mr. Suffecool, I will try to be there Monday."

"Yours fraternally
(Signed) Benj. F. Coon."

Concerning the complaint you made to this office about Benjamin Coon reaping benefits from the Margaret Bedell allotment, a letter dated Dec. 12, 1921, signed by Guy Zink and Leonard Coon, off Emporia, Kansas, was received and what they said follows:

"I received a letter from Ben Coon to day and he said that you had ordered him to stop cutting wood on that land. He said Bedell had instructed you that way. Now you know and I know what that land is worth in its condition now it isnt[sic] worth having unless it is cleared off or they strike oil, now you can take this from me, that man should receive pay besides what he cuts off that land, and Bedell knows it too, you can tell Bedell to go ahead and crack his whip I can get a lawyer mighty quick to fight this case, also tell him I have written into Washington, D. C. to find where he gets his claim, you said that would half[sic] to be fought out of the Indian Agency. These Coon men are a part Indian also this land is an Indian allotment you are there to protect them also see that they are not beat out of their land and as far as I can see you are doing nothing in that case, I say let him clear that land and let him get what he can out of the wood, I am glad to get out of it that easy. This is my understanding, that Bedell has marked himself off a certain third of this land and also it is the best part of 160, now what right has he to decide which is his third. If Bedell wants part of the money tell him to go help out the wood, also will you please tell me where Bedell get his rights at all."

"Yours Truly
(Signed) Guy Zink
(Signed) Leonard Coon"

In connection with agricultural leases covering these allotments, you are advised that the E/2 NE/4 24-8-4 is leased this year only to Daniel D. Kenyon for $90, $45 of which has been paid. $15.00 is now on the books to your credit for which check will in the near future be drawn and mailed to you. Balance of $45 will be due Oct. 1, 1922.

The W/2 of NE/4 24-8-4 is leased for improvement only to Joseph W. Bradburn this year.

If you can find an oil company that will take an oil lease covering the allotment, there should be no trouble in getting all the heirs to sign such a lease.

Mr. Edmister's report quoted above for your information would show that Benjamin F. Coon has not benefitted himself more than the other heirs, since, as reported he has done a great deal of work on the land himself. It would appear that he should have had some compensation for his work in clearing the land ready for the plow. This is shown by his own statements and that of the Farmer, Mr. Edmister.

It is believed the matter is reported to you in full and clearly sets for the status of the present condition of the allotment.

Very truly yours

J. L. Suffecool
Superintendent

JJ

Shawnee Indian Agency
Shawnee, Oklahoma
April 15, 1922

Mrs. Nellie F. Schmidlkofer
R #2, Shawnee, Oklahoma

Sac & Fox – Shawnee Estates
1920-1924 Volume VIII

My dear Madam:

With your letter of April 12, 1922 you returned the notices of hearing forwarded to you from this office stating that, you understood the hearing to be held was to determine the heirs of Clariese[sic] Tescier, your deceased mother, that you were not interested in the Rosalie Goyer estate.

The hearing to be held April 21, 1922 will be to determine the heirs to the estate of Rosalie Goyer, deceased. She, at the time of her death, had a 1/9th interest in the Clarisse Toecier[sic] estate. Therefore, her heirs should be determined to ascertain who would inherit her 1/9th interest in the Clarisse Tescier estate.

The Department, long ago, determined the heirs to the estate of Clarisse Tescier, deceased. You, your father and the other children were declared to be heirs to this estate.

Even though you have no interest in the Rosalie Goyer estate, it is necessary, to be legal, to notify all the relatives and prospective heirs, hence, the notice sent to you. The notices are returned herewith. Please keep one and date and sign the receipt on the other one and return it to this office in the envelope herewith which requires no postage. Do this so that this office may have proof that you received the notice.

Very truly yours,

J. L. Suffecool
Superintendent

Incls.
JJ

Shawnee Indian Agency,

Shawnee, Oklahoma, April 17, 1922.

Mrs. Anna Dibler[sic],
Chandler, Oklahoma, R# 4.

Dear Madam:
Referrence[sic] is made to your letter of the 15th instant, relative to the allotment of your deceased mother Hilda Pensoneau.

I have to advise you that this land is leased for the year 1922 only, to Jasper Buckmaster for $60.00 per annum, payable semi-annually on the first day of January and July and in addition to the cash rental the following improvements.

Sac & Fox – Shawnee Estates
1920-1924 Volume VIII

>Put BB flooring in W/2 of front room and level the floor, valued at $15.00. Patch roof with star A star shingles and put on saddle boards valued at $10.00. Replace rotten or missing boxing and bats valued at $15.00. Replace all broken window sash, panes and frames valued at $15.00. Flash upper edge of said roof valued at $3.00. Repair doors and frames valued at $2.00

I am enclosing you herewith my official check No. 10704 for $3.75, which represents you[sic] share in the above estate.

Very respectfully,

J. L. Suffecool,
Superintendent

TBA

Shawnee Indian Agency,
Shawnee, Oklahoma, April 17, 1922.

Mr. Thomas Bullfrog,

Tecumseh, Oklahoma, R# 4.

Dear Sir:

Referrence[sic] is made to your letter of the 14th instant, relative to al[sic] lease upon the allotment of Jim Bullfrog, deceased and above the money due you at this Agency.

I have to advise you that the check you received a few day ago is from the Billy Bullfrog allotment, leased by Charley Tyner for the year 1920, at $125.00 per annum. On march[sic] 28, 1921, Mr. Tyner paid $62.50 and on March 17, 1922, he paid $62.50 and your share in this estate is 11/36. In the year 1920 you was[sic] paid $19.10 and in March 28, 1922, you received $19.12 in the above estate. This is all the money you have placed to you[sic] credit at the time you got your check.

Mr. Stapp has paid on April 2, 1922, the sum of $40.00 on the allotment of Jesse Bullfrog, deceased, you[sic] share in this estate will be $12.47. This will be paid to you first Tuesday of[sic] in May.

Sac & Fox – Shawnee Estates
1920-1924 Volume VIII

There is $50.00 still due upon the allotment of Jim Bullfrog by Walter Philips. When this is paid you[sic] share will be $15.61, you[sic] share in this estate is 101/324.

Lease No. 3873, the allotment of Billy Bullfrog, dec. has not yet been paid by Decator Ogle, in the sum of $25.00. Your share in this estate is $7.63. Notice has been sent to both parties in the above estates.

I also note what you say about Walter Philip[sic] sub-leasing this land. I have taken this matter up with Mr. Philips before on the allotment of Little Captain. He advises that he is not subleasing this land, but that he has a hired hand on the places and that he looks after them himself. As to the improvements the lease reads as follows:

> The lessee further coveants[sic] and agrees that he will, at his own expense, within the first two years from the date of the approval hereof, A sufficient ditch along the west line, putting levee on the east side, about 120 rods long; cut three ditches from it to the east into the old creek bed, putting excavated dirt on the south saide[sic]; Keep the part of Pecan Creek Ditch now built from the bridge up, free from drift and well plowed out; Put a new ditch from end of one last named straight up to lines where it enters the allotment, making a good levee on the west side with the dirt; this ditch to be at least 15' wide at the top and 3-1/2' deep in center. All valued at $375.00

The above is what Mr. Philips has agreed to do. Please advise me what part of the improvements is not completed, so that I may be able to write to Mr. Philips in this matter.

Very respectfully,

TBA

J. L. Suffecool

Shawnee Indian Agency
Shawnee, Oklahoma
April 18, 1922

Mr. S. A. Doyle
1817 Wes 10th Street
Oklahoma City, Oklahoma

Sac & Fox – Shawnee Estates
1920-1924 Volume VIII

Dear Mr. Doyle:

    The Department, in response to our report on the application of the heirs, for a patent in fee to Josephine Bourassa allotment, states that the regulations provide that no patent on fee will be issued in the case where one of the heirs is not yet 21 years of age. Birdie Smith being only 19 years of age, the patent will not be issued, nor the regulations waived in the case.

    Mr. Fehlig from Kansas City was in the office to see about the matter yesterday. We informed him of the fact that patent cannot now be issued. He went on down to Maud and returned this morning with Mrs. Lewis, Birdie Smith, Eliza Colvin and Charlie Wiley to execute papers to acquire the small interests in the Josephine Bourassa allotment.

    Mr. Wiley purchased for his wife, Nellie Wiley, the inherited interest thru Martha Mullen of Birdie Smith in the Josephine Bourassa allotment. He also purchased for his wife Frank Smith's interest acquired thru Martha Mullen in the Josephine Bourassa allotment. He has deposited the consideration for the deeds executed to him.

    Mr. Fehlig purchased for his wife, Nancy Fehlig, Birdie Smith's inherited interest in the Josephine Bourassa allotment. He also purchased May Lewis' interest. He then purchased the interest of Eliza Colvin inherited thru Martha Mullen in the Josephine Bourassa allotment. Deeds covering these have been executed. He has deposited funds for these.

    Mr. Fehlig proposes to purchase the interest of Mrs. Rena Smith, now Richardson acquired thru Martha Mullen's interest. Also her interest in the original estate, Josephine Bourassa. Two deeds have been prepared for Mrs. Richardson and are herewith. He will send us the consideration to deposit to cover her share, $300.00 as soon as he reaches home. This is on the basis of $5,600 valuation of the allotment of Josephine Bourassa, deceased.

    If the transaction is satisfactory, it is desired that you have Mrs. Richardson to execute the two deeds herewith and return them to this office to be submitted to Washington for approval, or rather further consideration.

    The purchase of these interests eliminates all of the Sidney Smith and Martha Mullen heirs and leaves the Josephine Bourassa estate in the main heirs, except Zoa Denton and a deed has been prepared for her execution. Mr. Wiley proposes to purchase her interest thru Martha Mullen in the Josephine Bourassa allotment.

    Mrs. Richardson should be instructed to execute the deed, that is, sign her name as appears in the body of the deed.

Sac & Fox – Shawnee Estates
1920-1924 Volume VIII

Very truly yours

J. L. Suffecool
Superintendent

Incls.
JJ

Shawnee Indian Agency
Shawnee, Oklahoma

April 18, 1922

Mr. A. B. Collins,
U. S. Farmer
Cushing, Oklahoma

Dear Mr. Collins:

John Moses allotment is described as the W/2 of the NE/4 of Sec 24, Twp. 17 N., R. 2 East. Martha Lightfoot, daughter of prior deceased sister Mary Washburn, has a 1/4th interest in this estate. She has died and her estate is being probated now at Potawatomi Agency, Kansas, by Examiner of Inheritance, Mr. Paul L. Hallam. He desires an appraisement of the the[sic] John Moses allotment be forwarded to him. Please appraise this land and submit certificate of appraisement to this office in order that we may forward same to Mr. Hallam.

The heirs of John Moses were determined May 16, 1917, Probate 29631-1917 J R V. Allotment No. 101, Iowa. In order to expedite matters it might be well for you to forward to Mr. Hallam direct at Mayetta, Kansas, the appraisement certificate as soon as you complete it and forward a copy to us here showing your action in the matter. It appears that some of the heirs are very needy and the determination of the heirs of Martha Lightfoot, deceased, be made special is desired.

Very truly yours

J. L. Suffecool
Superintendent

JJ
cc to Mr. Hallam for his information.

Sac & Fox – Shawnee Estates
1920-1924 Volume VIII

Shawnee Indian Agency
Shawnee, Oklahoma
April 19, 1922

Mr. P. L. Hallam, Examiner of Inheritance
Potawatomi Indian Agency
Mayetta, Kansas

Dear Sir:

We have just succeeded in delivery notice of hearing, you sent to us with your letter of March 30, 1922, to Zow-num-kee, in the case of Ne-bow-a-sah, Kansas Potawatomi Allottee No. 242. The proof of service, duly signed on the reverse side of those you have marked "Returns" are herewith.

You will note that we delivered the copy of notice only to Zow-num-kee. The best we could get out of him was that Ko-was-me was his sister and that she died about 11 years ago.

Very truly yours

J. L. Suffecool
Superintendent

Incls.
JJ

****

DEPARTMENT OF THE INTERIOR

UNITED STATES INDIAN SERVICE

Potawatomi Indian Agency

Mayetta, Kansas.

March 30, 1922.

RECEIVED
MAR 31 1922
SHAWNEE INDIAN AGENCY

Mr. J. L. Suffecool,
Supt. Shawnee Indian Agency.
Shawnee, Oklahoma.

Dear Mr. Suffecool:

Enclosed herewith are notices of hearing in the case of Ne bow-o-sah, deceased Potawatomi allottee, for delivery to Zow-num-kee and Ke-Was-mo, of Shawnee, Oklahoma.

Sac & Fox – Shawnee Estates
1920-1924 Volume VIII

Kindly make returns of service on the extra notices and return same to me at your convenience.

Very truly,

PL Hallam
Examiner of Inheritance.

RSH

Shawnee Indian Agency
Shawnee, Oklahoma
April 19, 1922

Mr. A. B. Collins
U. S. Indian Farmer
Cushing, Oklahoma

Dear Mr. Collins:

Mr. P. L. Hallam, Examiner of Inheritance, Potawatomi Indian Agency, Mayetta, Kansas, is going to hold a hearing to determine the heirs of Chame[sic] Roubideaux, deceased allottee up the May 15, 1922. He has sent us, for delivery to Robert Roubidoux, notice of hearing.

Please deliver one of the copies of notices to Robert Roubidoux, and accomplish the proof of service on the reverse side of the other copies of notices and return directly to Mr. Hallam. Attend to this as soon as you can see Robert.

Very truly yours,

J. L. Suffecool
Superintendent

Incls.
JJ

Carbon copy of this letter
to Mr. Hallam.

****

DEPARTMENT OF THE INTERIOR

UNITED STATES INDIAN SERVICE

Potawatomi Indian Agency
Mayetta, Kansas.

RECEIVED
APR 17 1922
SHAWNEE INDIAN
AGENCY

April 13, 1922.

Sac & Fox – Shawnee Estates
1920-1924 Volume VIII

Mr. J. L. Suffecool,
Supt. Shawnee Indian Agency.
Shawnee, Oklahoma.

Dear Mr. Suffecool:

    Enclosed herewith is a notice of hearing in the case of Chame Roubideau[sic], deceased Iowa allottee No. 139, to be delivered to Robert Roubideau, whom I understand i under your jurisdiction.

    Kindly have this notice served and make your returns of service on the extra notices.

    Very truly,

    PL Hallam
    Examiner of Inheritance.

PLH-RSH

    Shawnee Indian Agency
    Shawnee, Oklahoma
    April 19, 1922

Mr. P. L. Hallam, Examiner of Inheritance
Potawatomi Indian Agency
Mayetta, Kansas

Dear Sir:

    We have just succeeded in delivery notice of hearing, you sent to us with your letter of March 30, 1922, to Zow-num-kee, in the case of Ne-bow-a-sah, Kansas Potawatomi Allottee No. 242. The proof of service, duly signed on the reverse side of those you have marked "Returns" are herewith.

    You will note that we delivered the copy of notice only to Zow-num-kee. The best we could get out of him was that Ko-was-mo was his sister and that she died about 11 years ago.

    Very truly yours

    J. L. Suffecool
    Superintendent

Incls.
JJ

Sac & Fox – Shawnee Estates
1920-1924 Volume VIII

Shawnee Indian Agency
Shawnee, Oklahoma
April 22, 1922

Mr. Chas. W. Edmister, Farmer
Shawnee, Oklahoma

Dear Mr. Edmister:

Please appraise the allotment of Clarisse Tescier and turn the certificate in to the office as soon as you can. Make it a very special case, for we are holding the report on heirship waiting on this appraisement.

The certificate in quadruplicate partially filled out is herewith. As soon as you have appraised the property turn the papers in promptly for we cannot hold up the report that must be made to Washington directly after conducting the hearing which was done April 21, yesterday.

Very truly yours

Incl.
JJ

J. L. Suffecool
Superintendent

Shawnee Indian Agency
Shawnee, Oklahoma
April 24, 1922

Mr. C. J. Griffinstein
2416 East Second Street
Wichita, Kansas

Dear Sir:

Your letter to John snake of this office of April 19, 1922 has been referred by him to this office for reply in connection with the action, if any, taken in the matter of the claim of Mrs. Emma Griffinstein against the estate of Catherine Griffinstein.

For a long time after the hearing which was held in this office the papers were held pending examination by the Attorneys.

After the papers were examined by the Attorneys and stipulations were agreed upon, they were mailed to the Commissioner of Indian Affairs, Washington, D, C. with our report.

Sac & Fox – Shawnee Estates
1920-1924 Volume VIII

We have not yet received any reply from the Indian Office.

Very truly yours

J. L. Suffecool
Superintendent

JJ

Shawnee Indian Agency
Shawnee, Oklahoma
April 25, 1922

The Commissioner of Indian Affairs
Washington, D. C.

Sir:

The inclosed carbon copy of a letter written to Mr. Fred Cobb, Assistant County Engineer, Cleveland County, Norman, Oklahoma, is self-explanatory.

Lawrence J. Bertrand was allotted as Citizen Pottawatomie Allottee No. 195 the E/2 of the NE/4 Sec. 20 and NW4 of Sec. 21 Twp. 6 N. of R. 1 East, containing 240 acres.

Only the part of this allotment described in the letter to Assistant County Engineer is affected by the proposed drainage ditch project of Cleveland County.

The Department determined the heirs to Lawrence J. Bertrand allotment on March 13, 1914 (Law-Heirship 68436-1913) to be:

Mary Bertrand, widow,	3/9
Lucy E. Cruse, daughter,	2/9
Laura Bertrand-Patrick, daughter	2/9
Nora Bertrand-Clark, daughter	2/9

It was thought, at the time the County Clerk of Cleveland County called the office up over the telephone, that a right of way for a ditch through this allotment was desired. It has, however, developed that not only a right of way across this allotment for the ditch is desired but that the County wants Government aid in paying the assessment that might be made against this Indian allotment which is restricted. The information as to the proper procedure to secure a right of way as contained in the General Land Office regulations concerning right of way over public lands and reservations for canals, ditches, and reservoirs, approved June 6, 1908 was given to the County Clerk in a letter from this office. The regulations referred to were

Sac & Fox – Shawnee Estates
1920-1924 Volume VIII

promulgated from the Act of Congress approved March 3, 1891 (26 Stat., 1095) entitled "An act to repeal Timber culture laws, and for other purposes."

What the county really want[sic] is information as to how it may secure payment of the assessment that may be made against the restricted Indian allotment which is in the course of the proposed ditch. The County officers are of the opinion that some way similar the Act of July 19, 1912 (37 Stats., L. 194) under which the Office paid to the ex-officio County Treasurer of Pottawatomie County $21,793.41, Claim No. 230670, Feb. 19, 1915, Little River Drainage assessments of the Indian allotments in its course, and the Act of July 21, 1914 (38 Stat. L. 555) under which $18,256.66 was paid Dec. 15, 1914 to the Pottawatomie County for assessments of Indian allotments in the course of the Salt Creek Drainage District, might be inaugurated to pay the assessment which might be made against the allotment involved in this project.

It is stated that by estimate the assessments against the owners of land within this proposed drainage project will average $15.00 per acre. This will make an estimated assessment of something like $5,000.00 against the Indian allotment in the course of the proposed ditch. This allotment is not leased through this office and it is not known what revenue is derived from it by the heirs. The widow lives in New Mexico and through her we will, it is believed, locate the other heirs. It is reported, however, that very little revenue is derived from it.

This matter is referred to the Office for final decision and information as to the proper procedure in view of the report herein made.

Very truly yours

J. L. Suffecool
Superintendent

JJ
CC to Assistant County Engineer,
   Mr. Fred Cobb, Norman, Okla.

Shawnee Indian Agency
Shawnee, Oklahoma
April 26, 1922

Mr. George Appletree
Prague, Oklahoma

My friend:

You mad inquiry of this office several times as to the reason that the Potawatomi Indian Agency has not transferred the funds amounting to about

Sac & Fox – Shawnee Estates
1920-1924   Volume VIII

$5,000.00 belonging to the estate of [??]m-ah-the-ah, deceased, and as you know we wrote to Supt. Snyder about it for you.

We now have a letter from Mr. Snyder, in which he states that there is to the credit of the estate $5,214.77. However this cannot be transferred or disbursed, as the Department has authorized a re-hearing in the case.

On May 25, 1912, he states, the Department decided Wah-the-quah to be sole heir. Since then, a large number of heirs have claimed, hence the authority for a re-hearing. He also states that the case is now before Mr. Hallam, Examiner of Inheritance and that he will take the matter up with Wah-the-quah, perhaps, thru this office.

Very truly yours

J. L. Suffecool
Superintendent

CC to Potawatomi Agency
Mayetta, Kansas

JJ

Shawnee Indian Agency
Shawnee, Oklahoma
April 27, 1922

Mr. Rufus Goyer
Choctaw, Oklahoma
Dear Sir:

The marriage license which you sent to this office to be copied and incorporated in the testimony is returned to you herewith as requested.

A copy has been made of it and will be filed with the other papers that will go to Washington as soon as the land of Clarisse Tescier is appraised.

Very truly yours

J. L. Suffecool
Superintendent

Incl.
JJ

Sac & Fox – Shawnee Estates
1920-1924 Volume VIII

Shawnee Indian Agency
Shawnee, Oklahoma
April 28, 1922

Mrs. Mary Gibson
Mounds, Oklahoma

Dear Madam:

Answering your letter of April 27, 1922 with reference to the estate of Willie Gibson, your deceased husband, you are advised that, as stated heretofore in the correspondence, this case was reported upon by the Examiner of Inheritance, Mr. E. A. Upton, on Jan. 15, 1919, but the heirs have not yet been determined by the Department.

It is probably the finding is being delayed in order to dispose of the matter of the rehearing in the case of Nah-wah-che-se-mo, deceased unallotted Shawnee, to which your deceased husband, Willie Gibson, was declared sole heir erroneously.

In any event, until the heirs to Willie Gibson, deceased have been legally determined, the funds to the credit of the estate cannot be legally paid out.

Very truly yours

J. L. Suffecool
Superintendent

JJ

Land-Sales
25918-04
46173-16
21348-22
30453-22
31409-22
J[?]H

Shawnee Indian Agency
Shawnee, Oklahoma
April 28, 1922

The Commissioner of Indian Affairs
Washington, D. C.

Sir:

Sac & Fox – Shawnee Estates
1920-1924 Volume VIII

With reference to Office letter dated April 25, 1922 in connection with the disposition of the proceeds of the sale of the allotment of Henry Kah-ah-sen-we, deceased, by Mr. P. S. Hoffman, legal Guardian of Fryor Franklin Brown, sole heir, the inclosed carbon copies of the letters from this office to both General Hoffman and the County Judge of Lincoln County will show the stage in the course of our investigation.

Any further developments will promptly be reported to the Office as the case progress[sic].

Very truly yours

J. L. Suffecool
Superintendent

JJ

Shawnee Indian Agency,
Shawnee, Oklahoma,
April 29, 1922.

Dr. J. E. Hughes,
14-16 East 9th St.,
Shawnee, Oklahoma.

Dear Sir:-

This is to acknowledge receipt of your account against the estate of Mrs. Jane Johnson, deceased.

I have to advise that at the present time there is no money at this office to the credit of the estate of Mrs. Jane Johnson, but just as soon as the money is paid in, your account will be taken care of.

Very respectfully,

J. L. Suffecool
Superintendent.

JLS:EV

Sac & Fox – Shawnee Estates
1920-1924 Volume VIII

Shawnee Indian Agency
Shawnee, Oklahoma
May 1, 1922

Mr. G. Letterman
Hominy, Oklahoma

Dear Madam[sic]:

Replying to your letter of April 26, 1922 requesting that some arrangement be made whereby you and the other children of Jane Johnson, your deceased Mother, be given a patent in fee in order that you may pay up the bills, you are advised that no patent in fee can be issued until the heirs of your Mother are legally determined by the Secretary of the Interior.

Even after the heirs are determined patent in fee can not be issued unless all the heirs are of age, past 21 years old. It is believed that Ada and Willie are under age yet. When an Examiner of Inheritance is assigned to this Agency, he will set the date of the hearing to take testimony in the case.

Very truly yours,

J. L. Suffecool
Superintendent

JJ

Shawnee Indian Agency.
Shawnee, Oklahoma,
May 1, 1922.

Miss Annie K. Shaw,
   Superintendent,
      Shawnee City Hospital,
         Shawnee, Oklahoma.

My dear Miss Shaw:-

I am in receipt of your statement of account of Mrs. Jane Johnson, deceased.

In reply, I have to advise that there is no money to the credit of the estate of Jane Johnson, at the present time; but just as soon as money is paid in to the credit of this estate, we will give your bill attention.

Sac & Fox – Shawnee Estates
1920-1924 Volume VIII

Very respectfully,

J. L. Suffecool
Superintendent.

EV.

Shawnee Indian Agency,
Shawnee, Oklahoma,
May 3d, 1922.

Mr. Thomas Lybarger,
524 S. Broadway St.,
Fort Scott,   Kansas.

Dear Mr. Lybarger:

    This has reference to your letter of April 4th last regarding patent in fee to the Caroline Fryer allotment.
    This land is located near Norman in Cleveland County. Therefore, all information regarding recording of land papers, etc., and tax matter can be procured from that office. Taxes are never attended to by this office for the reason that immediately after the issuance of a fee patent the authority of the Government over that land ceases. It is then the business of the owners of the land to attend to such matters. You will probably have to pay taxes beginning with the year of 1921.

    A representative of Company having an oil lease on this land was in the office recently for the purpose of cancelling their lease on this land. He was informed that patent in fee had been issued to the heirs of the deceased allottee, and that he will now have to take up such matters with the owners of the land. There is inclosed a list of the members of the Company, with the name of the Company. Mr. S. K. McCall and Mr. W. L. Eagleton have been the most active in the affairs of the company. You should write one of them. The oil lease has 5 more years to run. You may be able to have it cancelled at once. The rental due on oil lease should be paid direct to you heirs.

    Some one of you heirs should attend to the matter of collection of rents, agreeable to all of you. In fact attend to any thing connected with the estate.

Very truly yours,

5 od 3.

J. L. Suffecool, Supt.

Sac & Fox – Shawnee Estates
1920-1924 Volume VIII

Shawnee Indian Agency,
Shawnee, Oklahoma,
May 3, 1922.

Supt. H. B. Peairs[sic],
Haskell Institute,
Lawrence, Kansas.

Dear Mr. Peairs:

Inclosed herewith are land-sale papers in the sale of the allotment of Lizzie Crane, deceased Sac & Fox allottee No. 468 from the heirs to Sarah Ellis also one of the heirs.

All of the heirs have signed similar papers including the father of Mary Grant. The signature of said Mary Grant is desired. Will you please kindly explain the nature of these papers to Mary Grant and have her sign in the proper places if she approves of the sale of the land to Sarah Ellis. Please sign the acknowledgement both on acceptance of sale No. 5-110o, and petition for sale No. 5-110j in the event she signs them, mentioned above.

Very respectfully,

5 od 3.
Incl. Pet. & Accept.

J. L. Suffecool
Supt. & Spl. Disb. Agt.

Shawnee Indian Agency,

Shawnee, Oklahoma, May 4, 1922.

Mr. Leo Whistler,
    Stroud, Oklahoma.
Dear Sir:

Reference is made to your letter of the 30th ultimo, in which you wish to be informaed[sic] as to the amount of rental paid on the allotment of Phoebe Keokuk, deceased, Sac & Fox allottee No. 261.

I have to advise you that oil and gas lease No. 10303, the advance royalty and annual rental for the fourth year rental for $208.00 have been paid by A. L. Funk on August 10, 1921. The rental on this lease will not be due until July 31,

Sac & Fox – Shawnee Estates
1920-1924 Volume VIII

1922. Your share in the above estate is 1/6 or $34.66. This is the amount you received sometime ago.

The Agricultural lease No. 3927, is leased to Herman C. Wolf of Avery, Oklahoma, for a term of one year from January 1, 1922, consideration being $150.00 per annum, to be paid cash in lieu of bond. On April 3, 1922, Mr. Herman made the above payment. Your share in this estate is 1/6 or $25.00

I am enclosing you herewith my official check No. 11102 for $25.84. This money is derived from agr. lease No. 3957 including interest. This is all the money you have placed to your credit at this time.

Very respectfully,

J. L. Suffecool
Superintendent

TBA

Shawnee Indian Agency,

Shawnee, Oklahoma, May 4, 1922.

Mrs. Christine Tyner,

Skiatook, Oklahoma.

Dear Madam:

Referring you my letter of the 30 ultimo, wherein I advise you that Davis Tyner has made an application to lease the allotment of Ellen Tyner, dec. Abs. Shawnee allottee No. 567, the E/2 of the SE 1/4 & E/2 of SW 1/4 of section 30, township 9 north, range 2 east, for a term of three years consideration being $150.00 per annum and the following improvements.

In addition to the above, build a log crib 12 x 14 ft. 8 ft. high, with a shed on each side, to be covered with corrugated tin roofing valued at $50.00. Ceil overhead two front rooms 14 x 14 ft. each with shiplap ceiling valued at $40.00. Dig a ditch on the north boundry[sic] running east to the main ditch, 12 ft. wide, 4 ft. deep and 1/2 mile long valued at $100.00.

The above is for your consideration and it is requested that you please notify me by return mail if you will accept Mr. Tyner's application and a lease will be drawn in accordance with your wishes.

Sac & Fox – Shawnee Estates
1920-1924 Volume VIII

If you will authorized[sic] me to sign the lease for you the lease will be completed sooner and you will get your share sooner.

Very respectfully,

J. L. Suffecool
Superintendent

TBA

Shawnee Indian Agency
Shawnee, Oklahoma
May 5, 1922

Mr. P. L. Hallam
Examiner of Inheritance
Potawatomi Indian Agency
Mayetta, Kansas

Dear Mr. Hallam:

The notice of hearing in the case of Pam-ah-tho-ah, deceased Kickapoo Allottee No. 3 you sent us to be served on Wah-tho-quah is returned herewith with the proof of service duly stated on thereverse[sic] side.

The notice to be served on David Nioce has just been received. When this has been delivered it will be returned to you. The roads in the vicinity have been so bad that our field men have not been able to travel much. However, they are better now and we will place this in the hands of our farmer for delivery.

Very truly yours

J. L. Suffecool
Superintendent

Incls.
JJ

****

DEPARTMENT OF THE INTERIOR

UNITED STATES INDIAN SERVICE

Potawatomi Indian Agency
Mayetta, Kansas.

RECEIVED APR 29 1922 SHAWNEE INDIAN AGENCY

April 24, 1922.

Sac & Fox – Shawnee Estates
1920-1924   Volume VIII

Mr. J. L. Suffecool,
Supt. Shawnee Indian Agency,
Shawnee, Oklahoma.

Dear Mr. Suffecool:

Enclosed herewith are notices of hearing in the matter of the reopening of the estate of Pam-ah-tho-ah, deceased Kickapoo allottee No. 3, one for service upon Wah-tho-quah and two for returns of service.

>Very truly,
>P L Hallam
>Examiner of Inheritance.

RSH

>Shawnee Indian Agency
>Shawnee, Oklahoma
>May 6, 1922

Supt. A. R. Snyder
Potawatomi Indian Agency
Mayetta, Kansas

Dear Mr. Snyder:

This has reference to your inquiry for Mary Wabski, formerly wife of Sam Pemo, and perhaps she is the one who is one of the heirs to the Myra Hahksa estate known as Mary Wamego.

It was the Elizabeth Hahksa land which was sold. The proceeds of this sale was $735. This was sent to you Mar. 4, 1916 so we deposited to the credit of the heirs as follows:

Kahdot Pemo,	1/2	$367.50
Mary Wamego,	1/2	367.50

Myra Hahksa allotment is NW/4 of NW/4 of sec. 5 and NE/4 of NW/4 of Sec. 4, Twp. 5 N. R. 4 E. This is still held in trust. This land produces no revenue and it is not leased for any purpose; it is almost valueless for agricultural purposes. There are no funds on deposit to the credit of this estate.

We are sending you under this cover the testimony taken at the hearing to determine the heirs of Myra Hahksa, deceased, together with the Department finding, in order that Mr. Hallam, while you have him with you there, my post a hearing a take the testimony necessary to determine the heirs of the deceased heir,

Sac & Fox – Shawnee Estates
1920-1924 Volume VIII

Kah-dot Pe-mo. All the supposed heirs to Kah-dot Pe-mo appear to live up there in Kansas.

When a hearing has been held, reported upon, and file has served its purpose please return it to this office, with copies of the testimony and report necessary with the file.

Very truly yours,

J. L. Suffecool
Superintendent.

Incls. JJ

Shawnee Indian Agency,
Shawnee, Oklahoma,
May 7, 1923.

Mr. A. G. Wilson,
   Acting Superintendent,
   Kiowa Indian Agency,
   Anadarko, Oklahoma.

Dear Mr. Wilson:-

This will reply to your letter of April 27, 1923 regarding the sale of the Little Fish estate in which the Edmonds under your Agency are interested.

Please advise these heirs that in-as-much-as this allotment is of a very poor quality and as this office has not been able to sell land of this character, that this will not be sold for the present. However, if some party takes sufficient interest in the purchase of this land a sale will be attempted and the Edmonds will be notified and given opportunity to give their expression in regard to sale.

Very truly yours,

J. L. Suffecool,
Superintendent.

CD:EV.

Sac & Fox – Shawnee Estates
1920-1924 Volume VIII

Shawnee Indian Agency,

Shawnee, Oklahoma, May 8, 1922.

Supt. A. R. Snyder,
   Pottawatomi Agency,
      Mayetta, Kansas.

Dear Mr. Snyder:

    Referrence[sic] is made to your letter of the 20th ultimo, stating that the heirs of Non ne ko kat allotment No. 703, Nancy May Ke-dott and Anna Ke dott were in your Office inquiring about the rental of the allotment.

    On March 15, I instructed Chas. W. Edmister to see about the rental and he reports as follows:

> Regarding the collection of rent from the allotment if Mary Pandosh, for the tear 1921, from the occupant Thomas Rhodd. I wish to state that Thomas Rhodd occupied this land for two years 1920 and 1921. That in 1920 he paid $200.00 the highest price that we have gotten for this land and paid in lieu of bond.
>
> During the year 1921 he did not make a lease because he states he was unable at anytime to get the money. His crops was nearly all ate up with the worms, he says, and I guess there is no doubt of it.
>
> So I don't suppose we will be able to collect rental from this land for the year 1921.

    Very respectfully,

J. L. Suffecool
Superintendent

A
C.C. to Miss Anna Kahdot,
    Mayetta, Kansas.

Sac & Fox – Shawnee Estates
1920-1924 Volume VIII

Cushing, Okla.

May. 8 1922.

RECEIVED MAY SHAWNEE INDIAN AGENCY

Mr. Paul L. Hallam.

Examiner of Inheritance.
Pottawatomi Indian Agency
Mayetta Kansas.

Dear Sir.

Inclosed find a copy of Notice of Heirship hearing in the case of Chas Roubideaux. which was sent me for service on Robert Roubideaux. which I have completed.

Very, Respectfully,

Copy

U.S. Farmer.
****

(Edition of January, 1916.)

NOTICE OF HEARING TO DETERMINE HEIRS

RECEIVED APR 17 1922 SHAWNEE INDIAN AGENCY

DEPARTMENT OF THE INTERIOR
UNITED STATES INDIAN SERVICE.
Potawatomi Indian Agency
Mayetta, Kansas
April 13, 1922.

Robert Roubideau[sic], Perkins, Okla.
Mitchell Roubideau, C/o W.C. Margrave, Reserve, Kan.
Lucy Curley, Mayetta, Kansas.
Columbia Curley, Mayetta, Kan.

Notice is hereby given that on the   18th   day of   May   . 1922, at Potawatomi Agency, Kan. , I will take testimony to be submitted to the Secretary

of the Interior for the purpose of determining the heirs of   Chane-Roubideau   , Iowa allottee No. 139.
deceased.

All persons having an interest in the estate of the decedent are hereby notified to be present at the hearing and furnish such evidence as they desire. Bring with you two disinterested witnesses having full knowledge of decedent's family history.

Respectfully,

Paul L. Hallam
Examiner of Inheritance.

Notices posted at the following places:
Potawatomi Agency, Kan.
Kickapoo Agency, Horton, Kan.
Day School No. 1, Horton, Kan.
Post office, Mayetta, Kan.
First Natl. Bank, Mayetta, Kan.

****

DEPARTMENT OF THE INTERIOR

UNITED STATES INDIAN SERVICE

Shawnee Indian Agency
Shawnee, Oklahoma
April 19, 1922

Mr. A. B. Collins
U. S. Indian Farmer
Cushing, Oklahoma

Dear Mr. Collins:

  Mr. P. L. Hallam, Examiner of Inheritance, Potawatomi Indian Agency, Mayetta, Kansas, is going to hold a hearing to determine the heirs of Chame Roubideaux, deceased allottee up there May 13, 1922. He has sent us, for delivery to Robert Roubidoux[sic], notice of hearing.

  Please deliver one of the copies of notices to Robert Roubidoux, and accomplish the proof of service on the reverse side of the other copies of notices and return directly to Mr. Hallam. Attend to this as soon as you can see Robert.

Very truly yours

J. L. Suffecool
Superintendent

Sac & Fox – Shawnee Estates
1920-1924 Volume VIII

Incls.
JJ

Carbon copy of this letter
to Mr. Hallam.

Shawnee Indian Agency
Shawnee, Oklahoma
May 19, 1922

Mr. Paul L. Hallam,
Examiner of Inheritance,
Potawatomi Indian Agency,
Mayetta, Kansas.

Dear Mr. Hallam:

With reference to your letter of April 22, 1922, with which you sent to this office notices of the petition filed by Catherine Rice for re-opening of the case of Pah-nah-kah-tho estate, you are advised that the petition and notice have been served on all the parties except Mah-nim-mik-skuk, who, it is stated has gone back up to Kansas. The notice to his is out with the Farmer.

The proof of delivery of notices to the persons named are herewith, together with an affidavit we have taken from May Pen-a-tho, who protests that Catherine Rice is an heir; that she is the daughter of Na-ah-ga-be, but that Na-ah-ga-be is not the son of Pah-nah-kah-tho as claimed.

Very truly yours

J. L. Suffecool
Superintendent

Incls.
JJ

Shawnee Indian Agency,
Shawnee, Oklahoma,
May 12, 1922.

Conservative Loan Company,
Shawnee, Oklahoma.

Gentlemen: In Re: Ben Axey Loan.

Sac & Fox – Shawnee Estates
1920-1924 Volume VIII

This has reference to a portion of the allotment of Lilly Forman, Abs. Shawnee allottee No. 322, described as t he[sic] N/2 of NW/4, 31-9-4, information concerning which was requested for in your letter of the 8th instant.

The contention that Webster Alford might own 1/2 interest in this tract of land is impossible for the reason that he inherited, with his mother in equal shares, from his father, David W. Alford who inherited 1/2 interest in the Lilly Forman estate. Departmental Finding shows that Webster Alford's share in this estate to be 1/4.

All that we have concerning the sale of the foregoing mentioned tract of land is the report of the Examiner of Inheritance to the Secretary of the Interior which was approved. I am sending you a copy of a portion of this report; the part dealing with the allotment.

Cordially yours,

Sac & Fox Lease Clerk.

Shawnee Indian Agency,
Shawnee, Oklahoma,
May 18, 1922.

The Commissioner
  of Indian Affairs,
    Washington, D. C.

Sir:-

    Carbon copy of Office letter addressed to Miss Julia Davis, Oklahoma City, Oklahoma, concerning the estate of her mother, Dilcy Davis and other estates' has been received for report.

    Therwriter's[sic] letter is returned herewith with the report that there are no estates under this jurisdiction or Agency by the names she has mentioned in her letter; however, it is found that a Julia Davis holds 6/120ths[sic] interest in the Joseph Lewis Acton, Citizen Pottawatomie allottee No. 748 (Law Heirship 2661-1916); however, it is not known whether she is the same person as the writer.

Very truly yours,

J. L. Suffecool
Superintendent

JJ:EV
INCL. 2

Sac & Fox – Shawnee Estates
1920-1924   Volume VIII

Shawnee Indian Agency,
Shawnee, Oklahoma,
May 18, 1922.

Dr. Jacob Bried[sic],
  Supt. Sac & Fox Sanatorium,
    Toledo, Iowa.

Dear Dr. Bried:-

    Mr. C. J. Stevens with his letter of May 10, 1922, submitted an affidavit of a certain Indian woman on your reservation concerning Emily Nastowe, deceased; wherein, certain persons up there are claiming an interest in the estate.

    The affidavit and Mr. Steven's letter are herewith referred to you for investigation, and report to us what the contention is and who these people are. We have no one on the roll by the name of Emily Nastowe; however, it is believed that these people have reference to Emily Johnson, whose Indian name appeared to be Na taw we, Sac & Fox allottee No. 235.

    A hearing has been held in this case by the Examiner of Inheritance, and it has been reported to the Indian Office, and the case is now pending there.

    Upon your report as to what you find, the matter will be referred then to the Examiner of Inheritance for such action as may be necessary.

    Thanking you for your co-operation in these matters, I am

Very truly yours,

J. L. Suffecool
JJ:EV.   Superintendent.
INCL 2

Shawnee Indian Agency,
Shawnee, Oklahoma,
May 18, 1923.

Johnston & Robinson,
  Attorneys-at-Law,
    Famous Building,
      Perry, Oklahoma.

Sac & Fox – Shawnee Estates
1920-1924 Volume VIII

Gentlemen:-

In your letter of May 8, 1921, you state that a Mrs. Ada Perrit of Noble County, Oklahoma, claims to be interested in the estate of Sophia Embler, who subsequently went by the name of Sophia Embler Lincoln.

In this connection you are advised that the Department of the Interior has already determined the heirs to this estate. Tom Lincoln, with whom she lived until her death, has been declared the sole heir.

In connection with the decedents[sic] marriage relations considerable testimony has been submitted. Thomas Lincoln and Jennie Roubidoux had separated prior to March 12, 1897 at which time the Act regulating Indian marriages and divorces in Oklahoma became effective. The records show that Jennie Roubidoux after separating from Thomas Lincoln lived with several men. She began living with William Faw Faw, an Otoe Indian of Oklahoma, about 1904 and on November 2, 1909, she was married to him by ceremony and continued living with him until on her death, July 11, 1919. It was declared that since Thomas Lincoln and Jennie Roubidoux each had re-married after their separation, that a divorce could be presumed between them, and that each should be estopped from claiming to be the lawful spouse of the other, and that the marriage between Sophia Embler and Thomas Lincoln constituted a valid marriage.

You will note from the above that the Department has already decided the question and has declared Thomas Lincoln to be the sole heir.

Very truly yours,

J. L. Suffecool
Superintendent.

JJ:EV

Shawnee Indian Agency,
Shawnee, Oklahoma,
May 19, 1922.

Superintendent of the
  Indian School,
    Mt. Pleasant, Mich.

Dear Sir:-

David H. Abraham, of 319 South McKinley St. Shawnee, Oklahoma, called at this office a few days ago and requested that I write to you in regard to the Estate of John Mah-che-ne-na, in which he is one of the heirs. He stated that he was in receipt of a statement for $15.00 due as probate fees.

He appears to be under the impression that there is more that one heir and if there is more than one heir he thinks the others should pay some of the expenses connected with the probating of this Estate. He also requested that a copy of the findings be forwarded to him, so that he may know who are the heirs of this estate

If he is the only heir, he states that he will forward the $15.00.

Very respectfully,

J. L. Suffecool
Superintendent.

JLR:EV

Law-Heirship
106733-1914
Probate
51953-1917
EGT
JG McG

Shawnee Indian Agency
Shawnee, Oklahoma
May 19, 1922

The Commissioner of Indian Affairs
Washington, D. C.

Sir:

The above reference to files will refer the Office to the heirship cases of Josephine Bourassa, deceased Citizen Pottawatomie allottee No. 802, and Martha Mullins, deceased Citizen Pottawatomie Allottee No. 803.

Nellie Wiley and Nancy Smith Fehlig have purchased the interests of Birdie Smith, Eliza Colvin, May Coleman Lewis, Rena Smith Richardson, Frank Smith and Zoa Denton, in the allotment of Josephine Bourassa, deceased, inherited through Martha Mullins, deceased.

Sac & Fox – Shawnee Estates
1920-1924 Volume VIII

The deeds, with restrictive clause in each, in which various conveyances are made to the purchasers are inclosed herewith for approval, as follows:

1. Deed from Birdie Smith to Nancy Smith Fehlig conveying her 1/21st interest in the Josephine Bourassa allotment inherited through Sidney Smith, deceased (Law-Heirship 39912-15, 57936-15 F W S). Consideration $266.67.

2. Eliza Smith, now Colvin, conveying to Nancy Smith Fehlig, her 1/84ths[sic] interest in the Josephine Bourassa allotment acquired through Martha Mullin, deceased: viz:- Martha Mullin has a 3/21st interest in the Josephine Bourassa allotment; Eliza Colvin inherited and acquired 2/24ths interest in the estate of Martha Mullin, hence 2/24ths of 3/21st equals 1/84ths interest she is conveying. Consideration $66.66.

3. May Coleman, now Lewis, conveying to Nancy Smith Fehlig, her 1/21st interest inherited in the Josephine Bourassa allotment through her husband Sidney Smith, deceased. Consideration $268.67.

4. Rena Smith, now Richardson, conveying to Nancy Smith Fehlig, her 1/21st interest in the Josephine Bourassa allotment inherited through her father, Sidney Smith, deceased. Consideration $266.66.

5. Rena Smith, now Richardson, conveying to Nancy Smith Fehlig, her 1/168ths interest in the Josephine Bourassa allotment acquired through Martha Mullin, deceased. Consideration $53.34.

6. Birdie Smith, conveying to Nellie Wiley, her 1/168ths interest in the Josephine Bourassa allotment acquired through Martha Mullin, deceased. Consideration $55.54.

7. Frank Smith, conveying to Nellie Wiley, his 1/84ths interest in the Josephine Bourassa allotment acquired through Martha Mullin, deceased. Consideration $66.66.

8. Zoa Denton, conveying to Nellie Wiley, her 1/84ths interest in the Josephine Bourassa allotment through Martha Mullin, deceased. Consideration $66.66

It will be noted that Nellie Wiley purchased the interest of J. W. Mullin in the Josephine Bourassa allotment he inherited through his wife, Martha Mullin, deceased – Land-Sales 106722-14, 4619-19 O'N.

The above transactions eliminates all of the interests in the Josephine Bourassa allotment acquired through Sidney Smith, and Martha Mullin, except the purchasers' interests.

Sac & Fox – Shawnee Estates
1920-1924 Volume VIII

A partitionment proceedings attempted was unsuccessful. The heirs then applied for a patent in fee which could not be issued on account of one of the heirs being under the age of 21 years.

The object of the purchasing heirs at this time is to ultimately acquire through purchase all other interests, and then to request the approval of an unrestricted deed in order to have restrictions removed.

The transaction herewith submitted appear to be fair and just to all interests concerned. These people are practically white. Consideration name in the deeds have been paid in to this office and are being held as Special deposits. There are three documentary revenue stamps inclosed to be attached to the deeds wherein consideration exceeds $100.00.

The consideration named in the deeds herewith submitted have been based upon an appraised value of $5,600.00 placed upon the allotment of Josephine Bourassa, deceased. Appraisement certificate is also inclosed herewith.

In view of the many attempts on the part of the heirs to make an amicable settlement, and that it is difficult to secure the signatures of the scattered heirs, and for the further fact that the transactions submitted are all agreeable to the heirs and it is their desire to have the partial settlement made in the manner presented, it is recommended that the deeds be approved.

Very respectfully,

J. L. Suffecool
Superintendent.

Incls.
JJ

DEPARTMENT OF THE INTERIOR

UNITED STATES INDIAN SERVICE

Potawatomi Indian Agency,
Mayetta, Kansas,
May 20, 1922.

Mr. J. L. Suffecool, Supt.,
Shawnee, Okla.

Dear Mr Suffecool:

Sac & Fox – Shawnee Estates
1920-1924 Volume VIII

In answer to your letter dated May 16, 1922 in which you request information relative to the allotment of Naw-as-nose, in which estate Frank Smith and Philip Lee claim they have not received any benefit from this allotment for two years, I would say that the moneys transferred you each and every six months has included the rental from this allotment. This money was divided as per the Okla., findings and should have been divided according to the Kansas laws of descent. The money recently transferred you agency from the account of Frank Smith was the moneys held in the account of Stephen Harrison and other heirs (Okla). I am inclosing a copy of the Indian Office letter authorizing the correction of the errors that have been made. Philip Lee has nothing to do with the estate of Naw-as-nose.

        Very truly yours,
   A. R. Snyder
LLS.   Supt. & Spl. Disb. Agent.
        By L.S.

Explained to Frank Smith 6/8/22

Land-Sales
27555-22
43933-13
F I P

DEPARTMENT OF THE INTERIOR

RECEIVED
MAY 22 1922
SHAWNEE INDIAN
AGENCY

Office of Indian Affairs,
Washington May 10, 1922

Mr. Arvel R. Snyder, Supt.,
 Potawatomi School.
My dear Mr. Snyder:

   Referring to your letter of April 1, 1922 calling attention to the distribution of $1,000 of the proceeds of sale of Potawatomi-Kansas allotment No. 351, made to the Kack Kack Park Corporation, approved on April 30, 1921, it is noted that on September 14, 1921, you advised the Office that there was then to the credit of Stephen Harrison $166.66 under your jurisdiction. Since the amount was credited to him in pursuance of an erroneous order, reimbursement should be made to the

Sac & Fox – Shawnee Estates
1920-1924 Volume VIII

account of Frank Smith from any moneys on deposit to Harrison's credit under your supervision as soon as that can be done.

It is noted that the other ywo[sic] persons, Ida Nullake and Philip Lee, who likewise received under the same order $166.67, are under the supervision of the Shawnee Superintendent. You will please take up immediately with Superintendent J. L. Suffecool, the matter of reimbursement of this fund from any moneys on deposit to their credit under his supervision, or which may hereafter be deposited.

Concerning your suggestion "that a finding be made in the Jessie Lee estate covering the property in Kansas", you are advised that the findings of December 31, 1918, in the estate of Jessie Lee or Ka-tah-mah or Jessie Smith, contained the following paragraph:

> "In addition to her allotment (Sac and Fox, Oklahoma), she was possessed of the entire estate of her prior deceased husband, Nah-as-nose, (see 49703-13) and a one-fourth share in the estate of Quo-tose, the prior deceased father of her prior deceased husband, Nah-as-nose (see 43933-13), all of which passed under Sec. 2258 of the laws of Kansas, to her husband, Frank Smith."

The error made in this Office was in the use of the Oklahoma finding instead of the Kansas finding. As all the proceedings in these determinations were regular and formal, no further action in that regard is required.

Please inform the Office at an early date the result of your correspondence with Superintendent Suffecool, at Shawnee.

Very truly yours,

C. F. HAWKE
Chief Clerk.

****

Land-Sales
27555-22
43933-13
F I P

Shawnee Indian Agency
Shawnee, Oklahoma
May 20, 1922

Sac & Fox – Shawnee Estates
1920-1924 Volume VIII

Supt. A. R. Snyder
Potawatomi Indian Agency
Mayetta, Kansas

Dear Mr. Snyder:

This has reference to your letter of May 13, 1922, with which you [illegible] copy of Indian Office letter dated May 10, 1911, having reference to an erroneous distribution of funds received from Kack Kack Park Corporation for the Potawatomi-Kansas allotment No. 351.

It is presumed that you have adjusted the Stephen Harrison portion of this [illegible...] appears that you had funds to the credit there in your office. If not, he has funds here that may be transferred to you, upon advice to that effect from you.

Philip Lee has some income through this office, but he had withdrawn all he has at present. However, as funds accumulate to his credit we will transfer same to you from time to time to cover the reimbursement plan. He has an annual income of about $80.00.

Ida Nullake is not so fortunate as Philip. She has little income but to depend on her income through this office is about the only recourse and it will take her sometime to make the reimbursement. She has funds transferred from your office once in awhile. May be she will have some income through your office which might be used to liquidate the overpayment to her.

This matter will be kept in current file for proper attention from time to time as funds accumulate.

An extra copy of this letter is being attached which you might, if you like, use in reporting to the Indian Office.

         Very truly yours

JJ
         J. L. Suffecool
         Superintendent.

        Shawnee Indian Agency,
        Shawnee, Oklahoma,
        May 23, 1922.

Mr. S. Y. Tutwiler,
 Kiowa Agency,
  Anadarko, Oklahoma.

Sac & Fox – Shawnee Estates
1920-1924 Volume VIII

My dear Mr. Tutwiler;-

    Replying to your letter of May 15, relative to a re-hearing in the case of Jim Bullfrog, Doo-too, deceased Absentee Shawnee allottee No. 208 of this Agency; and in compliance with your request we are inclosing herewith the approved hearing to determine the heirs of this allottee together with certain affidavits that are on file in this office for your use in completing the case.

                Very truly yours,

                              J. L. Suffecool
                              Superintendent.

JJ:EV
ENCL.

                        Shawnee Indian Agency
                        Shawnee, Oklahoma
                        May 24, 1922

Mr. P. L. Hallam
Examiner of Inheritance
Potawatomi Indian Agency
Mayetta, Kansas

Dear Mr. Hallam:

    With reference to your letter of May 18, 1922 concerning the interest Cha-me Roubidoux has apparently in the estate of Thersa[sic] Big Ear, deceased, you are advised that one I-cha-ne or Mrs. John Waters, which we presume is Oha-me Roubidoux had 360/17640 interest in the Theresa Big Ear allotment. However, this allotment was sold thru this office and patent in fee was issued to[sic] Nov. 3, 1919 to George C. Miller, the purchaser of the land.

    Therefore, the Government has no further jurisdiction over the property. The funds derived from the sale were transferred to other Agencies having jurisdiction. In June, 1920 the portion belonging to Mrs. John Waters or Walters, was transferred to Mr. Snyder.

                Very truly yours

                              J. L. Suffecool
JJ   Superintendent

Sac & Fox – Shawnee Estates
1920-1924 Volume VIII

****

DEPARTMENT OF THE INTERIOR

UNITED STATES INDIAN SERVICE

Potawatomi Indian Agency
Mayetta, Kansas.

May 18, 1922.

Mr. J. L. Suffecool,
Supt. Shawnee Indian Agency,
Shawnee, Oklahoma.

RECEIVED
MAY 20 1922
SHAWNEE INDIAN AGENCY

Dear Mr. Suffecool:

Cha-me Roubidoux possessed an interest in the estate of her predeceased husband, Charles Roubidoux, Iowa allottee No. 85, under the jurisdiction of Supt. Snyder of the Potawatomi Agency, Kansas.

In looking up the Office findings in the matter of the estate of Charles Roubidoux I find that a modification of said findings recited that Charles Roubidoux had an undivided 360/17640 interest in the estate of Theresa Big Ear, allottee No. 43 of the Iowa tribe, reference being made to Indian Office file No. 79417-15. There is no such allottee under the supervision of Supt. Snyder and, upon inquiry, I am informed that this Theresa Big Ear had an allotment under your jurisdiction and that lease rentals are forwarded from time to time by you for deposit to the credit of various heirs of Charles Roubidoux.

If it is true that Theresa Big Ear is allotted under your jurisdiction, will you kindly advise me to that effect and forward to me an appraisal of the land involved. I had this case all written up, ready to forward to the Indian Office, when I discovered that the decedent possessed an interest in the estate of Theresa Big Ear, hence I will appreciate it if you will make the matter of submitting this appraisal special.

Very truly,
S/2 NW-22-17-3   PL Hallam
Examiner of Inheritance.

PLH-RSH   Sold to Geo C. Miller, Land patent Nov. 3, 1919
I-cha-ne or Mrs. John Waters
360/17640

****

Sac & Fox – Shawnee Estates
1920-1924 Volume VIII

Shawnee Indian Agency
Shawnee, Oklahoma
May 24, 1922

Mr. P. L. Hallam
Examiner of Inheritance
Potawatomi Indian Agency
Mayetta, Kansas

Dear Mr. Hallam:

    With reference to your letter of May 18, 1922 concerning the interest Cha-me Roubidoux has apparently in the estate of Thersa[sic] Big Ear, deceased, you are advised that one I-cha-ne or Mrs. John Waters, which we presume is Oha-me Roubidoux had 360/17640 interest in the Theresa Big Ear allotment. However, this allotment was sold thru this office and patent in fee was issued to[sic] Nov. 3, 1919 to George C. Miller, the purchaser of the land.

    Therefore, the Government has no further jurisdiction over the property. The funds derived from the sale were transferred to other Agencies having jurisdiction. In June, 1920 the portion belonging to Mrs. John Waters or Walters, was transferred to Mr. Snyder.

Very truly yours

J. L. Suffecool
Superintendent

JJ

Shawnee Indian Agency
Shawnee, Oklahoma
May 24, 1922

Mr. S. Y. Tutwiler
Examiner of Inheritance
Anadarko, Oklahoma

Dear Mr. Tutwiler:

    In compliance with your request for the amount of funds to the credit of John Wolf, Jane Wolf and James Wolf, all deceased Sac & Fox Allottees, the amounts carried in our books are as follows:

    James Wolf, $1,167.13

Sac & Fox – Shawnee Estates
1920-1924 Volume VIII

James and Jane Wolf,	3,011.04
John and Jane Wolf,	2,962.94
Total	$7,141.11

It appears that the funds were deposited to the accounts and has accumulated and carried, in some instanced, combined in one account, as you note here.

Very truly yours

J. L. Suffecool
Superintendent

JJ

Shawnee Indian Agency

Shawnee, Oklahoma, May 25, 1922.

Mrs. Sallie Tyner,

Paden, Oklahoma.

Dear Madam:

Referring to the agricultural lease upon the allotment of Lillie Foreman, deceased, described as the NE1/4 of SW1/4 of section 30, township 9 north, range 4 east of the Indian Meridian.

I have to advise you in looking over the Departmental finding, it appears that by a deed approved by the Department September 28, 1906 (84832-1906) one-half of the allotment of Lilly Foreman was conveyed to you and that patent in fee issued October 25, 1907 and the record shows that you have already received a larger share in the above estate than that to which you was[sic] entitled, consequently Sco-nay-se is entitled to two-thirds and Webster Alford to one-third of all that remains.

In February 1921 you received $25.00 and in November 25, 1921, you got $12.50 making a total of $37.50, which you are not entitled in accordance with the Departmental finding. This amount have[sic] been erroneously paid you.

It is requested that you send me a cashier's check for $37.50, by return mail, so that this amount be placed to the proper heirs.

Very respectfully,

J. L. Suffecool,
Superintendent

TSA

Sac & Fox – Shawnee Estates
1920-1924 Volume VIII

                              Shawnee Indian Agency

                              Shawnee, Oklahoma, May 25, 1922.

Mr. William S. Jackson,
    Shawnee, Oklahoma, R# 5.

Dear Sir:
        It has been reported to me that you have money deposited in Shawnee from three bales of cotton sold by you from the allotment of Thomas Buffalohorn, deceased, for the year 1921 rental.

        Please send me a cashier's check for the above rental and oblige.

                Very respectfully,

                          J. L. Suffecool,
                                  Superintendent
TSA

                          Shawnee Indian Agency
                          Shawnee, Oklahoma
                          May 25, 1922

Mr. Chas. W. Edmister
Agency Farmer, Shawnee, Okla.

Dear Mr. Edmister:

        Ka-dot Pemo, who resided in Kansas, had a 1/2 interest in the Myra Hahksa estate, is dead. Examiner of Inheritance, Mr. P. L. Hallam, has set June 12, 1922 for a hearing to determine the heirs of this old Indian.

        The inclosed notices should be delivered to the persons addressed prior to the date set for the hearing. Please do so as soon as possible.

        Pah-tose Pam-bo-go is believed to be John Baptiste Pambogo, of Lexington, Oklahoma. Correspondence on file in this office show that this man wrote about the case.

Sac & Fox – Shawnee Estates
1920-1924 Volume VIII

You stated that Sin-g-quah must be an Indian who lived near Sacred Heart, Oklahoma.

When notices are delivered, accomplish the proof on the reverse side of the copies retained and turn them in to the office to be forwarded to Mr. Hallam.

While you are on this trip it will be well for you apprise the allotment of Myra Hahksa, deceased and turn in the certificate of appraisement as it will be required. This land is described as NW/4 NW/4 of 3-3-4 and NE/4 NW/4 4-5-4.

Very truly yours

CC to Mr. Hallam.
Incls.   J. L. Suffecool
JJ   Superintendent

Shawnee Indian Agency,
Shawnee, Oklahoma,
June 1st, 1922.

Supt. A. R. Snyder,
Potawatomi Indian Agency,
Mayetta, Kansas.

Dear Mr. Snyder:

There is inclosed herewith petition for the sale of the allotment of John Moses, deceased, Iowa allottee No. 101 of this Agency.

If the heirs of Martha Lightfoot have been declared the petition should be submitted to them for such action as they may desire. I am informed that Dan Whitecloud, Sarah Whitecloud, and Louise Whitecloud are some where near Rulo, Nebraska, under your supervision. Will you kindly submit the petition to them for their signatures? Thanking you for the favor, I am,

Very truly yours,

6 od 1.   J. L. Suffecool
Incl. Pet.   Supt. & Spl. Disb. Agt.

Sac & Fox – Shawnee Estates
1920-1924 Volume VIII

Shawnee Indian Agency,
Shawnee, Oklahoma,
June 1, 1922.

Mr. A. R. Snyder,
  Supt. Pottawatomi Indian Agency,
  Mayetta, Kansas.

My dear Mr. Snyder:-

    Mrs. Lizzie Casteel Porter of Sparks, Oklahoma, who by the way is a lady of Indian blood and is affiliated with the Pottawatomie Tribe, came to the office this afternoon and requested that I write to you and secure, if possible, information concerning the allotment of Julia O'Brien and Edward O'Brien. It would appear from the information that she was able to give me that Julia O'Brien was her mother, and that Edward O'Brien is her brother, and that they were allotted on the Pottawatomie County, but she was unable to give me any description of the land. I[sic]

    I would be pleased to have you examine the old allotment roll and ascertain if you can as to whether the names of the parties given above are thereon, and if so give me the status s to the allotment number, description, location and etc.

    This same information is also requested by a lady named Mary Welfelt. Mrs. Welfelt was in the office with Mrs. Porter, and she stated that she had an allotment on the Pottawatomie reservation not far from Silver Lake.

    I would be pleased to have you make this request special.

    Thanking you for co-operation in this matter that these ladies may be informed, I am

                  Very respectfully,

JLS:EV.   J. L. Suffecool
                                            Superintendent.

Shawnee Indian Agency
Shawnee, Oklahoma
June 3, 1922

Mr. David Abraham
319 South McKinley St.

Sac & Fox – Shawnee Estates
1920-1924 Volume VIII

Shawnee, Oklahoma
My friend:

Regarding the bill you brought to the office recently and about which we wrote to Mr. Cochran, Supt. Mt. Pleasant, Michigan, we now have a letter from there stating that your share of the hearing fee, in the estate of John Mah-che-ne-na, deceased, to pay is $7.50 and states also that if you are in a position to pay it a post office money order will be appreciated.

Copy of the notice of the findings of the Department in the case is herewith for your information. You inherit 1/2 of the estate.

You may forward to Supt. Cochran money order for $7.50, or if you want to bring it out here and want us to forward ut[sic] for you we will be glad to do it for you. In any event, the money order should be payable to R. A. Cochran, Supt.

Very truly yours

J. L. Suffecool
Superintendent

Incl.
JJ

Probate
22986-14
V L D

Shawnee Indian Agency
Shawnee, Oklahoma
June 3, 1922

The Commissioner
of Indian Affairs
Washington, D. C.

Dear Mr. Commissioner:

Copy of the final adjudication in the matter of the heirship case of Kaseca, deceased Absentee Shawnee Allottee No. 395 which the Office mailed to this Agency with a memorandum attached, stating that the record in the case was inadvertently sent to this Agency on May 22, 1922, is returned herewith with the advice that only copy of the finding was received, with no other papers except the letter referring to the inclosure of modification of heirship.

Sac & Fox – Shawnee Estates
1920-1924 Volume VIII

Very truly yours

J. L. Suffecool
Superintendent

Incls:
JJ

Shawnee Indian Agency
Shawnee, Oklahoma
June 6, 1922

Mr. Charles J. Griffenstine[sic]
2416 Ease Second Street
Wichita, Kansas

Dear Sir:

The inclosed copy of Department letter of May 19, 1922 allowing Mrs. Emma Griffinstine $1100 for services rendered your deceased mother, Catherine Griffenstine is self-explanatory.

A credit of $300 has been given for the amount she received thru the Kansas Court, which leaves $800 to be paid with funds that may accrue to the credit of the estate in this office.

Very truly yours

J. L. Suffecool
Superintendent

Incl.
JJ

****

Shawnee Indian Agency
Shawnee, Oklahoma
June 6, 1922"

Mr. William T. Griffenstine
Mr. Burton G. Raymond
Mr. Charles W. Raymond
Care of Tulsa Shirt Company
Tulsa, Oklahoma

Dear Sirs:

Sac & Fox – Shawnee Estates
1920-1924 Volume VIII

The Department allowed Mrs. Emma Griffenstine $1100 for services rendered you deceased mother and grandmother respectively, of which she has already received $300 thru the Kansas Court, leaving the balance of $800 to be paid from funds derived from the estate thru this office.

Copy of Department letter is inclosed herewith for you information which authorized the payment of $800.

Very truly yours

J. L. Suffecool
Superintendent

Incl.
JJ

****

Shawnee Indian Agency
Shawnee, Oklahoma
June 6, 1922

Stanard & Ennis
Attorneys at Law
Conservative Loan Bldg.
Shawnee, Oklahoma

Gentlemen:

There is inclosed herewith, for your information and for the information of your client, Mrs. Emma Griffenstine, copy of the recommendation of the Commissioner of Indian Affairs as approved by the Department.

Mrs. Griffenstine has been allowed $1100 of which she has received $300, leaving a balance of $800 which is authorized to be paid from funds that may accumulate thru this office, for services she rendered Mrs. Catherine Griffenstine, deceased.

There are no funds to the credit of this estate in this office for settlement of the allowed claim at this time. A copy of the Department letter is being furnished the heirs of Mrs. Catherine Griffenstine, deceased.

Very truly yours

Sac & Fox – Shawnee Estates
1920-1924 Volume VIII

J. L. Suffecool
Superintendent

Incl.
JJ

Shawnee Indian Agency
Shawnee, Oklahoma
June 8, 1922

Mr. P. L. Hallam
Examiner of Inheritance
Potawatomi Indian Agency
Mayetta, Kansas

Dear Mr. Hallam;

    This has reference to your letter of May 4, 1922 in which you inclosed notices of hearing, one to be served on David Nioce in the case of Pam-ah-tho-ah, deceased Kansas Kickapoo allottee No. 3.

    The notice was served on David Nioce May 25, 1922 by our Field man and he just this morning turn[sic] in the papers. They are herewith inclosed.

    David Nioce came to the office recently and asked that an affidavit be prepared for him to execute in which he wished to waive any claim whatever in the estate. It was prepared for him and he executed it. The affidavit is herewith inclosed for your use in the case.

    Very truly yours

J. L. Suffecool
Superintendent

incl
JJ

a new affidavit revoking this one by Nioce made 6-12-1922 and given to Whitewate[sic] to take to Kansas.
    JHJ-

****

Sac & Fox – Shawnee Estates
1920-1924 Volume VIII

State of Oklahoma   (
County of Pottawatomie   (SS

Affidavit
being

I, David Nioce, of lawful age, upon first/duly sworn upon oath state that I received notice of re-hearing in the matter of the heirship case of Pam-ah-tho-ah, Kickapoo Allottee No. 3 of Kansas set for May 31, 1922; that I claimed an interest in this estate by claiming marriage to the decedent, but upon re-consideration I hereby withdraw my claim in the estate; that I further relinquish my claim waive same, and all my right, title and interest in said estate, if any there be.

                                                                                     His thumb
                                            David Nioce   [print]
Witnesses to thumb mark: Mark

John Jones
Shawnee, Oklahoma

Charles Dushane
Shawnee, Oklahoma

Subscribed and sworn to before me this 5th day of June, 1922.

                                                  SUPT. & S.D.A. Suffecool, Supt. & S.D.A.
                                                  S. D. Agent, Shawnee Indian
                                                  Agency, Shawnee, Oklahoma

a new affidavit made by Nioce revoking this one 6-12-22 and handed to Whitewate to take to Kansas with him. JHJ

****

DEPARTMENT OF THE INTERIOR

UNITED STATES INDIAN SERVICE
Potawatomi Indian Agency
Mayetta, Kansas.

RECEIVED
MAY 6 1922
SHAWNEE INDIAN AGENCY

May 4, 1922.

Mr. J. L. Suffecool,
Supt. Shawnee Indian Agency,
Shawnee, Oklahoma.

Dear Mr. Suffecool:

Sac & Fox – Shawnee Estates
1920-1924 Volume VIII

    Enclosed herewith are notices of hearing in the case of Pam-ah-tho-ah, deceased Kickapoo allottee No. 3, - one for service upon David Nioce, if he should now be under your jurisdiction, and two for returns of service.

    We tried to locate David Nioce on the Kickapoo reservation, but Mr. Thomas, the farmer in charge at Kickapoo, states that he is not in that vicinity and that the last heard of him he was at McCloud, Oklahoma.

                        Very truly,
                        P L Hallam
                        Examiner of Inheritance.

RSH

Mr Edmister:
    Please deliver notice as requested; accomplish proof of service and turn them & letter here into office.
                JHJ 5/6/22

                      ****

                        Shawnee Indian Agency
                        Shawnee, Oklahoma
                        June 8, 1922

Mr. P. L. Hallam
Examiner of Inheritance
Potawatomi Indian Agency
Mayetta, Kansas

Dear Mr. Hallam;

    This has reference to your letter of May 4, 1922 in which you inclosed notices of hearing, one to be served on David Nioce in the case of Pam-ah-tho-ah, deceased Kansas Kickapoo allottee No. 3.

    The notice was served on David Nioce May 25, 1922 by our Field man and he just this morning turn[sic] in the papers. They are herewith inclosed.

    David Nioce came to the office recently and asked that an affidavit be prepared for him to execute in which he wished to waive any claim whatever in the estate. It was prepared for him and he executed it. The affidavit is herewith inclosed for your use in the case.

Sac & Fox – Shawnee Estates
1920-1924 Volume VIII

Very truly yours

J. L. Suffecool
Superintendent

incl
JJ

Land-Sales
33658-13
69969-21
83465-21
92382-21
B D S

Shawnee Indian Agency
Shawnee, Oklahoma
June 8, 1922

The Commissioner
of Indian Affairs
Washington, D. C.

Sir:

    This has reference to Office letter of April 14, 1922 in connection [sic] the alleged double allotment of Wantay Davy, now deceased, who it appears was the same as Eugenia Tah-ho-ka-le-tha, Absentee Shawnee Allottee No. 467.

    We entered into correspondence with Superintendent Locke of the Five Civilized Tribes in this case. He has furnished certain testimony taken at Sapulpa, Oklahoma of John George on Oct. 12, 1915, together with copy of Creek census card.

    We have also secured, in this connection, affidavits of John Scott and Nancy French of this jurisdiction.

    All the papers stated herein are inclosed herewith for the information of the Office.

    From the testimony of John George, a Euchee Indian and the affidavits of Nancy French and John Scott, would appear to show that Wantay Davy and Eugenia Tah-ho-ka-le-tha is one and the same person. She is identified with the same people around Euchee Country in the Creek Nation as in the Shawnee Country under this jurisdiction. There appears to be no doubt of the double allotment, except that she was know under one name in the Euchee Country and under another in the Shawnee Country.

Sac & Fox – Shawnee Estates
1920-1924 Volume VIII

The father of Eugenia Tah-h-ka-le-tha[sic] is established to be a Euchee Indian. The affidavit of Nancy French show that Tah-ho-ka-le-tha means Euchee, a Shawnee word.

On April 20, 1922 this office addressed a letter to James or Jim Gibson at Depew, Oklahoma, setting forth the matter in detail as to the probable cancellation of one of the allotments. At the same time advising him the offer made by Mr. George Outcelt, Guardian of Jack Marhardy, the minor heir, to pay him 1/2 the value of the Shawnee allotment and to retain the Creek allotment. We requested him to advise us his wishes in the matter. We have not yet received any reply from him on the subject.

Should the Shawnee allotment eventually be cancelled, James Gibson could not inherit the Creek allotment not being a Creek Indian by blood. It is understood that old Creek law, excluding non-citizen of that Tribe from inheriting the allotment of a Creek, is still in force. Perhaps this is a matter Mr. Outcelt had in mind when he offered to pay James Gibson 1/2 the value of the Shawnee allotment should it be cancelled.

It has not been possible to obtain information from James Gibson as to his wishes in the matter. He lives at Depew, Oklahoma, over in the Creek country and seldom comes to this Agency and he does not respond to our letters.

Also report is made at this time in order that the Office may be informed as to the progress of the case. In the meantime, an effort will be continued to secure some expression from James Gibson.

Very truly yours

J. L. Suffecool
Superintendent

Incls.
JJ

Shawnee Indian Agency
Shawnee, Oklahoma

June 12, 1922

Mr. Paul L. Hallam
Examiner of Inheritance
Potawatomi Indian Agency
Mayetta, Kansas

Sac & Fox – Shawnee Estates
1920-1924 Volume VIII

Dear Mr. Hallam:

The appraisement certificate you requested in your letter of May 13, 1922, and with reference to your letter of May 22, 1922, I inclose herewith the certificate covering the appraisement of $4,600 on the allotment of Pah-pe-ach, deceased, to which estate John Butler has 1/6th interest thru Ke-ah-na, unallotted Kickapoo Indian.

Probate 3665-19, decision July 14, 191, John Butler 1/6th share, Ke-ah-na estate. Unallotted.

Probate 56195-1917, decision March 28, 1918, Ke-ah-na, sole heir, Pah-pe-ach estate, Mexican Kickapoo Allottee No. 189.

Very truly yours

J. L. Suffecool
Superintendent

Incl.
JJ

Shawnee Indian Agency,
Shawnee, Oklahoma,
June 12, 1922.

Mr. Philip George,
Quapaw, Oklahoma.

Dear Sir:

This is in reply to your letter of the 6th instant in which you inquire of the estate of your uncle whom you have not seen so long and cannot recall if he sold his land or not. It also appears that you have forgotten his name. For this reason we or[sic] unable to help you in any way but if you will tell us is name we do our best to put you next.

Very truly yours,

6 od 12.

J. L. Suffecool,
Supt. & Spl. Disb. Agt.

Sac & Fox – Shawnee Estates
1920-1924 Volume VIII

Shawnee Indian Agency
Shawnee, Oklahoma

June 12, 1922

Mr. Paul L. Hallam
Examiner of Inheritance
Mayetta, Kansas

Dear Mr. Hallam:

With reference to your letter of May 5, 2933 concerning notices of hearing you mailed to this office for delivery to Joseph Allen and Kish-kah-nah-kah-kah in connection with the hearing in the estate of Me-ahm-ne-noos-kuk and I-ah-tah, deceased Kansas Kickapoo Allottees, I have to advise that our Farmer turned in papers this morning with the note attached.

We have had Kish-kah-nah-kah-kah only under consideration with regard to the delivery of the notice. Joseph Allen you state lives near Ralston, Oklahoma and Ralston is in Pawnee County and it is probable that you will be able to reach him thru the Pawnee Agency Office.

The notices are returned herewith with the note attached thereto from our Farmer.

Very truly yours

J. L. Suffecool
Superintendent

Incls.
JJ

Shawnee Indian Agency
Shawnee, Oklahoma
June 12, 1922

Mr. George A. Hoyo, Supt.,
Ponca Indian Agency
Whiteagle, Oklahoma

Dear Mr. Hoyo:

Sac & Fox – Shawnee Estates
1920-1924 Volume VIII

With reference to your letter of June 8 inquiring about the share that Frances O. English holds in any estate under this jurisdiction, you are advised that:

He had a 1/2 interest in the estate of May Murray, deceased, Law-Heirship 76611-15, 59050-1916, 89336-16, but the allotment, the SW/4 of NE/4 of 19-15-2 was sold and the sale approved [illegible].

He has now a 1/4th interest in the estate of Kirwin Murray, deceased Iowa Allottee No. 66, Law-Heirship 120560-12, 75610-1916, the allotment described as W/2 of SE/4 of 11-27-5.

Very truly yours

J. L. Suffecool
Superintendent

JJ

Probate
36045-22
B W C

Shawnee Indian Agency
Shawnee, Oklahoma

June 12, 1922

The Commissioner of Indian Affairs
Washington, D. C.

Sir:

This has reference to Office letters of May 8, 1922 and June 9, 1922, in connection with outstanding hearing fees.

The records prior to 1918 had been kept poorly and in some[sic] instances no record was made as to payment of fees. There has been written up several pages of schedule of the proposed outstanding fees uncollected. By process of elimination of the fees paid from the records and from Individual files, we have been able to reduce the outstanding fees to what is believed to be the amount outstanding yet.

It is now necessary to further search the records to ascertain each outstanding fee as to the reason for non-collection; the shape the estate is in; if the heirs are able to pay it: and if the land involved brings in any revenue thru this office or if leased without supervision.

Sac & Fox – Shawnee Estates
1920-1924 Volume VIII

When the data has been completed a full report is expected to be made within the next few days. It is believed, however, that a report as given here should be give the Office.

Very truly yours

J. L. Suffecool
Superintendent

JJ

Shawnee Indian Agency
Shawnee, Oklahoma

June 12, 1922

Mr. Paul L. Hallam
Examiner of Inheritance
Mayetta, Kansas

Dear Mr. Hallam:

With reference to your letter of May 5, 2933 concerning notices of hearing you mailed to this office for delivery to Joseph Allen and Kish-kah-nah-kah-kah in connection with the hearing in the estate of Me-ahm-ne-noos-kuk and I-ah-tah, deceased Kansas Kickapoo Allottees, I have to advise that our Farmer turned in papers this morning with the note attached.

We have had Kish-kah-nah-kah-kah only under consideration with regard to the delivery of the notice. Joseph Allen you state lives near Ralston, Oklahoma and Ralston is in Pawnee County and it is probable that you will be able to reach him thru the Pawnee Agency Office.

The notices are returned herewith with the note attached thereto from our Farmer.

Very truly yours

J. L. Suffecool
Superintendent

Incls.
JJ

Sac & Fox – Shawnee Estates
1920-1924 Volume VIII

DEPARTMENT OF THE INTERIOR

UNITED STATES INDIAN SERVICE
Potawatomi Indian Agency
Mayetta, Kansas.
May 5, 1922.

RECEIVED MAY 8 1922 SHAWNEE INDIAN AGENCY

Mr. J. L. Suffecool,
Supt. Shawnee Indian Agency,
Shawnee, Oklahoma.

Dear Mr. Suffecool:

Enclosed herewith are notices of the joint hearing in the estates of Me-ahm-me-noos-kuk and I-ah-tah, deceased Kickapoo allottees, for service upon Kish-kah-nah-kah-kah and Joseph Allen, also two extra notices for returns of service.

The address of Joseph Allen is said to be Ralston, Pawnee Oklahoma, and is none of your employees are able to serve him, please return the notice and we will take other steps to get this service.

Very truly,

Paul L Hallam
Examiner of Inheritance.

RSH   RSH

  Kish-kah nah-kah-kah- Given to Edmister for Thursday 5/11/22
   another sent to Edmister 6/8/1921

Shawnee Indian Agency
Shawnee, Oklahoma
June 12, 1922

Mr. George A. Hoyo, Supt.,
Ponca Indian Agency
Whiteagle, Oklahoma

Dear Mr. Hoyo:

  With reference to your letter of June 8 inquiring about the share that Frances O. English holds in any estate under this jurisdiction, you are advised that:

Sac & Fox – Shawnee Estates
1920-1924 Volume VIII

He had a 1/2 interest in the estate of May Murray, deceased, Law-Heirship 76611-15, 59050-1916, 89336-16, but the allotment, the SW/4 of NE/4 of 19-15-2 was sold and the sale approved [illegible].

He has now a 1/4th interest in the estate of Kirwin Murray, deceased Iowa Allottee No. 66, Law-Heirship 120560-12, 75610-1916, the allotment described as W/2 of SE/4 of 11-27-5.

Very truly yours

J. L. Suffecool
Superintendent

JJ

DEPARTMENT OF THE INTERIOR
UNITED STATES INDIAN SERVICE
Ponca Indian Agency,
Whiteagle, Oklahoma
June 8, 1922

Mr. J. L. Suffecool, Supt.,
Shawnee Indian Agency,
Shawnee, Oklahoma.

RECEIVED
JUN 8 1922
SHAWNEE INDIAN
AGENCY

My dear Mr. Suffecool:-

I write to learn if Frances O. English owns any inherited interests on your reservation. If she does, I wish you would kindly furnish this office with the name of the deceased, allottee, the description of the decedent's land, allotment number and the file numbers of the heirship findings. For your information, I will state that we are now probating the estate of Frances O. English and it is for this reason, that we would like the foregoing information.

Very sincerely yours,

George A Hoyo
Superintendent

GAH:LS

Francis[sic] O. English owns
67 Iowa – May Murray 1/2 L.H. 76611-15, 39030-16, 89336-16
sold 4-29-21 SW NE ⎫
              SE NW ⎬ 19-15-2   Decision Oct 7, 1916

Iowa

Sac & Fox – Shawnee Estates
1920-1924 Volume VIII

66   Kirwin Murray   1/4   L H 120560-12, 76610-16
       W1/2 SE – 11-17-3

Shawnee Indian Agency,
Shawnee, Oklahoma,
June 13, 1922.

Mr. Arza B. Collins,
United States Farmer,
Cushing, Oklahoma.

Dear Mr. Collins:

       Inclosed herewith are[sic] the petition for partition of allotment of Samuel L. Moore, Sac & Fox allottee N.499 described as Lots 3 & 4 of NW/4 and S/2 of NW/4 of Sec. 2 Twp. 17 N., R. 6 E. I.M. in Oklahoma; the appraisements are also inclosed for your information. It is desired that an early return of these papers be made.

Very cordially,

6 od 13   J. L. Suffecool,
Incl. pet. part. & appr.   Superintendent.

Shawnee Indian Agency,
Shawnee, Oklahoma,
June 15th, 1922.

Mr. Thomas Lincoln,
Perkins, Oklahoma.

Dear Sir:

       Referring to the sale of the John Moses allotment, and to the partition proceedings requested for by the heirs of Ho-gra-ah-chey among them yourself and for which you signed the petition some time ago.

       This is to inform you that the heirs of John Moses living at Red Rock, Okla., namely Katie Roubidoux and English, and Lizzie R Homoratha refuse to sign the petition for sale. Therefore, the sale will not be made. After investigation by this office the partition of the Ho-gra-ah-chey allotment was found impracticable and the division inequitable. The division as requested would reduce the value of the

Sac & Fox – Shawnee Estates
1920-1924 Volume VIII

allotment to the extent of $500.00 or $600.00. Therefore the partition in this case is disapproved and cannot be made as requested.

Very truly yours,

6 od 15.   J. L. Suffecool,
                                                                        Superintendent.

Shawnee Indian Agency,
Shawnee, Oklahoma,
June 15th, 1922.

Mr. R. S. Hallam[sic],
Examiner of Inheritance,
Mayetta, Kansas.

Dear Mr. Hallam:

    This is in reply to your recent inquiry as to the progress made in the determination of the heirs in the estates of John, James, and Jane wolf[sic], deceased Sac & Fox allottees Nos. 206, 208 and 207. Please inform Mr. Thomas Oliver that the report of the Examiner has but recently been forwarded due to the fact that considerable time was required in assembling evidence.

Very cordially yours,

6 od 15.   J. L. Suffecool,
                                                                        Supt. & Spl. Disb. Agent.

Shawnee Indian Agency,
Shawnee, Oklahoma,
June 15th, 1922.

Mr. Robert Small,
Perkins, Oklahoma.

Dear Sir:

    Reference is made to you[sic] letter to this office in regard to the desire of the heirs of[sic] Hog gra ah chey, deceased Iowa allottee.

Sac & Fox – Shawnee Estates
1920-1924   Volume VIII

After an investigation made by this office it developed that the division was impracticable in as much as it would not equitable and that the allotment would lose in value to the extent of $500.00 or $600.00 by such division. This tract of land should never be divided up as it would be for the best interests of all that it remain as it is now.

Very truly yours,

6 od 15.   J. L. Suffecool,
                                                                          Superintendent.

Shawnee Indian Agency,
Shawnee, Oklahoma,
June 16th, 1922.

Supt. George A. Hoyo,
Ponca Indian Agency,
Whiteagle, Oklahoma.

Dear Mr. Hoyo:

This has reference to a certain deed inherited lands covering a portion of the allotment of Charles Murray, deceased, by the heirs in favor of Alice Murray of your supervision, wife of Kerwin[sic] Murray.

The above mentioned deed was made in the manner agreeable to all the heirs in order that Alice Murray and Kerwin Murray might build them a home from funds belonging to Alice at that time on deposit to her credit in your care, on this tract of land. The approved deed is now in this office but it was learned that the couple, Alice and Kerwin Murray, have changed their mind and no longer wish to carry out the proposition at first contemplated. In my opinion these two should be taught to cultivate stability character and as a suggestion I would recommend that hypothecations be made against the account of Alice Murray until such time as it will enable them to carry out their agreement, provided of course she has no funds available at the present time. I will be pleased to have your suggestions.

Very cordially yours,

6 od 16.   J. L. Suffecool,
                                                                  Supt. & Spl. Disb. Agt.

Sac & Fox – Shawnee Estates
1920-1924 Volume VIII

Shawnee Indian Agency,
Shawnee, Oklahoma,
June 21, 1922.

Mr. Frank T. Blair,
318 Lib. Nat'l Bk. Bldg.
Oklahoma City, Oklahoma.

Dear Mr. Blair:

    This has reference to the allotment of Philola Green, concerning which you made this office a visit, for the purpose of having restrictions removed, either by issuance of fee simple patent or by sale, preferably sale. The land in question is described as the S/2 of NE/4 of Sec. 32, and S/2 of NW/4, and the SW/4 of Sec. 33, Twp. 8 N., R. 1 E., I. M. in Cleveland County.

    A copy of the Departmental Finding of the Heirship matter is herewith inclosed which was promised you.

    This land has never been appraised for the reason that it never was offered for sale. But, the Superintendent directs that on Friday, 23 instant, he and I will proceed to the part of the country in which this land is located and make a complete investigation, as rentals, appraisement, etc. In as much as you expressed that you would like to make a visit to the allotment you are invited to join us in the trip. You could come via M. K & T. which arrives here about 9 a.m. This train will be set and in case you are not there we will make a visit to land just the same.

    Of the two methods, the sale of the allotment, or patent in fee to the heirs, the Superintendent prefers the latter provided none of the heirs are dead leaving minor heirs and undetermined. However, this matter can be gone over more fully later. It would appear that a sale could be arranged in view of the fact that the party in Kansas may be prospective bidder. We are anxious to consummate the removal of restrictions to this land thereby settle the estate in full.

    Very truly yours,
    J. L. Suffecool, Supt.
By   Charles Dushane
Sac & Fox Lease Clerk,

Sac & Fox – Shawnee Estates
1920-1924   Volume VIII

Pet. Part.
Sam Moore
Sac & Fox
No. 499.

Shawnee Indian Agency,
Shawnee, Oklahoma,
June 22, 1922.

The Hon. Com
of Indian Affairs,
Washington, D. C.

Dear Mr. Commissioner:

There is inclosed herewith petition for partition by the heirs of Samuel Moore, deceased Sac & Fox allottee No. 499, for which trust patents are to be issued.

The reason for the partition hereof is that one of these girls desires to build on the part set aside to her.

The partition is respectfully recommended for the purposes given by the heirs.

Very respectfully,

8 od 23
Incl. Pet. Part.

J. L. Suffecool,
Supt. & Spl. Disb. Agt.

Shawnee Indian Agency,
Shawnee, Oklahoma,
June 26, 1922.

Mr. P. L. Hallam,
   Examiner of Inheritance,
      Mayetta, Kansas.

My dear Mr. Hallam:-

This will acknowledge the receipt of your letter of June 14th, 1922 with reference to the matter of the estates of Meah-m-me-noose-kuk, and I-ah-tah-, deceased Kickapoo Indians; wherein it would appear that a Mr. A. E Crane, an Attorney for William White Water, presented depositions which he had taken in this neighborhood and from Indians under this jurisdiction. You request that I advise you the following facts in regard to the deponents: age, sex, tribe, address, means of knowledge, intelligence, and creditability.

Sac & Fox – Shawnee Estates
1920-1924 Volume VIII

In reply, I have to advise that I have been successful in getting three of the deponents to come to the office, and I have questioned them as to whether or not William White Water coached them in regard to their answers, and whether he offerred[sic] them more than a reasonable witness fee for their testimony.

In reply, I have to advise that it would appear that Ah ko the, Ah nah she meah, and Peck ke ah peah were each given $5.00 a piece for the testimony given; and they claim that no fee was offerred them for a future continuancy. Each appears to know but little about the case.

Ah ko the, who is now about 90 years of age, knew the deceased when he was 15 years of age.

Ah nah she meah has about the same knowledge as Ah ko the.

Also Peck ke ah peah. In fact I do not believe that any of the three mentioned knew definitely or have any definite knowledge as to the heirs of the deceased.

It was with considerable difficulty that I was able to develop anything concerning the deceased. They seemed to hesitate to tell for the reason that they said there was some crooked work going on. I was able to develop the fact, however, that they are of the opinion that William Whitewater[sic] is unscrupulous, and would not hesitate to do anything that would bring about additional compensation to himself through inheritance or any other way that he could.

Ah ko the, who seemed to do most of the talking said that William White Water spent most of his time in the pool hall and when an Indian died, he immediately set about to establish the heirship and in most of the cases, he was one of the heirs himself. Of course, I do not know whether the old man knows what he is talking about or not, but I supposed that he is basing what he says on what he has heard the other Indians say.

The file in the case sent to me is returned herewith.

Very respectfully,

JLS:EV.
INCL. file.

J. L. Suffecool
Superintendent.

Sac & Fox – Shawnee Estates
1920-1924 Volume VIII

Shawnee Indian Agency,
Shawnee, Okla.
July 8, 1922.

Mr. Paul L. Hallam, Examiner of Inheritance,

Mayetta, Kansas.

Dear Sir:-

  Herewith is testimony given by John B. Pambogo or Baptiste Pembogo and his sister Josetta Mego or Josetta Megah (Josetta Pembogo) before J. L. Riley, Clerk, stating their relationship to Kadot Pemo or Kahdot Pemo.

  Kahdot Pemo was heir in the estate of Elizabeth Hahk-sa, Citizen Pott., allottee No. 329--1/2 interest. (See: L.H. 132432-12; 29382-13, M.H.W.) This land was sold in 1916.

  He also held 1/2 interest in the allotment of Myra Hahk-sa, Citizen Pott., allotee[sic] No. 326 (See L.H. 128929014; 52191-15 W.S.) 40 acres of this land has been disposed and 40 acres still held in trust and same is not leased as it is very rough and undesirable for grazing or agricultural purposes.

  Notices were served to these people May 30, but they failed to report to this office any sooner than June 30, 1922.

Incls.   Very respectfully,
JLR.

           J. L. Suffecool,
           Superintendent.

Shawnee Indian Agency,
Shawnee, Oklahoma,
July 10, 1922.

Mr. C. H. Ennis,
 Attorney-at-law,
  Shawnee, Oklahoma.

My dear Mr. Ennis:-

  This will acknowledge the receipt of your letter of July 8th with reference to Catherine Griffinstein Estate and claim of Emma Griffinstein in the sum of $800.00 against this estate.

Sac & Fox – Shawnee Estates
1920-1924 Volume VIII

In reply, I have to advise that this has been made a matter of record at this office, and steps will be taken to see that the said amount is paid, as soon as possible.

The land in question will be leased through this office in the future, if found necessary, in order that the claim may be protected.

Very respectfully,

J. L. Suffecool,
Superintendent.

JLS:EV.

****

Shawnee Indian Agency,
Shawnee, Okla.
July 14, 1922.

Mr. C. J. Griffenstein,
    411 Ida Ave.,
    Wichita, Kansas,
Dear Mr. Griffenstein:-

    This will acknowledge receipt of your letters of the June 23 and July 7th, in which you make inquiry relative to matters pertaining to the Catherine Griffenstein estate.

    Replying to same I have to advise that after looking over correspondence in the case it appears that Emma Griffenstein did make a quit claim deed to you for the share of the portion of the estate you deeded her. As regards your former wife's lawsuit against you for breach of warranty I know of no assistance this office may be able to render you since this lawsuit is a matter of personal interest between you two.

    The Interior Department has allowed Mrs. Emma Griffenstein's claim for $1,100 as settlement in full against the estate of your mother.

Sac & Fox – Shawnee Estates
1920-1924 Volume VIII

JLR.

Very respectfully,

J. L. Suffecool, Supt.

Shawnee Indian Agency,
Shawnee, Oklahoma,
July 13, 1922.

Mr. A. R. Snyder,
Supt. Potawatomi Agency,
Mayetta, Kansas.

Dear Mr. Snyder:-

This afternoon George Appletree, a Sac & Fox Indian under the supervision of this Agency came into the office and requested that I take up a matter with reference to James Roubidoux.

The history of the family is as follows:

Joseph Roubidoux	(Father)
Ida Roubidoux	(Mother)

<u>Children</u>

Ka-Ke-Ke-Me-Qua	(son, dec'd)
Pearl Roubidoux, now Johnson	(daughter)
Helen Roubidoux, now Bass	(daughter)
James Roubidoux	(son)

The last child, James Roubidoux, who I understand is about 22 years of age does not know whether he is included on the rolls of the Sac & Fox Indians in Kansas, or not. He says that he can remember that his father, Joseph Roubidoux drew his annuity money one or two ties.

Will you kindly ascertain from the rolls in your office and advise George Appletree, Prague, Oklahoma, if James Roubidoux is carried on the roll and whether any trust funds is due him, as he claims he has never drawn this fund.

A prompt reply to this letter inclosing a carbon of your letter to this office will be appreciated.

Sac & Fox – Shawnee Estates
1920-1924 Volume VIII

Very respectfully,

JLS:EV.
cc to George Appletree,
    Prague, Oklahoma.

J. L. Suffecool
Superintendent.

Land-Sales.

106722-14
 51853-17
41805-23
JTH

Shawnee Indian Agency,
Shawnee, Oklahoma,
July 17, 1922.

The Commissioner of
  Indian Affairs
    Washington, D. C.

S I R;-

    Reference is made to Office letter of July 5, 1922, bearing above caption, regarding deeds returned to this office in matter of the estates of Josephine Bourassa and Martha Mullen, for minor corrections in several of the deeds.

    The Office is respectfully informed that the corrections requested for have all been made and the following deeds are returned; namely,

Deed	Amount
To-Nancy Smith	
	$266.67
From-Birdie Smith	
Deed	
To-Nancy Smith	$66.67
From-Eliza Smith, now Colvin	
Deed	

Charles Wiley and John B. Fehlig have been notified by card of the approval hereof today. 9-16-22 Charles Dushane

263

Sac & Fox – Shawnee Estates
1920-1924 Volume VIII

To-Nancy Smith

From-May Coleman, now Lewis $266.67

Deed

To-Nancy Smith

From-Rena Smith, now Richardson $266.67

Deed

To-Nancy Smith

From-Rena Smith, now Richardson $33.34

Deed	Amount
To-Nellie Wiley	$33.34
From-Birdie Smith	

Deed

To-Nellie Wiley

From-Frank Smith $66.66

Deed

To--Nellie Wiley

From-Zoa Denton $66.66

Very respectfully,

J. L. Suffecool
Superintendent

CD:EV.
INCLS.

****

Sac & Fox – Shawnee Estates
1920-1924   Volume VIII

                        Shawnee Indian Agency,
                        Shawnee, Oklahoma,
                        July 17, 1922.

Mr. John D. Fehlig,
   528 to 30 Delaware St.,
   Kansas City, Missouri.

Dear Mr. Fehlig:-

      This is in reply to your letter o f[sic] June 27, 1922 regarding deeds bearing on the settlement of the estate of Mrs. Josephine Bourassa.

      In connection with these deeds, you are advised that the Indian Office saw fit to return these deeds for some very minor corrections. These corrections have all been made in this office and the deeds will be re-submitted to the Office.

                                  Very respectfully,

                                  J. L. Suffecool
                                  Superintendent.
CD:EV.
                  ****

                        Shawnee Indian Agency,
                        Shawnee, Oklahoma,
                        July 17, 1922.

Mr. Charles Wiley,
   Maude, Oklahoma.

Dear Mr. Wiley:-

      Some two or three weeks ago, I promised to write you concerning the disposition of the Josephine Bourassa estate, and I instructed Mr. Dushane, of this office, to write you a card regarding the same. Since that time Mr. Dushane has been away and has neglected to write you at once.

      All of the deeds in the Josephine Bourassa estate and the Martha Mullen estate have been returned to this office for minor corrections in several of the deeds. The corrections have all been made and the deeds are now being re-submitted to the Department for approval.

Sac & Fox – Shawnee Estates
1920-1924 Volume VIII

Trusting that this will be satisfactory, I am,

Very respectfully,

J. L. Suffecool
Superintendent.

CD:EV.

****

REFER IN REPLY TO THE FOLLOWING:
Land-Sales.
106722-14
51853-17
41805-22
JTH

Rec'd July 8-22
Dushane
DEPARTMENT OF THE INTERIOR,
OFFICE OF INDIAN AFFAIRS,
WASHINGTON,
JUL -5 1922

ADDRESS ONLY THE
COMMISSIONER OF INDIAN AFFAIRS

Mr. J.L. Suffecool,
Supt. Shawnee School.

My dear Mr. Suffecool:

There are returned herewith deeds executed by the heirs of Josephine Bourassa and Martha Mullen.

In the deed which Frank Smith executes in favor of Nellie Wiley it is stated that the grantor conveys all of "the undivided 1/84ths (one eighty fourths) interest in and to the allotment of Josephine Bourassa, deceased, inherited through Martha Mullen, deceased". This should be changed to read "his undivided 1/84ths (one eighty fourths) interest in and to the allotment of Josephine Bourassa, deceased, inherited through Martha Mullen, deceased", and in the deed which Birdie Smith executes in favor of Nellie Wiley it is stated that the grantor conveys all of "the undivided 1/168ths (One and one hundred sixty fourths[sic]) interest in the allotment of Josephine Bourassa, deceased, inherited through Martha Mullen, deceased". This should be changed to read "her undivided 1/168ths (One – one hundred sixty eighths) interest in the allotment of Josephine Bourassa, deceased, inherited through Martha Mullen, deceased".

In the deed which Rena Smith executes in favor of Nancy Smith (the consideration being $33.34) the grantor conveys "all the undivided 1/168ths (One and one hundred sixty eighths) in and to the allotment of Josephine Bourassa, deceased, inherited through Martha Mullen, deceased". This should be changed to read "all her undivided 1/168ths (One – one hundred sixty eighths) interest in and to the allotment of Josephine Bourassa, deceased, inherited through Martha Mullen, deceased".

Sac & Fox – Shawnee Estates
1920-1924 Volume VIII

In the other deed which Rena Smith executes in favor of Nancy Smith (consideration being ($266.66) the grantor conveys "all the undivided 1/21st (One twenty first) in and to the allotment of Josephine Bourassa allotment". This should be changed to read "all her undivided 1/21st (One twenty first) interest in and to the allotment of Josephine Bourassa, deceased".

In the deed where Birdie Smith conveys certain lands to Nancy Smith (the consideration being $266.67) the grantor conveys "the undivided 1/21st (One twenty first) in the allotment of Josephine Bourassa allotment". This should be changed to read "her undivided 1/21st (One twenty first) interest in the allotment of Josephine Bourassa, deceased".

In the deed from Zoa Denton to Nellie Wiley the grantor conveys "all the undivided 1/84ths (One eighty fourths) interest in and to the allotment of Josephine Bourassa, deceased, inherited through Martha Mullen, deceased". It is requested that "the undivided" be changed to "her undivided".

Please return the deeds when above changes have been made.

6-RFP-29

Very truly yours,
CF Hauke
Chief Clerk.

****

Shawnee Indian Agency,
Shawnee, Oklahoma,
July 17, 1922.

Mr. John D. Fehlig,
  528 you 30 Delaware St.,
  Kansas City, Missouri.

Dear Mr. Fehlig:-

This is in reply to your letter of June 27, 1922 regarding deeds bearing on the settlement of the estate of Mrs. Josephine Bourassa.

In connection with these deeds, you are advised that the Indian Office saw fit to return these deeds for some very minor corrections. These corrections have all been made in this office and the deeds will be re-submitted to the Office.

Sac & Fox – Shawnee Estates
1920-1924 Volume VIII

Very respectfully,

J. L. Suffecool
Superintendent.

CD:EV.

****

J. B. FEHLIG. PRESIDENT AND TREASURER	**ESTABLISHED 1875** **INCORPORATED 1915**	**STEWART TAYLOR.** COUNSELOR-VICE PRES.-SECY.

Excelsior Heating Supply Company

WARM AIR FURNACES
PIPES AND REGISTERS
HEATING SUPPLIES

528-30 DELAWARE STREET

KANSAS CITY, MO.

[RECEIVED JUN 28 1922 SHAWNEE INDIAN AGENCY stamp]

June 27th, 1922

Mr. J. L. Suffecool, Agent,
Shawnee Indian School,
Shawnee, Okla.

Dear Sir:

    The latter part of April your office handled several deeds bearing on the settling of the estate of Mrs. Josephine Boursasa, and I would be pleased to be advised if this has been approved of by the department and if it is in line for payment to be made to the several different parties. Some of these have written me regarding this. They no doubt are in need of their funds, and I hope that you can advise that this is in such shape as to be finally closed.

    Thanking you in advance for your reply, I am

Very truly yours,

John B. Fehlig

****

Sac & Fox – Shawnee Estates
1920-1924 Volume VIII

Shawnee Indian Agency,
Shawnee, Oklahoma,
July 17, 1922.

Mr. Charles Wiley,
 Maude, Oklahoma.

Dear Mr. Wiley:-

Some two or three weeks ago, I promised to write you concerning the disposition of the Josephine Bourassa estate, and I instructed Mr. Dushane, of this office, to write you a card regarding the same. Since that time Mr. Dushane has been away and has neglected to write you at once.

All of the deeds in the Josephine Bourassa estate and the Martha Mullen estate have been returned to this office for minor corrections in several of the deeds. The corrections have all been made and the deeds are now being re-submitted to the Department for approval.

Trusting that this will be satisfactory, I am,

Very respectfully,

J. L. Suffecool
Superintendent.

CD:EV.

Ed-Ind.
53268-22
E S S

Shawnee Indian Agency,
Shawnee, Oklahoma,
July 18, 1922.

The Commissioner
 of Indian Affairs,
  Washington, D. C.

S I R:-

Sac & Fox – Shawnee Estates
1920-1924 Volume VIII

Referring to inclosed letter of Mr. Ed. Brown, Montour, Iowa, in which he makes inquiry concerning late[sic] rentals due him from the estate of his deceased wife, Pa-phia-na; I have to advise that at the present time there appears upon the books of this office a balance of $139.07 to the credit of this estate.

This amount will be transferred to Superintendent Breid, Sac & Fox Sanatorium, Toledo, Iowa, at an early date for proper distribution among the heirs.

Very respectfully,

J. L. Suffecool
Superintendent.

JLR:EV.
INCL. 1 let.

Ed-Ind.
53268-22
E S S

Shawnee Indian Agency,
Shawnee, Oklahoma,
July 18, 1922.

The Commissioner
of Indian Affairs,
Washington, D. C.

S I R:-

Referring to the inclosed letter written by one, Mr. Thomas Lybarger, Senior, sub-station No. 2, Kansas City, Missouri, in which he makes inquiry regarding money due him from the estate of his deceased wife, Caroline Frayer, and from the estate of Helen Cook; I have to advise that money in the amount of $123.08, which has been held here to Mr. Lybarger's credit on account of his addressbeing[sic] unknown, is forwarded to him today. This represents rentals derived from the two estates in question.

A patent in fee has been issued to the heirs on the Caroline Frayer allotment.

The Helen Cook allotment is still held in trust by the Government and at the present time there is no lease on it.

Sac & Fox – Shawnee Estates
1920-1924 Volume VIII

Very respectfully,

J. L. Suffecool
Superintendent.

JLR:EV.

INCL. 1.

DEPARTMENT OF THE INTERIOR

UNITED STATES INDIAN SERVICE

Shawnee Indian Agency,

Shawnee, Oklahoma, July 19, 1922.

Mr. J. H. Farley,

Cushing, Oklahoma, R# 3.

Dear Sir:

    This is to acknowledge the receipt of your letter of the 18th instant, relative to a bank draft for $100.00. I have to advise you that this check has been credited to the heirs and receipt have been issued and you will get it in a few days.

Very respectfully,

J. L. Suffecool,
Superintendent

TBA
ffffff

Probate
55584-22
WHG

Shawnee Indian Agency,
Shawnee, Oklahoma,
July 19, 1922.

Sac & Fox – Shawnee Estates
1920-1924 Volume VIII

The Commissioner
of Indian Affairs
Washington, D. C.

S I R:-

Referring to Office letter of the 13th inst., bearing file number as stated above, in which a report was requested on a letter received by the Office from M. Jacques from Delia, Kansas, concerning the allotment of Myra Hahk-sa; I have to advise that Mary Mego and Kahdot Pemo are her heirs in equal parts to the above named estate (LH 128929-14 and 52191-15 FWS). These two parties lived in Kansas under the jurisdiction of the Agency at Mayetta.

I understand that Kahdot Pemo is now dead and that a hearing was held to determine his heirs on June 12th, 1922.

I have further to advise that Kahdot Pemo and Mary [illegible] mego[sic] were also heirs in equal parts to the estate of Eliza Naohk-sa, a Citizen Pottawatomie allottee.

Perhaps if Mr. M. Jacques would go to the office at Mayetta, Kansas he could obtain the information he desires.

There remains in trust 80 acres of the original allotment of Myra Hahk-sa, which is not under lease at the present time as same is not desirable for grazing or agricultural purposes. The allotment of Elizabeth Naohk-sa was sold several years ago.

Very respectfully,

J. L. Suffecool
Superintendent.

JLR:EV. Incl. 1 let.

Sac & Fox – Shawnee Estates
1920-1924 Volume VIII

Shawnee Indian Agency,
Shawnee, Oklahoma,
July 21, 1922.

Dr. Jacob Breid,
   Sac & Fox Sanatorium,
   Toledo, Iowa.

Dear Dr. Breid:-

    This has reference to your letter of July 1st regarding the allotment of Hiram Gibbs which Gilbert Gibbs desires to deed his undivided 306/1620ths part.

    You are advised that inasmuch as there are several heirs to this allotment and the issuance of a deed to a tract of land precludes the issuance of a patent in fee thereafter.

    For this reason, you will please inform Gilbert Gibbs that it will be impracticable to have his part of this allotment deeded to his wife, Ina Gibbs.

Very respectfully,

J. L. Suffecool
CD:EV.   Superintendent.

Report &
Appraisement.
John McKuk
Sac & Fox Al-   Shawnee Indian Agency,
lotment No. 259.   Shawnee, Oklahoma,
                         July 25, 1922.

Supt. J. L. Suffecool,
Shawnee Indian Agency,
Shawnee, Oklahoma.

Dear Mr. Suffecool:

    Submitted herewith is a report and the appraisement on the allotment of John McKuk, with the view of division by partition

Sac & Fox – Shawnee Estates
1920-1924 Volume VIII

This allotment was visited on the 18th of July, 1922, and points of interest entering into the value of the farm were noted. It is located 2 miles southwest of Prague, Okla., on the Ft. Smith & Western Railroad. It is within the consolidated school district with the town of Prague. A small creek crosses the allotment along the East side which makes most of the bottom land in the East-Half, and, therefore, impossible of an equal division in value. The nearest approaching an equal division is as shown by the appraisements, viz., N/2 of DE/5, 32-12-6 E. and S/2 of SW/4 of 32-12-6 E. with a difference of $500.00 in favor of the South-Half. Both tracts lie along the main highway on the West side of the farm. The Improvements are on the South-Half but are if very little in value.

The appraisements submitted herewith are as stated before as nearly equal in value, according to legal sub-divisions, as practicable. It would appear that it will be necessary for the heirs to settle this difference.

Very respectfully,
Charles Dushane
Sac & Fox Lease Clerk.

Incl. 2 Appraisements.

Probate.
13157-19
WHG
                    Shawnee Indian Agency,
                    Shawnee, Oklahoma,
                    July 27, 1922.

The Hon. Com.
of Indian Affairs,
Washington, D. C.

Dear Mr. Commissioner:

There is transmitted herewith petition for partition of the allotment of Non-ne-ke-kat, deceased Citizen Pottowatomie[sic] allottee No. 703, described as the S/2 of the NE/4 of Sec. 8, Twp. 7 N., R. 4 E. I.M. in Pottawatomie County, Oklahoma.

Two of the heirs who own one-half of this allotment live in Kansas. The owner of the other half is living on the allotment but has been paying one-half of the proceeds of the farm to the other heirs until last year when he failed on account of the destruction of his crop by the bowl-weevel[sic]. Although he remitted rentals above the average the other two heirs are dissatisfied on account of the failure for the year of 1921.

Therefore, the partition of this allotment is respectfully recommended for approval.

Sac & Fox – Shawnee Estates
1920-1924 Volume VIII

Very respectfully,

7 od 27
Incl. Pet. Part.

J. L. Suffecool,
Supt. & Spl. Dis. Agent.

No. 86[?]9[?].
Re: Frank [Illegible]

Shawnee Indian Agency,

Shawnee, Okla.

July 27, 1922.

Bureau of Legal [Illegible]

City Hall,

Philadelphia, Pa.

Dear Sir: Attention Mr. H. W. Ko[???].

    This has reference to your letter of the 26 inst., making inquiry for Frank Kahdot as to why he does not receive any funds from the estate of his deceased mother, Emma Kahdot. I so reply to same I have to advise that at the time the heirs were determined in this matter, James Kahdot, the father of Frank Kahdot and the husband of the deceased allottee; was declared to have homestead rights in the estate, which gave him the use and occupancy of same for the remainder of his natural life or until the estate is otherwise disposed of according to law.

    Accordingly the children will not share in any of the proceeds derived from the rentals of the land, as long as the father, James Kahdot is alive. After his death the children will share in the proceeds.

JLR. Very respectfully,

J. L. Suffecool,
Superintendent.

Sac & Fox – Shawnee Estates
1920-1924 Volume VIII

Shawnee Indian Agency,
Shawnee, Okla.
July 27, 1922.

Mrs. Sarah Moxley,

Miami, Okla.

Dear Friend:-

I have your letter of the 21 inst., in which you made inquiry relative to heirship rights of several persons in the estate of your deceased father.

In reply to same I have to advise that this land is still held in trust by the U.S. Government and is not subject to terms. As regards the matter of certain ones sharing in the estate, I have to state that a hearing was held to determine the legal heirs sometime ago and it was found that in the [illegible] shown as heirs to the estate were so declared by the laws of Oklahoma. According to the law of decent in this state they were declared to be the legal heirs and cannot be prevented from sharing in the proceeds of the rental of the land. The heirship [illegible] involved several families, so their[sic] had been several marriages and deaths in the immediate family. Such conditions complicated matters and made the findings rather long, but the findings were made according to law.

You have a balance of $75.80 to your credit on the books of this office. This amount will be forwarded to you at an early date.

If you know the addresses of the other heirs, please inform us, so that their share of the funds may be sent to them.

The land of your father has been leased for this year for the amount of $96.00. The money has been paid into this office and you will soon receive your share.

JLR.   Very respectfully,

                                        J. L. Suffecool,
                                        Superintendent.

Sac & Fox – Shawnee Estates
1920-1924 Volume VIII

Shawnee Indian Agency,
Shawnee, Oklahoma,
July 31, 1922.

Supt. J. L. Suffecool,
Eagle Pass Hotel,
Eagle Pass, Texas.

Dear Mr. Suffecool:

Big Simon was in here this morning and called my attention to the fact that two of the heirs of Quen-nep-pe-thot and Kah-tuck-o-kah, his father and brother respectively, are at Eagle Pass. Their names are Tah-bah-she and Non-e-peach-e. All of the others are here.

It does not appear to me that we will be getting very far if we should accomplish dividing these two allotments but since he wants it done I thought it best to send you the petition for partition. It may arrive too late. There is a difference of about $1000.00 in the two tracts of land. This will necessitate the payment of $500.00 of one party of the heirs to the other. Big Simon is willing to pay $500.00.

Again hoping you and John will have good luck on your trip, I am,

Very cordially,

Incl. Pet. Part.   Sac & Fox Lease Clk.

Shawnee Indian Agency,
Shawnee, Oklahoma,
August 1, 1922.

Mr. Grover Wakole,
Mercier, Kansas.

Dear Sir:

This has reference to your inquiry recently in regard to your interest in the Rufus Wakole allotment, in which you say that you want a patent in fee for this allotment. In connection with this allotment you are advised that since this is inherited land and you own 2/3 of it, therefore it will be necessary that the other heir join you in an application for t he[sic] patent, There is another method, namely, by partition. This can be done only in the case of an equal division. By this I mean the part to each must equal your respective shares in the estate. The land will be appraised with that purpose

Sac & Fox – Shawnee Estates
1920-1924 Volume VIII

in view and the Superintendent at Mayetta Kansas will be notified of your wishes in this matter.

The description of the allotment is as follows:- S/2 of the NW/4, 3-11-4 E., and N/2 of the NW/4, 10-11-4E. If a purchaser could be found it might be sold to a better advantage than a division.

Very truly yours,

J. L. Suffecool,
Superintendent.
By

Sac & Fox Lease Clerk.

Order No. 110.

Shawnee Indian Agency,

Shawnee, Okla.

Aug. 7, 1922.

The Commissioner of Indian Affairs,

Washington, D.C.

Sir:-

Replying to the above named Order, I have to advise that heirs to deceased In dian[sic] allottee have been notified and that the regulations pertaining to the transfer of funds from the credit of the decedents to proper heirs, have been complied with.

Action is taken in these matters soon after the receipt by this office of notice from the Department that the heirs to the estates of deceased allottees have been determined.

JLR.   Very respectfully,

_____

J. L. Suffecool,
Superintendent.

Sac & Fox – Shawnee Estates
1920-1924 Volume VIII

Shawnee Indian Agency,
Shawnee, Okla.
Aug. 7, 1922.

Dr. Jacob Breid, Supt.,
Sac & Fox Sanatorium,
Toledo, Iowa.

Dear Dr:-

I am receipt of a letter from the Office advising me that if the Indians who feel like they are entitled to be heirs to the estate of E-sa-wi-si or Emma Red Rock or Abby Red Rock deceased allottee No 447 of the Sac & Fox tribe, wish the case re-opened it will be necessary for them to comply with Sections 39 and 40 of the Department Regulations.

There are several Indians living under your jurisdiction, I understand, are dissatisfied with the findings as they stand. The affidavits you sent with your letter of the 21st July have been forwarded to Washington. The pretending heirs have the name of the deceased wrong. It is Abby Red Rock or Au-saw-wau-se. Should these Indians care to take steps to have the case re-opened, please advise them what is neccessary [sic] and let this office know their purpose. According to the findings, Na-[?]a-ke-ko has been determined the sole heir.

JLR.

Very respectfully,

_____ J. L. Suffecool, Supt.

Shawnee Indian Agency,
Shawnee, Oklahoma, August 9, 1922.

Mr. Chas. W. Fear,
821 West Fourth St.,
Joplin, Mo.

Dear Sir:

Sac & Fox – Shawnee Estates
1920-1924 Volume VIII

Referring to your letter of the 5th instant, relative to the allotment of Phoebe Keokuk, deceased, Sac & Fox allottee #261, described as the lots 3 and 4 & E/2 of the SW1/4 of section 31, township 17 north, range 6 east.

I have to advise you that Herman C. Wolff, executed the lease on the above allotment February 23, 1922 and Supt. J. L. Suffecool, sign[sic] the lease for the heirs as they are all scattered, for a term of one year from January 1, 1922, to expire December 31, 1922, for a consideration of $300.00 per annum. Mr. Wolff paid to this Office on April 3, 1922 $150. and June 22, 1922 for $150.00 making the $300.00 for the year 1922.

Oil and gas lease No. 10303, was executed by the heirs June 5. 1918, in favor of A. L. Funk and he has made an assignment to this lease to Margay Oil Corporation of Tulsa, Oklahoma. This lease was approved by the Department July 31, 1918, for a term of ten years or much longer there after as oil and gas shall be found in paying quantities. This Office has written to the Company and the rentals will be fourth coming in a few days amounting to $280.00.

Hoping the information is satisfactory, I am

Very respectfully,

Clerk in Charge

TBA

Shawnee Indian Agency,
Shawnee, Oklahoma,
August 11, 1922.

Dr. Jacob B. Breid,
   Sac & Fox Sanatorium,
      Toledo, Iowa.

Dear Dr. Breid:-

There is inclosed herewith a copy of letter from the Office which has reference to the estate of Abby Redrock, or E-sa-wi-si, deceased Sac & Fox allottee No. 476, Oklahoma.

This letter is inclosed for the information of the parties interested in this estate.

Sac & Fox – Shawnee Estates
1920-1924 Volume VIII

Very respectfully,

J. L. Suffecool
Superintendent.

EV.
INCL. 1.

****

REFER IN REPLY TO THE FOLLOWING:
PROBATE
77289-1915
60787-1922
L A P
Heirship, Shawnee
Agency, Oklahoma.

DEPARTMENT OF THE INTERIOR,
OFFICE OF INDIAN AFFAIRS,
WASHINGTON,

AUG -7 1922

ADDRESS ONLY THE
COMMISSIONER OF INDIAN AFFAIRS

RECEIVED AUG 11 1922 SHAWNEE INDIAN AGENCY

Mr. J. L. Suffecool,
   Supt. Shawnee Agency.

My dear Mr. Suffecool:

    Your letter of the 24th of July, 1922, enclosing a certain petition and affidavits of Ke-ki-pa-no, and others, claiming interest in the estate of Abby Redrock, or E-sa-wi-si, deceased Sac and Fox allottee No. 476, Oklahoma, has been given consideration.

    Under date of July 31, 1922, you were advised that the petitioners by complying with Sections 39 and 40 of the Department Regulations might receive consideration by this Office. It is assumed that the petitioners and affidavits you submit are in response to this letter.

    The regulations require that notice of an application to reopen a determined heirship be served upon the adverse parties with a copy of all records, affidavits, or other evidence upon which the applicant relies for a reopening. No such notice or return thereof appears in the record you submit.

    You are directed to inform the applicants of the requirements as to notice and when such notices and proof of services thereof is received, this Office will give the matter careful consideration.

Very truly yours,

EB Meritt
Assistant Commissioner.

8-VR-3

Shawnee Indian Agency,
Shawnee, Oklahoma,
August 12, 1922

Dr. Jacob Breid,
Sac & Fox Sanitorium[sic],
Toledo, Iowa.

Dear Dr. Breid:

There are inclosed herewith the following papers concerning the allotment of John McKuk in which William Davenport is one-half owner:- The report of Charles Dushane, clerk from this office, for the purpose of making a division and an appraisement, the appraisements on form 5-110a, the petition for partition which is uncompleted.

According to records in this office the only heirs to John McKuk are as shown in the petition for partition. It appears that Ross Witonosee is an heir of John McKuk according to Departmental Finding submitted by you. Therefore, if the petition is at variance with your records it is to be hoped that it may be corrected by you.

If it is your purpose to report this to the Department please mail this office complete set of carbon copies of all papers for the files in the John McKuk estate.

Very cordially yours,

8 od 12.
Incl. Pet. Part. comp.

J. L. Suffecool,
Supt. & Spl. Disb. Agt.

Sac & Fox – Shawnee Estates
1920-1924 Volume VIII

Ke-wah-ko-uck
and
Pam-ah-to-quah
Kickapoo allotments Nos. 1 & 2.

Shawnee Indian Agency,
Shawnee, Oklahoma,
August 14th, 1922.

Supt. A. R. Snyder,
Potawatomi Indian Agency,
Mayetta, Kansas.

Dear Mr. Snyder:

There are returned herewith two sets of petition for partition, one of which was found to be incorrect as to description set aside for the Kansas heirs. The other one was presented to the Oklahoma heirs and to the heir in Mexico. All of the heirs belonging under this Agency have signed the petition and the issuance of a patent in fee need not be considered.

Very truly yours,

8 od 14.
Incl. pet. part.

J. L. Suffecool,
Supt. & Spl. Disb. Agent.

Shawnee Indian Agency,
Shawnee, Oklahoma,
August 25, 1922.

Mr Harry Wilson,
Route # 3,
Shawnee, Oklahoma.

Dear Sir;

Enclosed herewith official check No 12211, payable to your order for $14.67.

This check represents funds from the Nancy Billy estate.

Very truly yours,

J. L. Suffecool
Superintendent

MPG-encls

Sac & Fox – Shawnee Estates
1920-1924 Volume VIII

Shawnee Indian Agency,
Shawnee, Oklahoma,
Sept. 10, 1922.

The Commissioner
of Indian Affairs,
Washington, D. C.

Dear Mr. Commissioner:-

There is inclosed herewith in duplicate affidavit of William Pattequa and Dolly Pattequa, his wife, both allotted members of the Sac & Fox Tribe of Indians with reference to the heirs of Lula Duncan, deceased Sac & Fox Indian, in which they make affidavit, that, Lula Duncan died March 27, 1922; and that at the time of her death was survived by her father and mother, Richard Duncan and Allie Duncan—also two brothers, Marcellus Duncan and Richard Duncan; that, at the time of her death she was unmarried and without issue.

Lula Duncan has to her credit at this office the sum of $265.86 which it is respectfully requested that I be given the necessary authority to disburse the above amount in equal shares to the father and mother, if the same is consistent with the regulations.

Very truly yours,

J. L. Suffecool,
Superintendent.

JLS:EV.
encl.

****

State of Oklahoma
                        SS
County of Pottawatomie

William Pattequa and Dollie Pattequa, his wife, first being duly sworn depose and say as follows: concerning the heirs of Lula Duncan, deceased Sac & Fox Indian:

That, we are allotted members of the Sac & Fox Tribe of Indians, each of us being past sixty years of age, that, we were personally acquainted with Lula Duncan, deceased; that, we knew her from the time of her birth until her death, March 27, 1922; that, at the time of her death that she was unmarried and without issue; and that she left

Sac & Fox – Shawnee Estates
1920-1924 Volume VIII

surviving her Richard Duncan, her father, and Allie Duncan, her mother, and Marcellus Duncan, age 18, and Richard Duncan, age 14, brothers.

                                              His
                         William Pattequa
                         William Pattequa   mark

Witness to mark
John E. Snake [signature]   Her
John E. Snake   Dollie Pattequa
Elizabeth D Vogel [signature]   Dollie Pattequa   mark
Elizabeth D. Vogel

Subscribed and sworn to before me this 10th day of Sept; 1923.

                                    JLSuffecool [signature]
                                    J. L. Suffecool
                                    Supt. of the Shawnee
                                    Indian Agency.

                              Shawnee Indian Agency,

                              Shawnee, Oklahoma, Sept. 11, 1922.

Mr. Thomas Lybarger,
    Sub-Station No. 2,
        Kansas City, Mo.

Dear Sir:

    This will refer to your letter of the 4th instant, concerning the allotments of Caroline Frayer and Helen Cook, deceased, I have to advise you as follows:

    Caroline Fryer, dec. Cit. Pottawatomie allottee No. 303, was allotted the W/2 of SE1/4 & E/2 of SW1/4 of sec. 31, township 9 north, range 3 east containing 160 acres. The heirs in the above estate and their shares are as follows:

Thomas Lubarger[sic], Husb.		1/3
John Bogle	son	1/6
Geo. Lybarger	son	1/6
Charles Lybarger	son	1/6
Thomas R. Lybarger,	son	1/6

Sac & Fox – Shawnee Estates
1920-1924 Volume VIII

A patent in fee was issued to the heirs Oct. 20, 1920, and this land is not under the jurisdiction of this Office any longer, and any rentals due on this land, it will be collected by the hers.

Helen Cook, dec. Cit. Pottawatomie allottee No. 303, Lots 3 & 4 of section 31, township 9 north, range 1 east and the heirs to the above estate and their share are as follows:

Thomas Lybarger	2/12
John Bogle	1/2
Thomas R. Lybarger	1/12
George Lybarger	1/12
Charles Lybarger	1/12
Sarah Frayer	3/12
Earl Frayer	3/12

The oil and gas lease on this land expires July 3, 1922 and there is no money of any sourse[sic] to the credit to[sic] the heirs at this time.

Very respectfully,

TBA   J.L. Suffecool, Supt.

Shawnee Indian Agency,
Shawnee, Oklahoma,
September 12, 1022.

Mrs. Fred Harrison,
318 Illinois Ave.,
St. Joseph, Mo.

Dear Madam:-

This office is in receipt of carbon copy of letter written to you by the Indian Office, in which was enclosed your letter to the Indian Office under date of August 23, 1922, in which you make inquiry about the present location or whereabouts of one, Mr. H. C. Jones, a Sac & Fox Indian under this jurisdiction, and add that you are making this inquiry in behalf of his son, Edwin F. Jones.

Sac & Fox – Shawnee Estates
1920-1924 Volume VIII

In reply to same, you are advised that Mr. H. C. Jones died in the year 1912. Helen Jones, his daughter, was declared his sole heir by Departmental Finding.

In referring to the file in the case, it is noted that you wrote this office on July 15, 1920 and made inquiry about Edwin Fenton Penny, referred to in your recent letter to the Office as Edwin F. Jones, and you were informed by this office under date of August 24, 1920 that we had no evidence or knowledge of the adoption of Edwin Fenton Penny by Mr. H. C. Jones; this is to advise that at the present time we have no further information concerning the matter in question.

Very respectfully,

J. L. Suffecool
Superintendent.

EV.
CC to Indian Office.

Shawnee Indian Agency,
Shawnee, Oklahoma,
Sept. 12, 1922.

Supt. A. R. Snyder,
Potawatomi Ind. Agency,
Mayetta, Kansas.

Dear Mr. Snyder:

There are inclosed herewith the papers in the partition matter of the allotments of Pam-ah-to-quah and Ke-wah-ko-uck numbered 1 and 2, Kickapoo Reservation, Kansas.

It will be noted that the signature of Pe-ah-puck-o-he's signature does not appear for the reason that he is dead and that his heirs have not been determined.

The Oklahoma heirs request the sale of the part set aside for them after the approval of the petition for partition. The petition for sale by them is inclosed uncompleted as to the Superintendent's report.

This is a difficult proposition and if there is any thing further t hat[sic] we can help you with in connection [sic] this partition please call upon us.

Sac & Fox – Shawnee Estates
1920-1924 Volume VIII

Very truly yours,

9 od 12.
Incl. Part. Papers.

J. L. Suffecool,
Superintendent.

Mayetta Kansas
April 19, 1912

Supt. Shawnee Indian Training
    School,   Shawnee Okla.
Dear Sir:-

    In regard to the estate or the land, of Mrs. Caroline Frayer, I, the son, of her, acting as by the law, concerning the estate, I should also deem it my part to have a voice, in the said estate. I understand that the said estate is divided among the children of the said Caroline Frayer and also that her husband Mr. Thomas Larbarger[sic] also has a share in it. And, I, John Bogle the first son, and the oldest request you to sell the estate at a public sale, to the highest bidder, and I also request you to act as a guardian for the sons of the said Caroline Frayer until of age. And I John Bogle ask my share of the estate forwarded to me immediately when settled and I also ask you in concerning the other estate of Helen Cook.

    If I should also share in the Helen Cook estate, and I John Bogle am her Grandson.

    If it should cause any misunderstanding in regard to me sharing in the estate of my mother, Caroline Frayer, and Grandmother Helen Cook, I shall look into the case for I have many witnesses to testify my relationship as the son and the first and oldest son by first marriage. Would like to hear from you soon as possible in regard to the said estates and also your intentions and the settlements of the said estates for as any settlements have been made. Answer at once.
    Very Resp'

John Bogle
Mayetta
Kansas.

****

Sac & Fox – Shawnee Estates
1920-1924 Volume VIII

DEPARTMENT OF THE INTERIOR

UNITED STATES INDIAN SERVICE
SHAWNEE INDIAN AGENCY,

Shawnee, Oklahoma.
April 23, 1912.

Mr. John Boyle[sic],
Mayetta, KANSAS.

Dear Sir:

I have your letter of April 19, 1912, relative the heirs of Caroline Frayer, deceased. You state that she is your mother. In order that this office may know who the heirs are we will set a day for holding a hearing to determine the lawful heirs of Caroline Frayer. We will, in the course of a week or so, notify you of the date set and you will then please present any and all evidence showing how you claim to be an heir as well as setting forth the other heirs.

Very respectfully,
J.A. Buntin
RS Superintendent.

REFER IN REPLY TO THE FOLLOWING:
land-sales
58964-22
N R

DEPARTMENT OF THE INTERIOR,
OFFICE OF INDIAN AFFAIRS,
WASHINGTON,

ADDRESS ONLY THE
COMMISSIONER OF INDIAN AFFAIRS

SEP 12 1922

Mr. J. L. Suffecool,
 Supt., Shawnee School

My dear Mr. Suffecool:

Enclosed are eight approved deeds to the heirs of Josephine Bourassa, in partition of the allotment of the deceased.

As the deeds contain restrictions against alienation, you will please have them recorded before delivery. They have been recorded

Sac & Fox – Shawnee Estates
1920-1924   Volume VIII

in this Office in Deed Book inherited Indian Lands, volume 43, page 161 to 168, inclusive.

                        Very truly yours,

                        CF Hauke

9 MHF 9   Chief Clerk.

    Five deed belonging to the Fehligs – Recorded in Tecumseh by Dushane on Oct. 19-22.

                Shawnee Indian Agency,
                Shawnee, Oklahoma,
                Sept. 15, 1922.

Mr. George Spybuck,
Sperry, Oklahoma.

Dear Sir:

    This has reference to the estate of your deceased wife Ken-qua, or Kin-qua.

    Billy Hood and Billy Panther have been in this office and stated that they are or should be the heirs with you of your deceased wife named above. I do not know the facts in this matter but a promise was made to them that inquiry of you would be made as to who the heirs are if they have been determined.
    Therefore, I will appreciate the courtesy if you will inform me of the status of the estate of Ken-qua or Kin-qua, your former wife.

                Very truly yours,

9 od 15.   J. L. Suffecool,
                    Supt. & Spl. Disb. Agt.

                Montour, Iowa, Sept 16th 1922

Supt Sac & Fox Agency
Shawnee Oklahoma
Dear Sir
    I have a letter from the Assistant Commissioner of Indian Affairs at Washington D.C. dated July 31st 1922, advising me that the books at your Agency that there is a balance of 139.07 to te credit of my wifes[sic] estate. This amount will be

Sac & Fox – Shawnee Estates
1920-1924 Volume VIII

transferred to the superintendent of the Sac & Fox Sanatorium for proper distribution among the heisr[sic]

It has been six weeks since that letter was written and the agent here tells me that he has not received it yet.

I wish you would explain to me why I do not receive my share of this money. If the money has been sent will you please give the date it was sent how sent and to whom.

I am getting anxious about this money, for I need it very much I will send postage if it is necessary to get a reply

RECEIVED SEP 18 1922 SHAWNEE INDIAN AGENCY

Yours truly
Ed Brown

Shawnee Indian Agency,
Shawnee, Oklahoma,
Sept. 18, 1922.

Mr. Clarence Fox,
Wyandotte, Oklahoma.

Dear Mr. Fox:

Inclosed herewith are two copies of petition for the sale of your deceased mother's land. Mr. Timmie Harjoe was in the office recently and requested that a sale be made. If this is also your desire you will please sign and acknowledge the petition and return to this office for transmittal to the Department.

Very truly yours,

9 oe[sic] 18.
Incl. pet. sale.

J. L. Suffecool, Supt.

Shawnee Indian Agency,
Shawnee, Oklahoma,
Sept. 19, 1922.

The Owl Hardware Co.,
Bonner Springs, Kansas.

Gentlemen:

Sac & Fox – Shawnee Estates
1920-1924 Volume VIII

This is in reply to your letter of 31st ult. relative to the estate of Pete Sognah, deceased, asking if this party had any money or inherited interests under this Agency.

You are informed that an examination of the records in this office fails to disclose any money to the credit or nor any interest in any estate under this Agency.

Very truly yours,

9 od 19.

J. L. Suffecool,
Superintendent.

Shawnee Indian Agency,
Shawnee, Okla.
Sept. 20, 1922.

The Commissioner of Indian Affairs,
Washington, D.C.

Sir:-

Transmitted herewith is report of hearing fees collected at this agency during the fourth quarter 1922.

Also herewith is my report of the number outstanding hearing fees, which up to date have been uncollected for one reason or another. The accounts of the estates as well as the heirs to the same are being checked over to ascertain if there are any funds to their credit or determine whether the estates or heirs ever will have any funds passing through this office. When such investigation has been completed the Office will be notified as to the status of each outstanding fee.

Incls.
JLR.

Very respectfully,

J. L. Suffecool,
Superintendent.

Sac & Fox – Shawnee Estates
1920-1924 Volume VIII

Shawnee Indian Agency,
Shawnee, Oklahoma,
September 22, 1922.

Mr. A. R. Snyder,
  Superintendent,
    Pottawatomie Indian Agency,
      Mayetta, Kansas.

My dear Mr. Snyder:-

      Mrs. Louise Melott of Tecumseh, Oklahoma, Box 224, was in my office this morning and asked us to inquire of you concerning the estate of Black Wolf, in which she is one of the heirs. She wishes to know the number of acres in the estate; the amount of rental received each year; and a copy of Probate Findings.

      She also wishes to know the status of the estate of Julia A Nadeau, or she seems to think that the Indian name was probably Kitch-qua-me-quah. It was reported to her that they were unable to locate any of the heirs. She advises that she knows the location of several of them. Please give her the status of this case also.

      A letter in reply to this should be addressed to Mrs. Melott, address given above, and I would thank you for a carbon copy of such a letter to be sent to this office.

Very respectfully,

J. L. Suffecool
Superintendent

JLS:EV.
C. C. to Mrs. Louise Melott,
  Tecumseh, Oklahoma.
    Box 224.

Law-Heirship
Ken-qua, or
Kin-qua,
Cher. Shawnee

Shawnee Indian Agency,
Shawnee, Oklahoma,
Sept. 22, 1922.

Supt Victor M. Locke, Jr.,
Union Indian Agency,
Muskogee, Oklahoma.

Sac & Fox – Shawnee Estates
1920-1924 Volume VIII

Dear Mr. Locke:

This has reference to a certain estate consisting of some land near Sperry, north of Tulsa, Oklahoma, belonging to a Cherokee Shawnee woman, being the deceased wife of George Spybuck.

Two Indians of this Agency came into this office and requested that inquiry be made of the status of this estate. The statement was made by them that George Spybuck was the husband of the deceased during her last years. Therefore a letter was addressed to him and his reply is herewith inclosed.

Any information regarding this matter will be very greatly appreciated so that we will be able to inform the parties making the inquiry.

Very respectfully,

9 od 23.
Incl. letter

J. L. Suffecool,
Supt. & Spl. Disb. Agt.

Shawnee Indian Agency,
Shawnee, Oklahoma,
Sept. 23, 1922.

Supt. George A. Hoyo,
Ponca Indian Agency,
Whiteagle, Oklahoma.

Dear Mr; Hoyo:

This has reference to a tract of land allotted to Eliza White, deceased Iowa Indian, acquired by trust [illegible] by Sam Ellis who resides within your jurisdiction. Recently we received a letter from Ellis stating that he wanted to sell. Therefore, there is inclosed petition for sale partially filled for his use. Sam Ellis lives at Red Rock, Oklahoma.

It is desired that you fill out such portions of the Supt's. Report referring to the applicant, specially[sic] question 9.

Very respectfully,

9 od 22.
Incl. petition.

J. L. Suffecool, Supt.

Sac & Fox – Shawnee Estates
1920-1924 Volume VIII

Shawnee Indian Agency,
Shawnee, Oklahoma,
September 26, 1922.

Mrs. Gertie Pratt,
   Maud, Oklahoma.

Dear Madam:-

This is to advise you that I have been invited to meet the heirs of your deceased father, S. Pratt, at my office at 10 A. M., October 7, 1922. There are several matters of importance that we wish to look through pertaining to the disposition of his personal property, and it is requested that you be present at the date set.

Very respectfully,

J. L. Suffecool
Superintendent.

JLS:EV.

****

Shawnee Indian Agency,
Shawnee, Oklahoma,
September 26, 1922.

Miss May Pratt,
   Lexington, Oklahoma.

Dear Miss Pratt:-

This is to advise you that I have been invited to meet the heirs of your deceased father, S. Pratt, at my office at 10 A. M., October 7, 1922. There are several matters of importance that we wish to look through pertaining to the disposition of his personal property, and it is requested that you be present at the date set.

Sac & Fox – Shawnee Estates
1920-1924 Volume VIII

Very respectfully,

J. L. Suffecool
Superintendent.

JLS:EV.

****

Shawnee Indian Agency,
Shawnee, Oklahoma,
September 26, 1922.

Mr. Arthur Pratt,
Maud, Oklahoma.

My dear Sir:-

This is to advise you that I have been invited to meet the heirs of your deceased father, S. Pratt, at my office at 10 A. M., October 7, 1922. There are several matters of importance that we wish to look through pertaining to the disposition of his personal property, and it is requested that you be present at the date set.

Very respectfully,

J. L. Suffecool
Superintendent.

JLS:EV.

****

Shawnee Indian Agency,
Shawnee, Oklahoma,
September 26, 1922.

Mr. Earnest Pratt,
Maud, Oklahoma.

My dear Sir:-

This is to advise you that I have been invited to meet the heirs of your deceased father, S. Pratt, at my office at 10 A. M., October 7, 1922. There are several matters of importance that we wish to look through pertaining to the disposition of his personal property, and it is requested that you be present at the date set.

Sac & Fox – Shawnee Estates
1920-1924 Volume VIII

Very respectfully,

J. L. Suffecool
Superintendent.

JLS:EV.

****

Shawnee Indian Agency,
Shawnee, Oklahoma,
September 26, 1922.

Mrs. Jesse Powell,
  Maud, Oklahoma.

My dear Madam:-

    This is to advise you that I have been invited to meet the heirs of your deceased father, S. Pratt, at my office at 10 A. M., October 7, 1922. There are several matters of importance that we wish to look through pertaining to the disposition of his personal property, and it is requested that you be present at the date set.

Very respectfully,

J. L. Suffecool
Superintendent.

JLS:EV.

****

Shawnee Indian Agency,
Shawnee, Oklahoma,
September 26, 1922.

Mrs. Mandy Pratt,
  Maud, Oklahoma.

Dear Madam:-

    This is to advise you that I have been invited to meet the heirs of your deceased father, S. Pratt, at my office at 10 A. M., October 7, 1922. There are several matters of importance that we wish to look through pertaining to the disposition of his personal property, and it is requested that you be present at the date set.

Sac & Fox – Shawnee Estates
1920-1924 Volume VIII

Very respectfully,

J. L. Suffecool
Superintendent.

JLS:EV.

****

Shawnee Indian Agency,
Shawnee, Oklahoma,
September 26, 1922.

Mr. Walter Pratt,
  Maud, Oklahoma.

Dear Sir:-

    This is to advise you that I have been invited to meet the heirs of your deceased father, S. Pratt, at my office at 10 A. M., October 7, 1922. There are several matters of importance that we wish to look through pertaining to the disposition of his personal property, and it is requested that you be present at the date set.

Very respectfully,

J. L. Suffecool
Superintendent.

JLS:EV.

****

Shawnee Indian Agency,
Shawnee, Oklahoma,
September 26, 1922.

Mr. Charles Pratt,
  2217 W. Cedar,
  Oklahoma City, Okla.

Dear Mr. Pratt:-

    This is to advise you that I have been invited to meet the heirs of your deceased father, S. Pratt, at my office at 10 A. M., October 7, 1922. There are several matters of importance that we wish to look through pertaining to the disposition of his personal property, and it is requested that you be present at the date set.

Sac & Fox – Shawnee Estates
1920-1924 Volume VIII

Very respectfully,

J. L. Suffecool
Superintendent.

JLS:EV.

Shawnee Indian Agency,
Shawnee, Oklahoma,
Sept. 26, 1922.

Louis Melott,
Lookeba, Oklahoma.

Dear Sir:

    This has reference to certain papers submitted to you for your signature whereby Mary Alice Wynns would acquire in her own name the tract of land she inherited from the estate of Joseph Melott through her mother.

    Records in this office show that you and the other melot[sic] heirs of Joseph Melott disposed of the remainder of the allotment and hence this share belongs to Mrs Wynns but the title still vests in the heirs. You have on former occasions signed papers granting that complete title be granted to said Mrs Wynns. Therefore as man of honor repudiatet[sic] repudiate such action ~~by~~ made in writing. Of course if such honor is of no value to yourself the action you may take in the settlement matters very little.

    This as you are aware confers title to said land upon Mrs. Wynns which all of you admit rightfully belongs to her and the consideration in the sale papers reads " in settlement of estate " and that no cash will pass between the grantors and the grantee.

    I will thank you to reconsider the action you have taken, sign and return the papers so that this matter shall be closed.

Very sincerely,

J. L. Suffecool,
Supt. & Spl. Disb. Agt.

Sac & Fox – Shawnee Estates
1920-1924 Volume VIII

Shawnee Indian Agency,
Shawnee, Oklahoma,
Sept. 26, 1922.

Mr. A. B. Collins,
United Stated Farmer,
Cushing, Oklahoma.

Dear Mr. Collins:

The partition of the allotment of Jennie Faw-faw, Iowa No. 47, has been requested, described as S/2 of NE/4, 28-17-3, William Faw-faw and Harrison Rubidoux each share one-half in the allotment. Please make such appraisement according to governmental subdivisions that the two heirs will receive one-half in value of the allotment.

Very sincerely,

9 od 26.

J. L. Suffecool,
Superintendent.

Index

[??]M-AH-THE-AH 210
[?]ESUSHA 7
[?]EWASAMOQUA 7
[?]OLD, Mr 85
[?]ONACHEQUA 7
[ILLEGIBLE] MEGO, Mary 272
ABRAHAM
    David 239
    David H 226
ACTON, Joseph Lewis 224
ADA 213
AH CHE MA QUE 25
AH K THE 259
AH KIS KUK 66
AH KO THE 259
AH NAH SHE MEAH 259
AH-CHA-CO-GEESH, Angeline ... 48
AH-CHE-MA-QUE 24,28,29
AH-CHE-PEA-SE 90
AH-KISH-KUCK 34
AH-KISH-KUK 34
AH-KIS-KUCK 33
AH-NAH-THO-THE 24
AH-NH-THO-THE 24
AHN-WAH-NA-KA 193
AH-SHE-NEK 48
AH-SHE-PAH-KAH-SHE-NO-QUAH
.... 193
AH-SKE-PAH-KAH 193
AH-SKE-PAH-SHE-NO-QUAH .. 193
AH-THE-PAH-KAH-THE-QUAH…
.... 193
AH-THE-PAH-THE QUAH 193
AH-YAH-TAH 192
ALBRIGHT, Andy 156
ALFORD
    David W 224
    Mr 169
    Thompson 52
    Webster 60,224,236
ALLEN, Joseph 249,251,252
ANDERSON
    Mrs 52
    Mrs Marie 52
APPLETREE, George 209,262,263
ATKINS, Ellen 114,115
AU-SAW-WAU-SE 279
AXEY, Ben 223

BARKER
    Andew 38
    Andrew 35,36,37,38,41,44,45
    Minnie 150
BASS
    Helen 262
    Inez 122
    Inos 22
    Ione C 122
    Lee 122
BASSETT, Margaret 160,173
BATISTE, John 48
BEAUBIEN
    Nora 28
    Zora 26
BEDELL 197,198
    Margaret 61,72,73,112,195,
    196,197
    Mr W R 74,194
    W R 61,72,73,196
BERTRAND
    Lawrence J 208
    Lizette 176
    Mary 208
BERTRAND-CLARK, Nora 208
BERTRAND-PATRICK, Laura ... 208
BIG EAR
    Teresa 2
    Theresa 4,233,234,235
    Thersa 233,235
BIG JIM 116
BIG SIMON 277
BIG WALKER, Lelia 70
BIGWALKER
    Delia 189
    Dollie 90
    Esther 90,132,189
    Jennie 71
    Lelia 90,132
BILLY, Nancy 283
BLACK
    Earnest 109
    Emanuel 109
    Henry 109
    James 109
    Phoebe 138
    Phoeve 109
    Theodore 109

Index

BLACK WOLF 89,293
BLACKHAWK, Hoke S 160,173
BLAIR, Frank T 257
BOB
    Charley 116
    Sally 116
BOGLE, John 86,285,286,288
BONNET, W A 66
BOURASSA
    Josephine 181,202,227,228,229,
    263,265,266,267,269,289
    Mrs Josephine 267,268
BOYLE, John 289
BRADBURN
    Joseph Q 195
    Joseph W 198
BRANDON
    F E 114,116
    Mr F E 113
BRANNON
    Ed 116
    Mr 117
BREGANGE, Mrs Louisa 126
BREGONZE, Mrs L C 92
BREID
    Dr 35,37,44
    Dr Jacob 6,36,38,39,43,44,139,
    140,141,145,147,182,187,191,273,
    279,282
    Dr Jacob B 280
    Jacob 7,8,39,44
BRIED, Dr Jacob 225
BRODIE, Mrs [?] G 85
BROOKS
    Mr R A 54
    R A 118
BROWN
    Arthur 35,36,38,39,43,45
    Ed 270,291
    Fryor Franklin 150,212
    John 177
    Josephine 63,177
    Samuel 22
    Samuel L 150
BRUNER
    Ethel Shawnee 105
    Mrs Ethel 107
BUCKMASTER, Jasper 199

BUFFALOHORN, Thomas 237
BULLFROG
    Billy 201
    Jesse 200
    Jim 200,201,233
    Thomas 200
BUNTIN
    J A 13,289
    John A 85
    Mr J A 3,11,12
BURFORD, MILEY HOFFMAN &
    BURFORD 154
BURKE, Chas H 51
BUTLER, John 248
CADUE, John 45,47
CARSON
    George 2
    Joe 2
    Mr E T 117
CARTER
    Jos 152
    Madeline Houston 151,152
    Mrs 169
    Sadie 176
CATICK
    Blanche 127
    Louisa 127
    Rachel 127
CHAPMAN
    Mr W L 130
    W L 108,128,165
CHARLEY, Mark 109
CHISHOLM, Minnie 142
CHUCK, Thomas 35,36,38,39,43,
45,139,140,141,188
COBB, Fred 208,209
COCHRAN
    Mr 240
    Supt R A 240
COLEMAN, May 228,264
COLLINS 43
    Arza B 40,41,42,122,191,254
    Mr 36,39,66
    Mr A B 17,18,22,35,37,67,150,
    183,187,203,222,300
    Mr A G 205
    Mr Mattie 4
COLVIN, Eliza 202,227,228,263

Index

CONGER, Andre 122
CONNER & HAGAN 88
CONNOR & HAGAN 91,108
COOK, Helen. 71,86,270,285,286,288
COON
  Ben 195,196,197
  Benj F 197
  Benjamin 61,196,197
  Benjamin F 49,57,72,73,74,
  113,195,198
  Leonard 49,57,61,112,197,198
COOPER
  Joseph 48,153
  Mr 47,48
COPELAND
  Agnes 172
  Edward 172
  Eveline 172
  Florence 172
CORLISS
  A G 159
  Mr 160
  Mr A G 159
  Mr A O 173
  Mr O A 159
CRANE
  Edward L 92
  Lizzie 92,215
  Mr A E 146,258
  Viola May 22
CROCH, Fred 63
CRUSE, Lucy E 208
CUMMINGS
  Andrew J 155
  Helen 155,156,157,189
  Samuel 155,157,189
CUPPAWHE, Lee 151,152
CURLEY
  Columbia 221
  Lucy 221
DANIELS
  J W 162
  Mr 163
  Mr J F 162
DAVENPORT, William 7,147,282
DAVIS
  Dilcy 224
  Frank B 189
  Guss 3
  Harry 189
  James D 170
  Miss Julia 224
DAVY, Wantay 246
DEASON & MOODY 83
DEAVER
  Ira C 1,4,5,6,9,15,17,18,19,22,
  23,24,26,28,29,30,33,35,36,37,38,
  39,43,45,47,71,92,169
  Mr Ira C 52
  Supt I C 7
  Supt Ira C 7,20,32,34,39,44
DECKER, Mr H O 2
DEICHMAN, Peter 60
DEISTER, Mr 59
DELG, Mary 45,46
DENTON
  Madeline 143
  Zoa 227,228,264,267
DERADCLIFF, Mrs Julia 96
DEVAER, Ira C 3
DIBLER, Mrs Anna 199
DIMBLER
  Elizabeth 65
  Josephine 65
DODSON, Thomas S 185
DOO-TOO 233
DORIAN, Katherine 121
DOUD
  Nora 28
  Zora 26
DOWD, Bertha L 169
DOYLE
  Mr 202
  Mr S A 122,167,201
DUNCAN
  Allie 284,285
  Lula 284
  Marcellus 284,285
  Richard 284,285
DUPUIS, Osie 121
DUSHANE 290
  Charles 67,193,244,257,263,
  274,282
  Mr 265,269
EAGLETON, Mr W L 214
EASDY, Mrs Maria 4

Index

EC-AH-TAH-BE-AH 29
EDMISTER 252
   Charles W 161
   Chas F 52
   Chas W..............25,65,73,196,207, 220,237
   Mr 64,74,198,245
EDMONDS...................................219
ELLIS
   Sam 294
   Sarah 92,215
ELY, Maggie.................................160
EMBLER
   Sophia 226
   Sophie 16
ENGLISH
   Frances O 250,252,253
   Francis O.................................253
   Kate Roubedeaux 27,28
   Katie Roubidoux 254
   Minnie May..........................26,27
   Reuben 27
ENNIS
   C F 128
   C H..165
   Mr 51,166
   Mr C H..............................129,260
E-SA-WI-SI 279,280,281
FALK, John C................159,160,173
FARLEY, Mr J H........................271
FAW FAW, William....................226
FAW-FAW
   Jennie 300
   William 300
FEAR, Chas W............................279
FEHLIG 290
   J B..268
   John B 263,268
   John D 265,267
   Mr 202
   Nancy 202
   Nancy Smith 227,228
FOREMAN, Lillie 236
FORMAN, Lilly......................59,224
FOSTER
   Roy... 66
   Wm G.........................65,112,150
FOX, Clarence 291

FRANKLIN, Osmond 58
FRAYER
   Caroline 71,86,270,285,289
   Earl...286
   Mrs Caroline............................288
   Sarah..286
FRENCH
   Joe 85
   John A 85
   Nancy 246,247
FRYER, Caroline 214
FUNK, A L..........................215,280
GARBER, Mr J A......................... 115
GEORGE
   John 246
   Philip 248
GIBBS
   Gilbert......................................273
   Hiram.......................................273
   Ina..273
GIBSON
   Alex.. 60
   Annie.. 90
   James 247
   Jim 247
   Mary... 60
   Mrs Mary................................. 211
   Willie......................... 60,142,211
GIVENS
   Gertrude............................ 139,141
   Matilda 66
GOKEY
   Augustine 70
   Dollie............................70,90,189
   Dolly..132
   Frank 70
   Lily 135
GOODE, Mark 117
GOYER
   Lula 136
   Rosalie................ 136,158,174,199
   Rufus 210
GRANT
   Mary 16,215
   Mary O 145
GRASS, Silas 112
GRAYSON, Watt 194
GREEN

Index

Mr 14
Mr O J 10,157
Philola 257
GRIFFENSTEIN
    Catherine 51,56,58,261
    Chas J 56
    Emma 56,58
    Mr 51
    Mr C J 261
    Mrs Emma 51,261
GRIFFENSTINE
    Catherine 241
    Charles J 241
    Mrs Catherine 242
    Mrs Emma 242
    William T 241
GRIFFINSTEIN
    Catherine 56,74,75,76,77,78,
    79,128,129,164,165,166,207,260
    Charles J 165,166
    Chas J 76,83
    Emma 83,128,129,164,165,
    166,260
    Mr C J 207
    Mrs 165
    Mrs Emma... 74,75,76,77,78,79,80,
    81,82,83,84,166
    Mrs Enna 207
    William T 75,82
GRIFFINSTIEN, Mrs Catherine ...166
GRIFFINSTINE, Mrs Emma 241
GUTHRIE, Mollie 64
HAGAN, Horace H 88
HAHK-SA
    Elizabeth 260
    Myra 260,272
HAHKSA
    Elizabeth 218
    Myra 218,237,238
HAH-WAH-CHE-SE-MO 142
HALE, Bessie 175
HALL, Harry 129
HALLAM
    Mr 203,210,218,222,238
    Mr P L 204,205,206,217,222,
    233,235,237,243,245,258
    Mr R S 255
    P L 205,218,234,245

    Paul L 203,221,222,223,247,
    249,251,252,260
HALLUM
    Beanktrice.................................. 4
    Mr Q V 4
    Wodard 4
HAMPTON, L J 151
HANAN, Boe 195
HANEY, Zoa H 163,164
HANON
    B 197
    Bee 197
    Mr 196
HARDIN
    Davis 164
    Lizzie 163,164
    Thomas 164
HARJOE, Timmie 291
HARRAGARRA, Mary 2
HARRIS 67
    Sarah Turner 67
HARRISON 231
    Mrs Fred 286
    Stephen 230,232
HARROLD, Hon J W 54
HARRY, Harry 85
HART
    J C 28
    Supt J C 26
HARVEY, Mrs Malinda 87
HAUKE, C F 16,267,289
HAWKE, C F 231
HENRY, Mr J W 88
HIGGINS & BARTON 158,160,
161,173
HO NO KO KAT 63
HOFFMAN
    General 212
    Mr P S 212
HOG GRA AH CHEY 255
HO-GRA-AH-CHEY 254
HOMORATHA, Lizzie R 254
HOOD
    Billy 290
    Rachel Tyner 15
HOUSTON, Samuel 151,152
HOW, Ellen 48
HOYO

Index

Geo A 124,167,168
George A 1,2,138,145,159,249,
252,253,256,294
Mr 17,109,173
Superintendent 173
Supt 135,159,168
HUDSON, Mrs Dora E 26,27
HUGHES, Dr J E 212
HUNTER
    Henry 191
    Robert 191
I-AH-TAH 249,251,252,258
I-CHA-NE 233,234,235
I-OSH-SUCK 31,32
JACKSON
    Oliver 22,111,149,182
    Taylor 4
    William S 237
JACQUES, M 272
JAGER, Dr Thor 56
JEFFERSON, Esther B 70
JEPSEN, George 170
JESSEPE
    Mrs Susie 171
    Susie 172
JOCELYN, Mrs Dorothy 56
JOHN 277
    J H 193
JOHNSON
    Edith 144
    Emily 18,131,132,133,152,
153,154,189,225
    George 144
    Harry 187,191
    Horace J 48,90
    Jane 213
    Miss Edith 143
    Mr 47,48
    Mrs 48
    Mrs Emily 132
    Mrs Horace J 131,133
    Mrs Jane 212,213
    Mrs Mary 90,153
    Orlando 187
    Oscar 144
    Pearl 262
    Scott 90
    Silas 144

JOHNSTON & ROBINSON 225
JONES
    Edwin F 286,287
    Helen 287
    John 137,138,139,140,141,
142,143,244
    Mr 88,91
    Mr H C 286,287
KAH-AH-SEN-WE, Henry 212
KAH-AH-TAH-BE-AH 179
KAHDOT
    Frank 275
    James 275
    Miss Anna 63,220
KAH-E-SHAH 193
KAH-TUCK-O-KAH 277
KA-KE-KE-ME-QUA 262
KASECA 240
    George 53
    Joe 52
KASSON 119
KA-TAH-MAH 231
KE DOTT, Anna 220
KE SHA SAH 36,43,45
KE TUM WA 161
KE TUM WAH 151
KE WA SO NO QUA 36,45
KE-AH-NA 248
KE-AH-TAH-BE-AH .. 29,30,144,178
KE-DOTT, Nancy May 220
KEESIS, Frank 32
KEESIS-FRANK 31
KE-KI-PA-NO 281
KEN-QUA 290,293
KENT, Inspector 155
KENYON, Daniel D 198
KEOKUK, Phoebe 215,280
KE-SAH-ASHA 7
KE-SE-NAH 48
KE-SHA-SAH 35,36,38,39
KE-TAH-NAH 193
KE-TUM-WA 147
KETUMWA 68
KE-TUM-WAH 57
KE-WAH-KO-UCK 283,287
KE-WAH-YAH-KA-QUAH......
.... 192,193
KE-WAS-MO 204

Index

KE-WA-SO-NO-QUA 35,36, 38,39,43
KIAH-KAH-HAH-KAH-KAH 193
KICKAPOO, Roy 34
KIHEGA, Jefferson 138
KI-HEG-A-ING-A 4
KING
    Etta 185,186
    John 185
KIN-QUA 290,293
KISH-KAH-NAH-KAH-KAH
    192,249,251,252
KISN-TAH-CHE-UM 16
KITCH-KUM-ME-QUA 124
KITCH-QUA-ME-QUAH 293
KO[???], Mr H W 275
KO-CHE-SHIN-QUAH 193
KO-CHE-SHIN-WAH 193
KOH-ZE-QUA 48
KO-NO-CHE-PEA-NE 90
KON-ZE-WIN 153
KO-TA-NAH 192
KO-WAS-ME 204
LA CLAIR
    John Moses 13
    Oliver 13
LACLAIR
    John Moses 11
    Mr P O 14
    Oliver 10,13
    P O 11,12,14
LADUE, Amarbe 1
LANSDOWNE, J H 176
LARBARGER, Thomas 288
LECLAIR
    Monroe 9
    Oliver 9
    P O 8
LEE
    Jessie 231
    Philip 47,230,231,232
LETTERMAN, Mr G 213
LEWIS
    J Harmon 144
    May 228,264
    May Coleman 227
    Mrs 202
    Mrs Charles 183

Mrs Chas 52
Mrs May 167,181
Mrs May Smith 180
LIGHTFOOT
    Martha 203,238
    Mrs 48
    Peter W 47,48
LINCOLN
    Alice 139,140,141,188
    Mr Thomas 254
    Sophia 5
    Sophia Embler 226
    Sophie 16
    Thomas 5,226
    Thomas C 5
    Tom 226
LITTLE CAPTAIN 201
LITTLE DOCTOR 28
    Martha 28
LITTLE FISH 110,111,126,219
LITTLE JIM 116
LOCKE
    Mr 294
    Supt Victor M, Jr 293
LONGHAT, Nancy 126
LOWE, Mrs Eveh S 93
LOYD, Mr S W R 3
LUBARGER, Thomas 285
LUTHIE, Walter L 148
LUTHYE
    Fred 50,68
    Walter 68
    Walter L 50
LYBARGER
    Charles 285,286
    Geo 285
    George 286
    Thomas 71,86,214,285,286
    Thomas R 285,286
    Thomas, Sr 270
M AT MA PA KA WE 171
M, ... 282
MA KA SE AH 162
MACKINNON, Mrs D 85
MAGAY OIL CORP 280
MAH CHA WA 46
MAH MAH QUA CHE 174
MAH MAH QUA CHO 146

Index

MAH THE WAS... 45
MAH-CHA-WAS... 47
MAH-CHE-NE-NA, John... 226, 227,240
MAH-NIM-MIK-SKUK... 223
MAH-SEE-WAS... 45,47
MAH-TASH-KUK... 193
MAH-THE-WAS... 47
MA-KA-THE-QUAK... 33
MAMECHE... 7
MA-NAH-THE-QUAH-AH... 29
MANATOWA, George... 169
MANSUR, Rhoda... 122
MARGRAVE, W C... 221
MARHARDY
  Billie... 84
  Jack... 247
  Oscar... 84
MARTIN
  Michael... 110,111
  Mr J H... 183
MASHNO... 57,67
MASON
  Helen... 56
  Lena... 56
MATCHIE, Patrick... 124
MA-THA-AH-QUA-TWA... 193
MATTHEWS
  Ann... 18
  Annie... 18
  Edward... 18
  Mrs... 18
MCCALL, Mr S K... 214
MCCLELLAN, Edward... 122
MCCOONSE
  Francis... 68
  James... 68
  Joseph... 68
  Peter... 68
MCGLASLIN
  Charles... 2,135
  Elizabeth... 135
  John... 2
  Mary Vetter... 135
  Robert... 2
  Robert, Jr... 135
  Walter... 2
MCINTOSH, Mr W C... 169

MCKEE
  Bessie... 133
  Eddie... 134
  Edward... 133
  Gertrude... 133
  John B... 133,134
  John T... 133
  Ruby... 133
MCKEOWN, James F... 151
MCKINNEY, John... 61
MCKUCK, John... 6,7
MCKUK, John... 7,35,36,38,39, 43,45,147,273,282
MCLANE, William... 92,126,127
ME-AH-ME-NO SKUK... 193
ME-AH-ME-NO-SKUK... 192,193
MEAH-M-ME-NOOSE-KUK... 258
ME-AHM-ME-NOOS-KUK... 252
ME-AHM-NE-NOOS-KUK.. 249,251
MECK KE THE QUAH... 34
MEGAH, Josetta... 260
MEGO
  Josetta... 260
  Mary... 272
MELOT, Mrs Louise... 89
MELOTT
  Joseph... 299
  Louis... 299
  Mrs Louise... 293
  William W... 172
ME-NAH-QUAH... 33,34
MERITT, E B... 24,26,282
ME-SHE-KA-TA-NO-QUAH... 193
ME-THAH-QUAH... 192,193
MH ME AH... 68
MI-AH-KE-PE-AH... 193
MI-E-NAH-QUA... 33
MI-E-NAH-QUAH... 34
MILES, Thomas C... 62
MILLER
  Earle T... 183
  Geo C... 234
  George C... 233,235
MINE, John... 174
MO NA CHE QUA... 36,45
MO NA-CHE-QUA... 35,38
MODOC, John... 21
MOHEE

Index

Charley 59
Christian 59
MO-NA-CHE-QUA 36,43
MO-NO-CHE-QUA 39
MOORE
   Sam 258
   Samuel 258
   Samuel L 254
MORRIS
   Edward L 92
   Mrs Lena 4
   Mrs Lena Kihegainga 5
MOSES, John 203,238,254
MOTLEY, John C 171
MOXLEY, Mrs Sarah 276
MULLEN
   Marth 202
   Martha 202,263,265,266,269
   Mrtha 267
MULLIN
   J W 228
   Martha 228
MULLINS, Martha 227
MURDOCK
   Jesse 175
   Joseph 33,34
MURRAY
   Alice 125,139,181,256
   Charles 125,139,256
   Charles C 125,181,182
   Franklin 181,182
   Kate 181,182
   Kerwin 125,256
   Kirwin ... 125,181,182,250,253,254
   Kirwin, Jr 182
   May 250,253
   Pearl 181,182
   Velinda 181,182
   Vestina 181,182
NA TAW WE 225
NA-[?]A-KE-KO 279
NA-AH-GA-BE 223
NADEAU, Julia A 293
NAH-AS-NOSE 231
NAH-KAH-E-QUAH 193
NAH-NIM-MIK-SKUK 20,21
NAH-WAH-CHE-SE-MO 211
NAN-I-TOKE 174,175

NAOHK-SA
   Eliza 272
   Elizabeth 272
NASTOWE, Emily 225
NA-THA-AH-QUA-TWA 193
NAW-AS-NOSE 230
NE BOW-O-SAH 204
NEAL
   John A 148
   Lily 135
NE-BOW-A-SAH 204,206
NIOCE, David 217,243,244,245
NIX, John 146
NO-DE-NO QUA 48
NO-DE-NO-QUA 153
NON NE KO KAT 220
NON-E-PEACH-E 277
NON-NE-KE-KAT 274
NULLAKE, Ida 231,232
O'BRIEN
   Edward 239
   Julia 239
OGEE, Mrs 85
OGLE, Decator 201
O-KETCH-E-SHOW-O-NOW 127
OLIVER
   Thomas 149,255
   Thomas K 23,111,182
O'SHEA, Mr 48
OUTCELT, George 247
OWENS, Fredonia 94,97,99,103
PA PA NINE 36
PA PHIA NA 45
PAH MAH MIE
   Pete 151
   Peter 67
PAH NAH KAH THO 19
PAH NAH KOH THO 19
PAH-AH-THE-QUAH 193
PAHMAHMIE, Pete 57
PAH-NAH-KAH-THO 20,21,223
PAH-NAH-KE 21
PAH-NAH-KETHO 66
PAH-NAH-KOH-THO 18
PAH-PAH-ME-TO-THAH-QUAH
.... 193
PAH-PAH-ME-TO-THA-QUAH. 192
PAH-PE-ACH 248

309

Index

PA-KOTA 162
PAM-AH-THO-AH 217,218, 243,244,245
PAM-AH-TO-QUAH 283,287
PAM-BO-GO, Pah-tose 237
PAMBOGO
   George F 175,184
   John B 260
   John Baptiste 237
   Mr A B 184
PANDOSH, Mary 220
PANTHER
   Billie 89
   Billy 290
   Mrs Sally 89
PA-PA-HINE 39
PA-PHIA-NA 36,43,270
PA-PHIS-NA 35,38
PARKER, Gabe E 2
PARKMAN, Harrison 57
PATE, Rachel Hall 129
PATTEQUA
   Charlotte 139,141
   Dollie 284,285
   Dolly 284
   William 284,285
PE-AH-PUCK-O-HE 287
PE-AH-TAH-TAH-NO-QUAH 193
PEAIRS, Supt H B 215
PECAN, George 55
PECK, Herbert M 5
PECK KE AH PEAH 259
PECK-KE-AH-PEAH 192,193
PEMBOGO
   John Baptiste 260
   Josetta 260
PE-MO, Kah-dot 219
PEMO
   Ka-dot 237
   Kadot 260
   Kahdot 218,260,272
   Sam 218
PEN-A-THO 20,21
   Mary 21
   May 223
PENATHOQUAH 120
PENNOCK
   David 122

   Hester 122
   William 122
PENNY, Edwin Fenton 287
PENSONEAU
   Hilda 199
   Narcisse 175
   Steve 175
PEQUA 33
PE-QUAH 34
PERRIT, Mrs Ada 226
PETITT, Mrs Ada 30
PETTIT, Ada 31
PE-TUN-WAH 193
PHIA TUS NA 45
PHIA-TAU-NA-NA 44
PHILIP, Walter 201
PHILIPS
   Mr 201
   Mrs Susan 4
   Walter 201
PHIS-TAU-NA-HA 35,36,38
PHISTAUNAHA 37,38
PICKERING, Nellie 160,173
POOLE, Daniel L 63
PORTER
   Mrs 239
   Mrs Lizzie Casteel 239
POST MASTER 49
POWELL, Mrs Jesse 297
PRATT
   Arthur 296
   Charles 298
   Earnest 296
   Ernest 195
   Miss May 295
   Mrs Gertie 295
   Mrs Mandy 297
   S 295,296,297,298
   Walter 298
QUA TO 47
QUAH-QUA-CHE-QUA 142
QUAH-TAH-KAH-ME-SHECK 21
QUEN-NEP-PE-THOT 277
QUINTARD, Mabel G 148
QUO-TOSE 231
RAGSDALE, Mrs Lydia 94
RAYMOND
   Burton C 82

Index

Burton G 77,241
Charles W 241
Chas W 78,81
REASOR
  Mr 180
  Mr E D 179
RED ROCK
  Abby 279
  Emma 279
REDROCK, Abby 280,281
REED
  F B 79,137
  F E.. 80
  Mr 69,138
RHODD
  Alexander................................171
  Enos 172
  Inez 172
  John...172
  Lizze 172
  Mary.....................................63,64
  Peter 172
  Thomas 220
  Zoa...172
RICE
  Catherine.................................223
  Edith..172
  Edward...................................... 66
RICHARDSON
  Mrs 123,167,181,202
  Mrs Rena.................................202
  Rena 180,228,264
  Rena Smith.......................167,227
  Renal 123
RIGGS, Mrs Catherine................. 56
RILEY, J L...................................260
ROBERTS, Mr W O 112
ROUBIDEAU
  Chane 221
  Mitchell...................................221
  Robert 206,221
ROUBIDEAUX
  Chame 205,222
  Chas 221
  Robert 205,221
ROUBIDOUX
  [Illegible] 121
  Cha-me 233,234,235

Charles.......................................234
Charlie 121
Charlie..2
Emily 181,182
Felix.. 121
Helen 262
Ida...262
James 262
Jennie..226
Joseph 262
Katie 27
Mrs 121,134
Oha-me 233,235
Pearl..262
Robert 222
Sophie 16
RUBIDOUX, Harrison 300
RUTLEDGE, Mr H C.................. 171
SA-KE-NA-WE-QUA.... 139,140,141
SAS-QUE-QUOT 39
SCHMIDLKOFER
  Mrs Nellie F............................. 198
  Mrs Nellie Frances 174
SCO-NAY-SE 60,236
SCOTT
  Dollie... 70
  Jim 35,36,38,39,43,45,139,
  140,141,188
  John 246
  Susie 40,45
  Susie Grant 139,141
SELLS, Hon Cato........................... 51
SHA QUE QUOT
  Cora...................................... 36,45
  Henry... 36
SHA-QUE-QUOT
  Cora 35,38,42,43
  Henry 35,38,43
SHAW, Miss Annie K 213
SHAWNEE
  David 101,105
  Dudley 93,94,96,97,99,100,102,
  103,104,105,107
  Emeline.................................... 105
  Evah... 105
  Fredonia................................... 105
  George 93,94,96,97,99,100,102,
  103,104,105,107

Index

Julia........ 69,79,80,93,95,96,97,99,
 100,102,103,104,105,107,137
Lafayetta 105
Lafayette 104,105
Lydia 105
Mrs Myrtle 100
Myrtle 105
Rebecca..................................105
Walter 93,94,96,97,99,100,102,
 103,104,105,107
William, Sr..........................69,137
Wm 79,93,94,96,97,99,100,
 102,103,104,105,107
SHENRESHQUAH
 Edith................................114,115
 Edward.............................114,115
 Theresa.............................114,115
SHI-AHN-WAH 193
SHI-AHN-WH 193
SHIVES
 [Illegible] 156
 Clarence..................................156
 Florence 156
SHOPWETUCK, James...............143
SHO-WAH-KAH......................... 29
SIN-G-QUAH............................238
SMALL, Robert..........................255
SMITH
 Bertie...............................167,180
 Birdie 202,227,228,263,267
 Eliza................................228,263
 Ella.. 2
 Frank 47,202,227,228,230,
 231,264,266
 James E 133,134
 Jessie 231
 Mrs Rena.................................202
 Nancy 263,264,267
 Rena 228,264,267
 Sidney 123,167,180,202,228
 Theresa.................................... 66
 Thurma....................................112
 William 92,93
SNAKE
 Joe... 23
 John..175
 John E 66,88,285
 Mr 19,91,112

SNAKE MAN 23,24
SNAKEMAN 28
SNYDER
 Arvel R 230
 Mr 45,47,113,135,233,235
 Mr A R . 31,32,33,47,113,119,120,
 121,127,134,144,178,239,262,293
 A R 4,27,34,47,230
 Superintendent........................ 111
 Supt 179,180,210,234
 Supt A R 5,89,149,191,218,220,
 232,238,283,287
SOGNAH, Pete...........................292
SOLDIER, Peter 147
SOPHIA 31
SO-SAH 143
SPEAR, Charley 193
SPRINGER
 J 121
 Joseph.............................. 121,134
 Josie....................................... 121
SPURLOCK
 Clarence................................... 54
 Clarence Z 118
 Lizzie 54,118
SPYBUCK, George 290,294
STANARD 128
STANARD & ENNIS 51,56,58,74,
 75,76,77,78,79,80,83,242
STARR, Mrs Sarah F..................... 50
STEVENS, Mr C J 225
STINCHECUN
 Mr... 111
 Supt C V 110
STRUBLE, Isaac 22,66
SUCK-KO-PE-AH, Annie................ 2
SUFFECOOL
 J L......49,50,51,52,53,55,56,57,58,
 59,60,61,62,63,64,65,66,67,68,69,70,
 71,72,73,74,75,76,77,78,79,80,81,
 82,83,84,85,86,87,88,89,90,91,92,93,
 94,95,97,98,100,101,103,104,105,
 106,108,109,110,111,112,113,116,
 118,119,120,121,122,123,124,125,
 126,127,128,129,130,131,132,133,
 134,135,144,145,146,147,148,149,
 150,151,152,153,154,157,158,159,
 161,162,163,164,166,167,168,170,

Index

171,172,173,174,175,176,177,178, 180,181,182,183,185,186,187,189, 191,192,193,194,198,199,200,201, 203,206,207,208,209,210,211,212, 213,214,215,216,217,219,220,222, 223,224,225,226,227,231,232,233, 235,236,237,238,239,240,241,242, 243,246,247,248,249,250,251,254, 255,256,257,258,259,260,261,262, 263,264,265,268,269,270,271,272, 273,275,276,278,279,280,281,282, 283,284,285,286,287,288,290,291, 292,293,294,295,296,297,298,299, 300
  J S 64
  Mr 196,197
  Mr J L 204,206,218,229, 234,244,252,253,266,268,281,289
  Supt J L 139,140,141,276,277
SULLINS, Walter D 145
SWARTZLANDER, Supt E L 84
TAH HO KA LA THA, Eugenie ..108
TAH-BAH-SHE..........................277
TAH-COM-E 192,193
TAH-H-KA-LE-THA, Eugenia 247
TAH-HO-KA-LA-THA, Eugenie .. 88
TAH-HO-KA-LE-THA, Eugenia..246
TANKERSLEY, Mrs Gertrude 58
TAYIAH, Emmett........................176
TAYLOR
  Flora 87
  John 87
  Stewart 268
TECUMZEE 127
TENNESSEE............................... 3
TESCIER
  Anthony 136
  Claricse 199
  Clarisse 136,158,199,207,210
  Lula 136
  Robert 136
THACKERY, Frank A................... 14
THA-COM-E 193
THOMAS..................................... 3
  Cam 4
  Mr 245
  Mrs Cornelia 4
  Willie 4

THOMPSON
  Angeline 114,115
  James 114,115,116,120
  Jim 115,116
  Peter................................... 114,115
THORN
  J R...................................... 155,156
  Mr 155,156,157
  Mr J R 189
THORNE
  Mr 157
  Mr J R 155
THUMA, Mrs Osie........................ 56
THURMAN
  Lucy................................... 139,141
  Mary 139,141
TOECIER, Clarisse 199
TOHEE
  Annie Perry................................ 54
  David 16,54
TO-HE-KE-LA-THA, Eugenie 91
TOWNSEND................................. 54
TROMBLA 8
  Ozetta 8,9
  Rosetta...................................... 10
TROMBLY
  Ozette 9
  Rozetta...................................... 11
TUSSINGER, Jessie Guam 85
TUTWILER
  Mr 90,132,152,184,233
  Mr S Y 19,29,126,131,135, 146,174,175,232,235
  S Y 18,20,21,30,62,90
TYNER
  Charley 200
  Davis 15,216
  Ellen 15,216
  Mrs Christine 216
  Mrs Sallie 236
  Sallie.. 59
UPTON
  A E 20
  Mr E A 19,211
VARNER, Mrs Minnie.................129
VETTER
  Joe 54,118,167,168
  Nesojame........................... 54,118

Index

VETTERS, Nesojame ... 54
VOGEL, Elizabeth ... 285
WA SE NAH ... 189
WABAUNCE ... 115
   Louis ... 114
   Luis ... 114
WABSKI, Mary ... 218
WAFFORD, Mrs Emmaline ... 99
WAH NAH BE QUAH ... 175
WAH QUE TAH NO QUAH ... 19
WAH-AH-NAH-PE-QUAH ... 178
WAH-PAH-KE-AH-SHE-KA ... 193
WAH-PAH-KO-THE-QUAH ... 21
WAH-PAH-MAH-PE-QUAH ... 29
WAH-PAH-NAH-PE-AH ... 144
WAH-PAH-NAH-PE-QUA ... 30
WAH-PAH-NAH-PE-QUAH ... 144,179
WAH-PAH-SEAP-TO ... 116
WAH-QUE-TAH-NO-QUAH ... 18
WAH-THAH-KO-KO-QUAH ... 21
WAH-THAH-QUE ... 21
WAH-THE-QUAH ... 210
WAH-THEY-THE-QUAH ... 135
WAH-THO-QUA ... 21
WAH-THO-QUAH ... 217,218
WAHTHOUQUAH ... 120
WAKOLE
   Grover ... 277
   Rufus ... 277
WALKER, Mrs Rebecca ... 97
WALTERS, Mrs John ... 233,235
WAMEGO, Mary ... 218
WARD, Mr ... 169
WARRIOR, Jim ... 55
WASHBURN, Mary ... 203
WASHINGTON
   Franklin ... 12
   Mary ... 142
   Nannie ... 142
   Stella ... 142
   Walter ... 142
WATERS, Mrs John ... 233,234,235
WE WE NAS, Grant ... 111
WEISS, Anna ... 56
WELD
   Hiram ... 186
   Joseph ... 186

WELFELT
   Mary ... 239
   Mrs ... 239
WELLS
   Charles E ... 137
   Chas E ... 79,104
   Chas K ... 69
   Hon W E ... 170
   Mr ... 138
WE-SHO-KE-QUA ... 182
WEST, Benjamin ... 55
WE-WE-NATH ... 193
WHIPPLE
   Alice ... 114
   Andrew ... 114
   Angeline ... 114
   Joe ... 113,114,115,116,120
WHISTLER, Leo ... 215
WHITE
   Corbett ... 167,168
   Eliza ... 294
   Ruth ... 168
   Ruth Vetter ... 168
WHITE WATER, William ... 258,259
WHITECLOUD
   Dan ... 34,238
   Louise ... 34,238
   Phoebe ... 109
   Sarah ... 34,238
   Susan ... 34
WHITEHORN, Maggie ... 173
WHITEWATE ... 243
WHITEWATER, William ... 259
WILEY
   Charles ... 263,265,269
   Charlie ... 202
   Mr ... 202
   Nellie ... 202,227,228,264,266
WILKINS, Wade ... 3
WILLAHAN, Mr W C ... 123
WILLIAMS ... 3
   Angeline ... 53
   Peter ... 53
   W Henry ... 4
WILLIE ... 213
WILLINGHAM
   William M ... 116
   Wm M ... 117

Index

WILMETH
   Examiner 18
   Mr 132
   Walter L 16
   Warner L 23,90
WILSON
   Aaron 55
   Harry 55
   Mary 170
   Mr A G 219
   Mr Harry 283
WITONESSE, Mose 7
WITONOSEE
   John 7
   Ross 282
WOLF
   Herman C 216
   James 149,235,236,255
   Jane 149,235,236,255
   John 149,235,236,255
WOLFE 150
   James 145
   Jane 145
   Jerome 183
   John 145
WOLFF, Herman C 280
WORCESTER, Thomas 110,111
WUKET, Nellie 267
WHITECLOUD-BLACK, Phoebe ... 16
WYNNS
   Mary Alice 299
   Mrs 299
YEGER, Ed 4
YOUNGBLOOD, Mr 59
ZAHN-QUA
   John 68
   Louis 68
ZINK, Guy 197,198
ZOW-NUM-KEE 204
ZOW-NUM-LEE 206
ZUGG, Josephine 65

ramcontent.com/pod-product-compliance
ource LLC
30426
0010B/623